W9-BUL-859

TEACHING GLBALLY

TEACHING GLOBALLY

GLOBALLY

Reading the World Through Literature

Edited by Kathy G. Short, Deanna Day, and Jean Schroeder

Stenhouse Publishers

Portland, Maine

Stenhouse Publishers
www.stenhouse.com

Library of Congress Cataloging-in-Publication Data

Names: Day, Deanna, 1963- editor. | Schroeder, Jean, 1948- editor. | Short,
    Kathy Gnagey, editor.
Title: Teaching globally : reading the world through literature / [edited by]
    Deanna Day, Jean Schroeder, and Kathy G. Short.
Description: Portland, Maine : Stenhouse Publishers, [2016]
Identifiers: LCCN 2016000417 | ISBN 9781571107923 (pbk. : alk. paper)
Subjects: LCSH: Children's literature--Study and teaching (Elementary) |
    Children--Books and reading. | Multicultural education.
Classification: LCC LB1575 .T39 2016 | DDC 372.64/044--dc23 LC record available at
http://lccn.loc.gov/2016000417

Cover and interior design by Lucian Burg, Lu Design Studios, Portland, ME
www.ludesignstudios.com

Manufactured in the United States of America

PRINTED ON 30% PCW
RECYCLED PAPER

22 21 20 19 18 17 16   9 8 7 6 5 4 3 2 1

Contents

131967

Acknowledgments

This book grew out of our participation in Worlds of Words, a community in which we have the privilege of thinking with one another about the potential of global literature for building intercultural understanding. We want to acknowledge the important role of colleagues in this community in challenging our thinking, introducing us to new global books, and asking questions that cause us to pause and reconsider. We also want to express our appreciation to the publishers who have been willing to take a risk and publish and distribute global children's and young adult literature in an uncertain market. These books create a context of possibility by inviting readers to enter into life spaces that go across cultures.

Contributors

Seemi Aziz is an instructor and specialist in global cultures, literacy, and literature at Worlds of Words in the College of Education at the University of Arizona. Her research and writing is on multicultural children's literature, particularly Muslim representations in young adult and children's literature.

Jennifer Hart Davis is a biology and earth science teacher at the middle and high school levels in the Corvallis 509J School District in Oregon. Before becoming a teacher, she was a research soil scientist with the US Department of Agriculture–Agricultural Research Service.

Deanna Day is an associate professor in the Department of Teaching and Learning at Washington State University, Vancouver. Her research is in children's literature and technology.

Jeanne Gilliam Fain is an associate professor at Lipscomb University in Tennessee. Her research and teaching interests are classroom-based research, literacy, and linguistically and culturally diverse learners, family literature discussion, critical literacy, and international, informational, and global texts used in elementary and middle school classrooms.

Angeline P. Hoffman is the Student Support Service director and the teacher assistant team coordinator for Dishchii'bikoh Community School in Arizona. She is interested in multicultural literacy and Indigenous children's literature, both in the United States and internationally, and their role in the lives of children and teachers in classrooms.

Holly Johnson is a professor in the Literacy and Second Language Studies program at the University of Cincinnati. Her interests include reader response theory, young adult literature, disciplinary literacy, and the effect of international literature on young people's understandings of the world. She has coauthored books including *Essentials of Young Adult Literature, Creating Confident Adolescent Readers,* and *Developing Critical Awareness at the Middle Level.*

Sandy Kaser retired after working thirty-five years for the Tucson Unified School District as a classroom teacher and curriculum specialist. She also taught at the University of Arizona in teacher preparation and is interested in identity construction.

Wen-Yun Lin teaches in the Teaching Chinese as a Second Language graduate program in the Department of Language and Creative Writing at the National Taipei University of Education in Taiwan. She works with local teachers to integrate literature circles and children's literature into their curriculum.

Julia López-Robertson is an associate professor of language and literacy at the University of South Carolina. Her scholarly agenda is built on a commitment to working with children, families, teachers, and preservice teachers in public schools, universities, and communities to advance understandings about emerging bilingual/multilingual students and their families and on the transformation of teacher education to support equitable teaching for all children, particularly English language learners.

Prisca Martens is a professor of elementary education at Towson University in Maryland, where she teaches courses on reading/literacy and children's literature. Her research is on picturebooks and children's literature, early literacy, miscue analysis, retrospective miscue analysis, and learners' eye movements while reading.

Ray Martens is an associate professor in the Department of Art + Design, Art History, Art Education at Towson University in Maryland, where he teaches courses in art education. His research explores readers' eye movements when they are transacting with the written and pictorial texts in picturebooks.

Janelle Mathis is a professor of literacy and children's literature at the University of North Texas. Her research interests include critical content analysis of literature; international literature, especially in light of art and culture; and multimodal strategies in using children's and adolescent literature.

Genny O'Herron is a founding teacher of Mountain Mahogany Community School in Albuquerque, New Mexico. As a National Writing Project Fellow and SEED (Seeking Educational Equity and Diversity) School Leader, she is passionate about the intersection of literacy and social justice in her classroom.

Jean Schroeder taught and served as an instructional coach in the Tucson Unified School District for forty-two years. She is on the board of the IDEA School, a nonprofit, noncharter school with an inquiry-based curriculum, and chaired the Notable Books in the Language Arts award committee.

Kathy G. Short is a professor in the Language, Reading and Culture program at the University of Arizona with a focus on global children's and adolescent literature, intercultural understanding, and critical content analysis. She has coauthored many books, including *Essentials of Children's Literature*, *Essentials of Young Adult Literature*, and *Stories Matter: The Complexity of Cultural Authenticity in Children's Literature*. She is director of Worlds of Words and is past president of the National Council of Teachers of English.

Tracy Smiles is a professor of literacy education at Western Oregon University, where she teaches literacy courses. Her scholarly interests include English language arts/literacy education, children's and adolescent literature, teacher preparation and professional development in elementary/middle school education, and case methods with an emphasis on teacher research.

Yoo Kyung Sung is an associate professor in the Department of Language, Literacy and Sociocultural Studies at the University of New Mexico in Albuquerque. She teaches a range of children's literature courses.

Whitney Young is a fourth-grade teacher at an elementary school in Texas and is working on her doctorate in the Department of Teacher Education and Administration at the University of North Texas. Her scholarly focus is multimodality, arts integration, and critical literacy.

PART 1

The Transformation of Curriculum Through Global Literature

Chapter 1

A Curriculum That Is Intercultural

Kathy G. Short

"Children today are growing up in a different world than we did" is a common refrain among adults. These words often reflect nostalgia for the "old days" when life was supposedly simpler and more straightforward. The world that children live in today is not all that different in complexity and societal issues—except that our knowledge of, and connection to, that world has changed. The fundamental change for children is that the world is visibly present in their daily lives through technology, mass media, economic interdependency, and global mobility. Even if children never leave the small communities in which they were born, their everyday lives are constantly influenced by global societies and peoples. Globalization touches every part of their daily activities and relationships.

An understanding of global cultures is thus a necessity, not a luxury. Although children can no longer decide whether they will lead global lives, the way in which they live those lives is open to question. That tension is what led us to this book and to our concern with curriculum that supports and challenges children to develop open-minded perspectives toward ways of living that differ from their own.

Global education has existed as a field of study for many years, but often as a strand within social studies or an emphasis in international schools. Explorations of global cultures and the development of intercultural understanding are increasingly essential as perspectives that weave across the curriculum. This possibility creates both tension and excitement. On one hand, teachers feel constrained by the standardization of curriculum through prescriptive programs and high-stakes tests. On the other hand, the lack of existing curriculum around global issues and cultures provides a potential space for innovation. The challenge is how to locate and use that space within mandates and schedule overload. The good news is educators do not have to fight to replace an established global curriculum and can adapt response strategies to integrate a global focus into existing literacy and social studies curricula.

Although there are many possibilities for opening up global spaces, our particular interest is the integration of global children's and adolescent literature. Our goal is the use of literature to build intercultural understanding as a stance or perspective that permeates the curriculum and students' lives, not to add a new content area to a crowded curriculum. Of course, moving from beliefs and goals into actual action in classrooms is always the more difficult step, but it's one we are committed to as educators.

Our strength as educators is our knowledge of global children's and adolescent literature and our long-term involvement in bringing children and books together through dialogue and inquiry. This book grows out of putting theory into practice in classrooms around our interest in encouraging intercultural understandings through critical engagements with global literature. We wrote this book as a community who has been working together for many years through Worlds of Words, an initiative we created as a network of educators who share the vision of bringing global literature and children together to create intercultural understanding. We work together to create resources for educators on the Worlds of Words website (wowlit.org) and meet regularly face-to-face as well as online. In addition, we meet in a summer workshop to think together about an issue of common concern around global literature. We wrote this book as a community who think and work together across diverse contexts.

This chapter contextualizes the classroom inquiries shared in this book through a discussion of global literature and intercultural understanding and an introduction to the curriculum framework around which we organize our work in classrooms.

Building Bridges Across Cultures Through Literature

One important resource for building bridges across cultures is global children's literature. Literature provides an opportunity for children to go beyond a tourist perspective of gaining surface-level information about another culture. Because literature expands children's life spaces, they travel outside the boundaries of their lives to other places, times, and ways of living to participate in alternative ways of being in the world. Readers are invited to immerse themselves into story worlds to gain insights about how people around the world live, feel, and think—to develop emotional connections and empathy as well as knowledge. These connections go beyond the surface knowledge of celebrations, food, and facts about a country to the values and beliefs that lie at the core of each culture. Readers also go beyond the mass media emphasis on catastrophe, terrorism, and war that often results in superficial views, fear, and stereotypes.

Our goal in integrating global literature into classrooms is to challenge students to understand and accept those different from themselves, thus breaking cycles of oppression and prejudice between diverse cultures. As students read these books, they come to recognize the common feelings and needs they share with children around the world, as well as to value the unique differences each culture adds to the richness of our world. Through reading books from global cultures, students come to know their own cultures as well as the world beyond their homes. They see how people of the world view themselves, not just how we view them.

We use the term *global literature* to refer to any book that is set in a global context outside the reader's own global location, which for most of us means the United States (except for Wen-Yun Lin, for whom any book outside of Taiwan is global). For those of us from the United States, global literature includes books authored by Americans and by insiders to a global culture. We recognize that this definition needs to remain flexible based on how readers define their cultural location, not how we define them; for example, children who are recent immigrants to the United States may have a primary affiliation with their home country and so see US books as global literature or see themselves as binational with both the United States and their home country as their cultural location and any other location as global.

One type of global literature is *international literature*, books that were first written and published in another country for the children of that country before being published in the United States. International books include those from English-speaking countries, such as the Harry Potter series, and books that are translated before being published in the United States. *Multicultural literature* refers to books that highlight the lives of people from marginalized and underrepresented groups within the United States.

Issues of Availability and Authenticity

Although global literature has always been present through well-loved characters, such as Heidi and Pippi Longstocking, their numbers were so small that they had little influence. For years, many global books were so-called "travel books," books written by Americans who traveled to a country for several weeks, and so were often superficial stereotyped representations of those cultures. This context is quickly changing as increasing numbers of authentic books from global cultures are distributed and published in North America.

Despite recent increases in the amount of global literature, these books are still a small minority of the total books being published for children in the United States. The Cooperative Children's Book Center documents children's books about characters of color published each year in the United States. The CCBC (2015) found that out of 3,500 children's books published in 2014, only 11 percent were about multicultural or global characters of color. Only 1–2 percent of the children's books available in the United States each year are translated books, because many international books come from English-speaking countries, especially the United Kingdom and Australia. So, although books are available, they remain such a small portion of the total number of books published that educators need to prioritize them or their classroom and library collections will not reflect global diversity. Appendices A and B list the award lists, websites, and resources we have found helpful in locating global literature and other global resources.

Once a book has been located, another issue is evaluating cultural accuracy, authenticity, and representation. *Accuracy* refers to the details of everyday life and language portrayed in the text and illustrations, and *authenticity* refers to the extent to which a book reflects the core values and beliefs at the heart of a cultural group. *Representation* examines the relationship of an individual book to images of a specific culture within a collection of books, such as whether particular images are over- or underrepresented. Picturebooks on Mexico, for example, overwhelmingly depict rural life and small villages rather than urban cities. Another example is that the genres of folklore and historical fiction dominate the books available in the United States for most global cultures, leading to misperceptions of those cultures as set back in time.

Educators often feel uncomfortable evaluating books from unfamiliar cultures, but there are resources available, including the review sites and questions to ask in considering authenticity noted in Appendix C. We have found it particularly helpful to research the backgrounds of authors, illustrators, and translators to determine their relationship to the content of a book. Given the many resources available online, we often find information on author websites, interviews, and videos in which they talk about their lives and the stories behind specific books. Translators are the most difficult to locate information on. We check the book jacket and author notes or acknowledgments for information on research processes and sources. In addition, we examine the copyright information to find out where and when a book was initially published.

Our purpose in engaging in this research is to determine the questions we want to ask as readers in interacting with children around a book. We are not trying to make a yes/no decision about whether a book is authentic, because there are always multiple perspectives and issues. We want to raise questions about issues of accuracy, authenticity, or representation for discussion, not remove the book from student use. Books reflect societal perceptions and biases, and so discussing issues within these texts supports critique of societal issues. Sometimes the questions we raise are not ones that we can answer, because we lack background knowledge on a culture, but raising the question is a first step and can help in developing a critical lens for reading global literature as well as lead to further inquiry.

For us, cultural authenticity refers to the responsibilities of both readers and authors. Typically, discussions of authenticity have focused on the text and the responsibilities of authors in writing texts that are culturally accurate, authentic, and representative. We do need to ask difficult questions about the text as readers, but we are also responsible for asking those same questions about the cultural match between our responses and the text. The responsibilities of readers are discussed in greater depth by Holly Johnson in Chapter 2, and questions related to both author and reader responsibility are included in Appendix C.

The issues of availability, access, and authenticity can feel overwhelming to educators who want to integrate more global literature into classrooms and libraries. Initially, many of these obstacles seem insurmountable, but our belief in the powerful role that literature can play in creating intercultural understanding helps us persevere. Over time, we have located a range of useful resources and developed other resources through our work with Worlds of Words. We created the following online resources at wowlit.org:

- *WOW Books*: A database, searchable by geographical region, genre, age, theme, author, illustrator, and so on along with My Take/Your Take Dialogues highlighting different perspectives on a book
- *WOW Review*: An online journal of reviews of culturally diverse children's and adolescent literature that include comments on content, themes, and authenticity

- *WOW Stories:* An online journal of stories from K-16 classrooms on the ways in which teachers have used global and multicultural literature to support classroom inquiries
- *WOW Currents*: A weekly blog on issues around global and multicultural literature

Many of us are also involved with the International Board of Books for Young People (IBBY) and the US national section (USBBY) and make extensive use of the resources available on their websites, including award lists.

Issues of Engaging Readers

Once educators access global books, the tension remains of how to engage children and adolescents thoughtfully with this literature. Global books often focus on ways of living that seem far removed from children's immediate experiences and contain unfamiliar stylistic features, names, and terms. Some international books are written in unfamiliar story structures and assume knowledge of distant cultural contexts and historical events. One danger is that children will come to view this literature as "exotic" or "weird" or "boring" and fail to connect in significant ways. The use of global literature can actually establish stereotypes and misunderstandings and lead to feelings of pity or superiority. Knowing the books is only a first step; educators also need examples of thoughtful engagement around these books.

This book highlights our work in classrooms to engage K-8 readers with global literature and our thinking about a curriculum framework that is theoretically based and guides our planning to provide a range of experiences with books and global perspectives. Our goal is not just to engage students with global literature but to integrate literature into inquiries to encourage the development of intercultural understanding. This framework, A Curriculum That Is Intercultural, is based in our beliefs about intercultural understanding.

The Development of Intercultural Understanding

The first question we are often asked is how interculturalism relates to multiculturalism, and although there are many connections, some important distinctions exist as well. Banks (2001) and Nieto (2002) note that although the specific definition and list of qualities for multiculturalism may vary, there is consistency across theorists on the goals and purposes of multicultural education. Those goals emphasize the sociopolitical nature of education through challenging and rejecting racism and discrimination and affirming pluralism, particularly for individuals and groups considered outside the cultural mainstream of society. They argue that, from the beginning, multicultural education has had reforming education as its goal so that students from diverse racial, ethnic, and social class groups can experience educational equality. Issues of inequity, discrimination, and oppression cannot be excluded from multiculturalism without changing its very nature. Sleeter (1991) writes, "Multicultural educators give voice and substance to struggles against oppression and develop the vision and the power of our future citizens to forge a more just society" (22).

Underlying this focus on sociopolitical goals is the belief that multiculturalism is not a special unit or piece of literature, but a perspective that is a part of all education. Sleeter and Grant (1987) argue for using the phrase *an education that is multicultural* to indicate that multiculturalism is an orientation that pervades the curriculum.

These understandings about the underlying sociopolitical nature of multicultural education provide an important backdrop for interculturalism. Interculturalism is based in the work of European theorists and educators, and developed out of the racism and genocide of World War II (Fennes and Hapgood 1997). This movement precedes and parallels the multicultural movement in North America and positions itself as more broadly concerned with issues and perspectives related to cultures across national borders as well as between ethnic groups within a country. Cushner (2015) points out that *multicultural* generally refers to knowledge about an underrepresented group within a specific country and so attends to issues of power within that country. In contrast, *intercultural* focuses on knowledge about the world, cognitive elements of a global perspective, and the skills needed to successfully interact within cross-cultural exchanges.

As is true for multiculturalism, teaching for intercultural understanding involves far more than lessons on human relations and sensitivity training or adding a book or unit about a country into the existing curriculum. These approaches typically lead to superficial depictions of cultural differences that reinforce stereotypes instead of creating new understandings and open-minded perspectives.

Interculturalism is an attitude of mind, an orientation that pervades thinking and permeates the curriculum. This orientation is based on a broad understanding of culture as ways of living and being in the world that serve as designs for acting, believing, and valuing. Geertz (1973) defines culture as "the shared patterns that set the tone, character and quality of people's lives" (216). These patterns include language, religion, gender, relationships, class, ethnicity, race, disability, age, sexual orientation, family structures, nationality, and rural/suburban/urban communities, as well as the values, symbols, interpretations, and perspectives held by a group of people. González (2005) argues for a dynamic view of culture as funds of knowledge, the cultural knowledge and skills that households accumulate over time and that are essential to the well-being and functioning of the household and the individuals in the household. Funds of knowledge put an emphasis on the cultural resources of households and social practices of families, rather than individual interests or identity.

Fleck (1935), a Polish scientist and philosopher, argues that cultures consist of thought collectives that form whenever groups of people learn to think in similar ways because they share a common interest, exchange ideas, maintain interaction over time, and create a history that affects how they think and live. These thought collectives can be constraining, particularly when individuals within them are unable to think in any other way, but they also function as generative "think tanks" that facilitate collaborative thinking and work. Since most individuals think and act within several thought collectives at a time, this view captures the dynamic, evolving nature of culture as each person interacts with, and is changed through, transactions with other cultures, as well as the multiple cultural identities within each person's life. Fleck argues that the movement between thought collectives or cultures opens up a generative potential for tension and learning. This movement between cultures disrupts the commonplace and leads to a reexamination of assumptions about oneself and the world, leading in turn to intercultural understanding.

Our work is based in a definition of intercultural understanding as "a stance of openness to multiple ways of thinking and being in the world and to differences as resources for our shared humanity and responsibility in working together to create a better and more just world." I developed this definition through reading scholars on culture (Geertz 1973; González 2005) and intercultural education (Allan 2003; Fennes and Hapgood 1997; Hofstede 1991) as well as global education (Begler 1996; Case 1991) and cosmopolitanism (Choo 2013; Rizvi 2009). Many of these researchers use different terms, particularly *intercultural* or *global competence*, but I prefer *intercultural understanding* to signal the ongoing lifelong process of developing these perspectives. Our abilities in one situation shift in each new cultural context, so competence is never achieved but is always in flux. Intercultural understanding is a process of "becoming" that continues throughout our lifetimes, just as our identities remain dynamic and evolve over time.

Given this definition of intercultural understanding as an orientation that pervades our interactions and thinking, this stance plays out in our lives through the following ways:

- Exploring our cultural identities and developing conceptual understandings of culture.
- Developing an awareness and respect for different cultural perspectives as well as the commonality of human experience.
- Examining issues that have personal, local, and global relevance and significance.
- Valuing the diversity of cultures and perspectives within the world.
- Demonstrating a responsibility and commitment to making a difference to, and in, the world.
- Developing an inquiring, knowledgeable, and caring perspective on taking action to create a better and more just world.

Since curriculum involves putting our beliefs into action (Short and Burke 1990), these theoretical beliefs provided a foundation for our work in classrooms. What we still need, however, is a curricular framework to guide the planning and implementation of engagements with children.

A Framework for a Curriculum That Is Intercultural

The curricular framework used in this book is one that I developed through action research with teachers from Van Horne Elementary School in Tucson (Short 2009). Over a four-year period, I met with teachers in a study group to examine student work and plan instruction for children in a demonstration classroom. The goal of this action research was to explore the components of a global curriculum and how these components play out across grade levels. Teachers from the school wrote vignettes about their classrooms that are published in *WOW Stories* (Volume 1, Issues 1-3).

We have made a few adaptations in the framework to reflect our current work. The framework highlights multiple ways of engaging with intercultural perspectives to support children's critical explorations of their cultural identities, ways of living within a specific cultural community, multiple global perspectives on a theme, and complex local and global issues. The curricular components interrelate and build on each other to highlight different aspects of intercultural understanding. Surrounding these components is an environment in which students are encouraged to inquire from a critical stance. This framework supports teachers in exploring the ways in which global perspectives and literature can be integrated across the curriculum. (See Figure 1.1.)

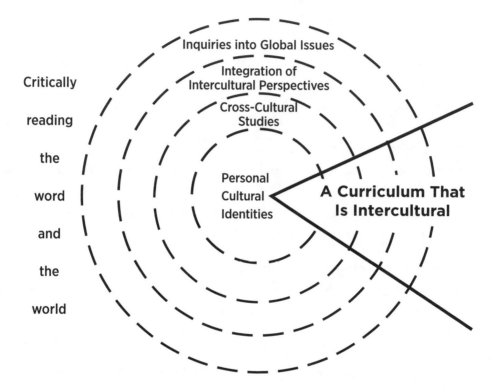

Figure 1.1 **A Curriculum That Is Intercultural**

This book is organized around the components of the framework, and each component is introduced here with examples from chapters to provide an overview of the framework. The chapters, of course, provide in-depth discussions and descriptions of curricular engagements and inquiry units. Many of these classroom inquiries involve several of the components, not just one. For example, Sandy Kaser's chapter explores how students gained insights into their personal cultural identities through their inquiry into Mexican American culture, but this study also involved inquiries into global issues of migrant workers and undocumented immigrants. The dotted lines between the components signal the fluid and interconnected nature of each part of the framework.

We placed each chapter into the section that was the major intent of that inquiry, but recognize that classroom inquiries involve multiple components.

The chapters highlight inquiries from classrooms that cut across geographical settings and communities in the United States, including one chapter set in Taiwan, and across grade levels, from prekindergarten to grade eight. The details of each inquiry are shared, including the responses of children, along with titles of global literature that were most significant for that classroom. Because of our focus on interactions with literature, we used response strategies to encourage dialogue about these books, and a description of these dialogue strategies is in Appendix D. Each chapter also includes a section on negotiating district and state mandates in that particular context to provide space for global curriculum.

Critically Reading the World and the Word

The components of this framework are permeated with critically reading the world and the word—a phrase used by Freire (1970) to indicate the importance of raising issues of power and social justice through problem-posing. Without a focus on critically reading the world and the word, the four components could easily become a superficial tour of culture where students are tourists picking up isolated pieces of information. A tourist curriculum is based on the assumption that "if we all just learned more about each other, we would like each other and the world's problems would be solved." This approach does not consider difficult issues of social justice, so students are unable to make real change in how they think about and relate to others.

Reading critically by naming the world is the stance that race, class, and gender matter in how we interpret and analyze our experiences in the world as well as the texts we encounter. Freire (1970) argues that students need to wrestle with ideas and words, not just walk on top of them. Reading the world and the word from a critical stance provides the opportunity to question "what is" and "who benefits" as well as to consider the "what if" of new possibilities. Students often avoid talking about racism by taking a position of color blindness, saying, "It doesn't matter what you look like on the outside; it's the inside that counts." These statements deny that skin color is essential to cultural identity for people of color and matters in how they are treated. Color blindness allows students to walk on top of words, and they need to be challenged to wrestle with the difficult issues of racism in their lives as well as the broader world.

Critically reading the world and the word involves students in questioning power relationships and the status quo to consider multiple cultures, perspectives, and ways of taking action. We encourage students to take this critical stance whether they are looking at their own personal cultural identities, engaging in a cross-cultural study, considering multiple perspectives about a theme, or examining a global issue.

Holly Johnson positions this critical stance in her chapter as the social responsibility of the reader when engaged with global texts, based on the theoretical frame of transactional theory and reader response. She argues that discussions of cultural authenticity often call for the social responsibility of authors and publishers, but that readers also have a responsibility to bring a critical and open stance to a text. She describes the different aspects of this stance both theoretically and practically as it plays out in the lives of readers. The social responsibility of readers is a theoretical framework that cuts across all of our chapters in moving beyond naïve or biased thinking toward intercultural understanding.

Personal Cultural Identities

An understanding of why culture matters in the lives of people around the world is rooted in the realization that we each have cultural identities that shape our thinking and actions. If we do not see culture as integral to our identities, but as present only in "others," culture becomes exotic and divisive. We cannot recognize and consider multiple points of view unless we first acknowledge that each of us has a point of view based in our experiences within a particular community. Intercultural understanding is built on a close examination of our own cultural identities and the ways these identities influence our beliefs, values, and actions.

Children bring their personal experiences of living in the world as members of specific cultural groups and social contexts to school. By examining their histories, they can explore how those experiences and interactions determine their view of the world. When students recognize the cultures that influence their thinking, they become more aware of how and why culture is important to others. They no longer see culture as about the "other," but recognize that it is at the heart of defining who they are as human beings. In addition, they need the opportunity to find their lives and identities reflected in books in order to value literacy as relevant to their identities.

Interactions with literature can encourage students to focus on themselves as cultural beings and go beyond "Who am I?" activities where children make lists of favorites and interests but do not examine *why* these exist in their lives—their origin and significance. Many of our chapters include examples of engagement around children's own identities, often as a beginning experience within a larger unit, but the chapters on personal cultural identities highlight inquiries where children's identities are the major focus.

One curricular engagement that we often use is cultural x-rays in which students label the outside of their bodies with visible aspects of their culture that are evident to others, such as language, age, ethnicity, gender, and religion, and the inside with the values and beliefs that they hold in their hearts. Ray and Prisca Martens share how teachers worked with young children to create x-rays, noting that first creating cultural x-rays of favorite characters from books provides children with a demonstration of what they might consider in creating their own x-rays.

The literature we choose to read aloud can invite students to consider their identities through making connections to characters. We particularly look for books that are close to children's lives and in which characters struggle with some aspect of their identities. Many of the chapters include lists of picturebooks and novels. These read-alouds served as invitations for children to talk about their lives and reflect on their experiences. A book like *Marisol McDonald Doesn't Match* (Brown 2011), about a biracial child, engages children in considering the need to belong and the struggle of maintaining multiple cultural identities.

One issue is that sometimes the literature that is available is either full of misrepresentations or has large gaps. Wen-Yun Lin worked with teachers to gather books showing immigrant and Indigenous cultures in Taiwan. Teachers found very few books, so they created a project in which children from those cultures wrote, drew, and told their stories, as well as critiqued the few published books. Indigenous children were upset that books on Indigenous cultures in Taiwan were historical and did not show contemporary images, and children from China challenged the stereotypes held by Taiwanese children and teachers about China. This critique led to an inquiry comparing the shared Chinese cultural heritage but differing political identities of Taiwanese and Chinese peoples.

Another curricular engagement involves children in gathering and displaying collections of artifacts that are significant to who they are, such as each child creating a museum display with labels for four or five artifacts that reflect different aspects of their identities. Ray and Prisca had young children collect artifacts for a Marvelous Me bag to share the ways in which they were each marvelous after reading *Marvelous Me* (Bullard 2003).

Sandy Kaser found that the novel *Esperanza Rising* (Ryan 2000) created a space for students to discuss their identities as Mexican Americans and their connections to family members in Mexico. Mapping Esperanza's life journey led to mapping their life journeys and changes over time. They also reflected on their bicultural identities as Mexicans and Americans, creating a T-chart of those identities after reading Francisco Jimenez's books in which he writes about moving across two cultures. Their many connections to these books led to new questions and global inquiries into social issues surrounding migrant farmworkers and undocumented immigrants.

Literature can also be a means for students to go beyond their immediate local community and identify as members of a broader cultural community. Angeline Hoffman discussed international Indigenous literature with White Mountain Apache students and found that these books created a sense of belonging to a larger global Indigenous community of many tribal nations. They were able to see their connections to the ways of life in other Indigenous groups as well as to identify unique aspects of their Apache heritage and ways of life.

Families are the basis of children's cultural identities, and involving them in cultural explorations is an immediate and strong connection. Ray and Prisca Martens describe surveying families about their cultural backgrounds at the beginning of the year and using world maps to plot their countries of origin. They also found that nonfiction books highlighting the diversity of families provoke interesting discussions about the unique aspects of children's families. In addition, children used an adaptation of the cultural x-ray to create heart maps filled with images of what they loved and considered special about their families.

When children come from families with histories of marginalization and oppression within mainstream society, issues of cultural identity become more complex. Julia López-Robertson started a literature discussion group with Latina mothers, recognizing that they needed to explore their own identities and value their funds of knowledge to challenge society's deficit views of Latino/as and to support their children.

Engagements around personal cultural identities help students realize that their experiences within families and communities shape how they think and act. Many of the books that support these cultural explorations are multicultural and closely related to children's lives to encourage reflection on their identities. The discussions around global literature focus more on universals, what connects people as human beings across cultures, because of our focus on understanding self; however, this focus on self needs to be balanced with in-depth inquiry into the differences across cultures.

Cross-Cultural Studies

Although intercultural understanding is grounded in awareness of one's own cultural perspective, students need to consider points of view beyond their own so they come to recognize that their perspective is one of many ways to view the world, not the norm against which to measure other viewpoints. In-depth studies of specific global cultures can broaden students' perspectives and provide a window on the world. Unfortunately cross-cultural studies often take the form of theme units built around superficial aspects of a culture through a limited study of the five *F*s: food, fashion, folklore, festivals, and famous people.

A cross-cultural study should provide an opportunity to examine the complexity and diversity that exists within a particular cultural group to avoid essentializing that group through generalizations. Focusing on food or folklore is a beginning but can lead to stereotypes and superficial understandings unless students also examine the deeper values and beliefs that are significant within that culture. A cross-cultural study should highlight the complexity of economic, social, political, aesthetic, moral, historical, and geographical contexts within a cultural group (Begler 1996). Knowing that a particular food is eaten or clothing is worn within a culture should be embedded in understanding *why* that food or clothing is significant given the history, geography, and social values for that group.

We found that because students already recognized the complexity of culture within their own lives, we could use the same engagements of cultural x-rays, life journey maps, and cultural museums to explore experiences of children from a new culture as depicted in literature. For example, Yoo Kyung Sung and Genny O'Herron engaged students in charting the ways in which their culture was depicted in books about New Mexico before asking them to use the same charts to look at books about South Korea and to compare similarities and differences between the two ways of life. Seemi Aziz notes that teachers engaged students and families in exploring the story of each child's name before moving into books, such as *My Name Is Sangoel* (Williams and Mohammed 2009), to understand the cultural and personal significance of names that sounded "foreign."

Choosing a powerful novel as a read-aloud or shared reading is particularly significant in providing an in-depth depiction of characters within a cultural context. Yoo Kyung and Genny were able to get beyond students' initial resistance to a Korean inquiry through reading aloud *A Single Shard* (Park 2001) as students came to care about and be concerned for the main character. Deanna Day read *The No. 1 Car Spotter* (Atinuke 2011) with struggling readers to challenge stereotypes of Africa and develop children's awareness of connections and differences between their lives and those of children in Nigeria.

Locating a range of genres and settings to represent the diversity and complexity of a culture can make it challenging to create text sets around that culture. We often find that these sets are missing contemporary images, so we use online images, videos, and guests from that culture as resources. The books available on global cultures are primarily historical fiction and folklore with several informational books, but there are very few books about everyday contemporary life. Deanna engaged students in a larger set of picturebooks set in African countries with which they interacted while reading a short novel. She also found that online news reports provided access to current events, and more deeply engaged children in feeling empathy for and connection to Nigeria.

We always include books written in the language of that culture, whether Hanguel from the Korean inquiry or Arabic from the Middle East inquiry, so that students understand that language is integral to that culture, not an add-on. In addition, picturebooks published from those countries in the language of that country often provide more authentic images and raise many questions for students.

Encountering a range of images across books can challenge stereotypes and misunderstandings. Initially, children reading books about Arabic cultures in the Middle East had many misunderstandings about the hijab, but Seemi found that the images of different types of head coverings and of Muslim women who chose not to wear them created an interest in why the hijab is worn and an understanding of different options for women.

Families can become involved in these cross-cultural studies by sharing resources when they have connections to the culture or by coming into the classrooms as guests. Families can also be invited to join the inquiry. Yoo Kyung and Genny sent home a Korean backpack containing bilingual audiobooks, Hanguel letter magnets, Korean schoolbooks, and Korean snack food to invite families into their inquiry.

Cross-cultural studies encourage a critical lens by examining the ways in which images in the books differ from images available from other resources or by examining images that are overrepresented in books and have the potential of becoming stereotypes. Yoo Kyung and Genny note that students commented on the depictions of Korean children in special masks and dresses in American informational books, whereas those images did not dominate picturebooks from Korea. Not surprisingly, Seemi encountered many stereotypes of Muslims, equating them with terrorists, which were challenged by stories of everyday life in Muslim families. Students also had stereotypes of Arabic countries in the Middle East as full of sand and camels, set back in time. Several teachers presented *Mirror* (Baker 2010), which compares rural Morocco with urban Australia, along with Internet images of the Australian desert and modern Moroccan cities, leading children to critique the way in which the book unfairly compares the two countries.

The value of a cross-cultural study is that students have time for in-depth inquiry to understand the complexity within a culture and to go beyond the surface-level explorations that often characterize this type of study. These studies not only provide a window on a culture, but also encourage insights into students' own cultural identities. Students come to deeper understandings about their cultures and perspectives when they encounter alternative possibilities for thinking about the world. Many times they do not realize that their actions or values are cultural until they encounter another way of life. Cross-cultural studies thus provide both a mirror and a window for children as they look out on ways of viewing the world and reflect on themselves in a new light.

We believe that cross-cultural studies and explorations of personal cultural identities work together to construct a conceptual understanding of culture. Looking at their identities develops an understanding of culture as dynamic and complex. At the same time, a deep understanding of culture as a way of thinking and living in the world includes the realization that there are alternative ways of being in the world. Both in-depth cross-cultural and personal cultural studies are also essential to understanding the connections shared across cultures that unite us as human beings while also valuing the differences that make each culture unique and add to the rich diversity of our global community.

Integration of International Perspectives

Although an occasional cross-cultural study is important, literature reflecting a wide range of cultural perspectives needs to be woven into *every* classroom study, no matter what the topic or curriculum area. The stories, languages, lifestyles, and ways of learning from many cultures need to be integrated into all units of study across the curriculum, not just one or two special units each year. Whether the classroom focus is folklore, family, conflict, the moon, or fractions, we look for literature reflecting a range of global perspectives. Otherwise, interculturalism can be viewed as a special unit instead of an orientation that pervades our thinking.

Whitney Young and Janelle Mathis developed an intercultural unit around forced journeys that examined different types of forced journeys in students' lives and in people around the world, bringing in many global perspectives. They began with books from the United States that included familiar journeys to encourage children to think conceptually about the journeys in their lives. They moved into a broader range of global and multicultural literature to distinguish between chosen and forced journeys and then into a global set of picturebooks on forced journeys. These books were selected to encourage children to try on new perspectives and used in engagements where children took on the voice of the main character, such as writing a first-person journal entry, to more fully immerse themselves in that perspective. They also looked closely at the authorship of books and considered the author's point of view and positionality in relation to a book's cultural context and authenticity.

This emphasis on a range of cultural perspectives and experiences across multicultural and global contexts is evident in Jeanne Fain's description of an intercultural inquiry on diverse languages and stories with young children. Her text set carefully paired fiction and nonfiction picturebooks and involved children in constructing charts and Venn diagrams to make comparisons of linguistic and cultural differences across the books. These interactions engaged children in close reading as they made comparisons and thought critically about the issues that emerged in their discussions.

Integrating literature from diverse cultures into student inquiries provides for a wider range of perspectives on a theme and encourages more complexity in the issues that students consider. They cannot settle comfortably into their own cultural perspectives but are challenged to go beyond that worldview. These text sets thus contain books that are close to children's own identities as well as books that take them beyond their views to perspectives that are both multicultural and global. We see these inquiries as highlighting a conceptual understanding of perspective to support their developing insights into culture.

Inquiries into Global Issues

Another curricular component that is significant for building intercultural understanding is inquiries into global issues, many of which highlight difficult social, political, and environmental concerns, such as violence, human rights, environmental degradation, overpopulation, poverty, language loss, racism, and economic imperialism (Collins, Czarra, and Smith 1999). Students need to occasionally study a global issue in-depth and over time to understand the local and global complexity of these issues and to consider ways of taking action. These studies are essential in encouraging students to go beyond talk and inquiry to accept responsibility as global citizens and take action to create a better and more just world.

Inquiries into global issues can establish stereotypes about violence and poverty as located in global cultures in comparison to the privileged life of children in the United States unless those inquiries are based in local as well as global contexts. Jennifer Hart Davis and Tracy Smiles had students report on their water use before looking at water use globally. An inquiry on human rights that I was involved with began with an exploration of unfair events in students' lives in school and an inquiry on hunger began with identifying issues of power in children's lives and the influence of "tight times" on the lives of families in their community.

These inquiries into global issues depend on a strong knowledge base so that students take action based on a deep understanding of the underlying issues and not on surface problems. They also involve combining nonfiction sources to gain information with fiction sources to create empathy. Jennifer and Tracy immersed students in scientific activities around water as well as had them read a novel set in the Sudan and a nonfiction book on water around the world. In the hunger inquiry that I describe, children examined the many reasons that people go hungry before they considered possible action. Students engaged with different types of informational materials and nonfiction books to build their knowledge of the different causes of hunger.

The action developing out of an inquiry into global issues can take the form of changes in thinking and beliefs, greater awareness of current events, or involvement in social action. Jennifer and Tracy saw a significant shift in their students' thinking about water use moving from a lack of concern to an awareness of the interconnectedness of their lives with others around the world. In the inquiries that I documented, students took action on their rights in school and engaged in local and global community projects out of their inquiry on hunger.

Inquiries into global issues highlight global citizenship and the responsibility of each person to work with others in taking action to make a difference in the world. This sense of global responsibility and interconnectedness is essential to intercultural understanding but is often the component that is overlooked in a global curriculum or addressed at a superficial level, leading to charity to raise money for a remote cause rather than social action for change.

So What? Are We Making a Difference?

One of the fears we all face as teachers when engaging in curricular innovation is whether or not what we are doing actually makes a difference in student learning and thinking. Any innovation requires a great deal of energy and commitment to make a change from "how things have always been done," and concerns about whether that effort leads to change need to be addressed, especially in the high-pressure context of tests and standards. In our case, our concern was the influence of curricular engagements and inquiries on children's intercultural understandings. We had to face the dreaded "so what" question about whether our work resulted only in an enjoyable experience or led to more significant learning and thinking.

Prisca and Ray Martens met with teachers to examine the oral, written, and artistic responses of young children around global literature. They identified three key learnings indicating that young children evidenced deeper understandings of their cultural identities, appreciated and respected the ways they are similar to and different from others, and identified themselves as responsible citizens of their communities and world.

Along with a group of teachers at Van Horne Elementary School, I examined transcripts from literature discussions in K-5 classrooms around books that reflected the four components of our curriculum framework. Specific categories were identified for intercultural understanding as knowledge, perspective, and action that can be used as a tool for evaluating intercultural understanding within student talk.

Final Reflections

The curriculum framework that is the organizational structure for this book provides a means for us to evaluate the curricular engagements and units occurring in a classroom context and whether they support intercultural understanding. What is working well in the curriculum can be identified along with what is missing or needs to be strengthened. Although all aspects of this framework will not be in place at one particular moment in time, we believe that each component plays a different role and should be available to students at some point in the school year. The interrelationships of these components work together across the framework to build complex intercultural understandings. Inquiries of personal cultural identity and cross-cultural studies focus students on conceptual understandings of culture, the integration of global books across the curriculum develops conceptual understandings of perspective, and inquiries on global issues highlight conceptual understandings of social action. All of these understandings are essential for interculturalism as an orientation, both inside and outside of school, for socially responsible readers and global citizens.

References

Allan, Michael. 2003. "Frontier Crossing: Cultural Dissonance, Intercultural Learning, and the Multicultural Personality." *Journal of Research in International Education* 2 (1): 83–110.

Banks, James. 2001. *Cultural Diversity and Education.* 4th ed. Boston: Allyn and Bacon.

Begler, Elsie. 1996. "Global Cultures: The First Steps Toward Understanding." *Social Education* 62 (5): 272–276.

Case, Robert. 1991. "Key Elements of a Global Perspective." *Social Education* 57 (6): 318–325.

Choo, Suzanne. 2013. *Reading the World, the Globe, and the Cosmos.* New York: Peter Lang.

Collins, H. Thomas, Frederick Czarra, and Andrew Smith. 1999. "Guidelines for Global and International Studies Education." *Social Education* 62 (5): 311–317.

Cooperative Children's Book Center. 2015. *Children's Books by and About People of Color Published in the United States.* http://ccbc.education.wisc.edu/books/pcstats.asp.

Cushner, Kenneth. 2015. "Development and Assessment of Intercultural Competence." In *The Sage Handbook of Research in International Education,* ed. Mary Hayden, Jack Levy, and Jeff Thompson. Thousand Oaks, CA: Sage.

Fennes, Helmut, and Karen Hapgood. 1997. *Intercultural Learning in the Classroom.* London: Cassell.

Fleck, Ludwick. 1935. *The Genesis and Development of a Scientific Fact.* Chicago: University of Chicago Press.

Freire, Paulo. 1970. *Pedagogy of the Oppressed.* South Hadley, MA: Bergin and Garvey.

Geertz, Clifford. 1973. *The Interpretation of Cultures.* New York: Basic Books.

González, Norma. 2005. "Beyond Culture: The Hybridity of Funds of Knowledge." In *Funds of Knowledge: Theorizing Practices in Households, Communities, and Classrooms,* ed. Norma González, Luis Moll, and Cathy Amanti. Mahwah, NJ: Erlbaum.

González, Norma, Luis Moll, and Cathy Amanti. 2005. *Funds of Knowledge: Theorizing Practices in Households, Communities, and Classrooms.* Mahwah, NJ: Erlbaum.

Hofstede, Geert. 1991. *Cultures and Organizations.* London: Profile Books.

Nieto, Sonia. 2002. *Language, Culture, and Teaching.* Mahwah, NJ: Erlbaum.

Rizvi, Fazal. 2009. "Global Mobility and the Challenges of Educational Research and Policy." *Yearbook of the National Society for the Study of Education* 108 (2): 268–289.

Short, Kathy G. 2009. "Critically Reading the Word and the World: Building Intercultural Understanding Through Literature." *Bookbird* 47 (2): 1–10.

Short, Kathy G., and Carolyn Burke. 1990. *Creating Curriculum*. Portsmouth, NH: Heinemann.

Short, Kathy G., and Jerome Harste, with Carolyn Burke. 1996. *Creating Classrooms for Authors and Inquirers*. Portsmouth, NH: Heinemann.

Sleeter, Christine. 1991. "Multicultural Education and Empowerment." In *Empowerment Through Multicultural Education,* ed. Christine Sleeter. Albany, NY: SUNY Press.

Sleeter, Christine, and Carl Grant. 1987. "An Analysis of Multicultural Education in the United States." *Harvard Educational Review* 57:421–444.

Children's Books Cited

Atinuke. 2011. *The No. 1 Car Spotter: Best in the Village—Maybe in the World!* London: Walker.

Baker, Jeannie. 2010. *Mirror*. Somerville, MA: Candlewick.

Brown, Monica. 2011. *Marisol McDonald Doesn't Match/Marisol McDonald no combina*. Illus. Sara Palacios. New York: Children's Book Press.

Bullard, Lisa. 2003. *Marvelous Me: Inside and Out*. Illus. Brandon Reibeling. Mankato, MN: Picture Window Books.

Park, Linda Sue. 2001. *A Single Shard*. New York: Clarion Books.

Ryan, Pam Muñoz. 2000. *Esperanza Rising*. New York: Scholastic.

Williams, Karen Lynn, and Khadra Mohammed. 2009. *My Name Is Sangoel*. Illus. Catherine Stock. Grand Rapids, MI: Eerdmans.

Chapter 2

The Social Responsibility of the Reader: Becoming Open to Intercultural Perspectives

Holly Johnson

Students often engage with literature across cultural and international boundaries in classrooms as well as in outside reading. When reading global literature, readers are confronted with characters and situations representing cultures outside their own, and they respond to these stories in ways that are unique but also culturally situated. Reading interculturally with an aim of developing more intercultural understanding invites readers to expand their responses by critically examining how those responses are conditioned by their cultural values and experiences. Without such examination, we may limit our compassion for and understanding and recognition of those unlike ourselves.

Authors and publishers are frequently called upon to be responsible for creating authentic and accurate narratives. If these expectations exist on the production side of creating texts, what are the responsibilities of those who consume the texts? St. Pierre (1996) suggests that readers must be responsible for their products just like writers. If this is the case, the tension becomes how readers can be responsible in attempting to understand a narrative from another cultural perspective and whether this responsibility can be taught. What is the connection to reading and social responsibility, especially if and when readers find themselves "outsiders" to the culture highlighted in a text?

This chapter addresses the concept of the social responsibility of readers along with cultural authenticity and accuracy. I also include a discussion on transaction theory (Rosenblatt 1938), an unseen but crucial aspect of reading where intercultural understandings are created. I then suggest ways in which educators might create curriculum to teach young people about the role of the reader when responding to literature across geographies and cultures.

Role of the Reader—Transactional Theory and Codification

Readers respond according to their knowledge, value systems, understandings of a particular literary genre, and experiences of the world—all of which are grounded in cultural ways of being. Most readers do not scrutinize the ways their experiences, knowledge, and culture play an active role in their responses. Readers know what they like, what they don't, what was interesting, and whether they want to read more books in the same genre or from the same author.

Rosenblatt (1978) asserts that readers "transact" with a text on a subconscious or unconscious level, and that their experiences, cultural understandings, and knowledge of the book's content shape the text to connect with their understandings. If readers don't make these connections, they may have difficulty understanding the book. At the same time, what they read has the potential to expand their intercultural understandings as well as themselves as members of particular cultures.

This "conditioning" or shaping highlights what meanings or understandings readers might focus on or give to the text, which is why different readers get different understandings of a story or want to talk about different aspects of a story. This is readers shaping the text. Similarly, the meanings that might be taken from the text either emotionally or cognitively allow for the narrative to work on readers in various ways. This is the text shaping readers' understandings, which typically differ from reader to reader. And because this conditioning takes place on an unconscious level, readers might be unaware of how much the text "spoke" or didn't speak to them unless they examine their responses more closely.

The author's text and the reader "meet" in transaction, and through this transaction readers create their unique understandings of the text, which is influenced by who they are and what they noticed in the author's work (see Figure 2.1). Every reading and understanding of the narrative is filtered through the reader's value system and cultural reality and is what readers respond to when talking about a book. Freire (1970) suggests that by *codifying* (making concrete) their own experiences, or in this case responses to what has been read, readers are better able to reflect critically upon their reading experiences by questioning why they had a particular response. Through questioning their responses, readers gather deeper understanding of the situations within the text as well as their *culturally situated understandings* of the text and its assumptions. It is the reactions against or assimilations of narratives outside readers' particular cultural situations that facilitate their responses to the world and, thus, bring to the forefront how important it is to address reader social responsibility.

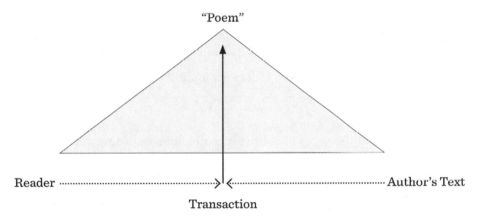

Figure 2.1 Rosenblatt's Transactional Theory

The Social Responsibility of Readers

The concept of reader responsibility has been discussed in relation to literary, pedagogical, or theological studies, and termed in ways that include ethical reading (Attridge 1999), reader responsibility (St. Pierre 1996), and cosmopolitan reading (Jollimore and Barrios 2006). The term *social responsibility* aligns with these concepts, which Booth (1988) interprets as entering into "serious dialogue with the author" about how their value systems as reader and writer conflict or assimilate. He argues that not entering into this invitation is irresponsible (135). The author and reader come together and agree to be answerable to each other in their attempts to work toward communicating and understanding each other in honest and authentic ways. Thus, authors must write authentic and accurate texts, and readers agree to recognize those texts as valid and authentic while sincerely trying to understand the author's perspective and the ways of life and cultures represented within the text.

Reader responsibility is similar to having a discussion with the author's text that draws on other works we have read and our life experiences. Readers who enter into this dialogue bring together their understandings of the world and the world created in a story. I read Arnaldo's (2014) *Arto's Big Move,* a picturebook about a young Canadian boy resisting his family's move to the US Southwest, to a group of second graders from Cincinnati. The book is from Canada, but most details in the story, including the illustrations, would be familiar to many young people in the Southwest region of the United States. But because the second graders were unfamiliar with cactus and the desert landscape, many of them asserted that the book could not be about the United States. The United States—to them—was Cincinnati and what they knew about tree-lined streets, paved sidewalks, and green lawns. It was through talking with them about the larger geography of the United States that they eventually accommodated the possibility that *Arto's Big Move* involved their country, thus expanding their thinking about the text. Without this discussion about geography, however, they would have dismissed the book as lacking relevancy.

Discussions across differences of culture often include opposing viewpoints. There are times readers encounter and respond to characters or situations in a story that have them wondering why the character did such and such, or why the author created a plot that doesn't match what the reader would do or what the reader knows. In talking with others about their responses, readers expand not only a discussion, but a worldview. By expanding their understandings of others and their worldviews about cultures or individual stories outside their experiences, readers become socially responsible. When readers accept this responsibility, they are not necessarily responsible for fully understanding what the author meant, but rather acknowledging that other people and cultures are represented behind and within the story being read. Socially responsible readers understand and try to learn from perspectives and understandings of the world that differ from their own. Furthermore, they acknowledge that the text creates or frames possible worlds with which they may be unfamiliar, but nonetheless exist and hold value.

When considering literature from an intercultural stance, readers frequently encounter differences. Differences are often considered "other." Attridge (1999) wrestles with ethical considerations of relating to "the other" in reading, asserting that "the other in these accounts is primarily an impingement from the outside that challenges assumptions, beliefs, habits, and values and that demands a response" (23). This impingement is not negative, but rather a nudging to recognize alternative ways of thinking and living.

The demand for response suggests that readers don't simply say okay to these differences, but examine those differences and learn from them.

Returning to *Arto's Big Move,* I talked with second graders about how the book was a unique experience that came from an author in a different country and so, although there were similarities they could relate to, there were also differences they could learn from. They noted the different landscapes, clothing styles (one of the characters had a hat that might be considered a traditional Cordova hat), and the ways they might have responded to a "big move." I encouraged them to see the differences and similarities found not only in *Arto's Big Move* but in all the literature from other cultures we read together. As a class they read twenty books from global cultures so we could discuss how the books were similar to and different from what they knew. Attridge (1999) asks readers to rethink their ideas so they can understand what the story might reveal about another culture and those who live within it. Readers can then appreciate and respect the author's creativity and be open to changes in their worldview that might include drastically new ways of thinking and living.

Just as readers are embedded in a cultural context, the stories being read are cultural artifacts that reflect aspects of a larger culture but are still unique and individual. Thus, when engaging with a story that reflects cultural situations outside a reader's experience, readers recognize several things: (1) their transaction with the text will create something new (the poem), and therefore (2) they accept the risk that their thinking might change them in unexpected ways, which (3) is an opening that allows them to respect, learn from, and preserve difference as well as the individuality of the other (Attridge 1999).

Reading responsibly compels readers to respond to the otherness within a literary work and to do justice to that work by affirming it. Furthermore, readers examine their responses more objectively and recognize that those responses are culturally conditioned. Jollimore and Barrios (2006) suggest reading literature as a *cosmopolitan,* which "helps develop the capacity to view oneself objectively, to enter into other people's minds" (364). Rizvi (2009) argues that the focus shifts to citizenship as an orientation, rather than membership to a physical place in the world. This orientation involves a willingness to engage the other, to imaginatively enter into their world, to focus on difference over uniformity, and to value diversity within sameness. The purpose of engaging with literature is to develop a responsibility to the other through narrative imagination, which allows us to perceive the world through their eyes. Readers then engage with a text with a sense of obligation and responsibility to others and to become more conscious and committed to others, rather than to personally connect to the text. Reading for pleasure is no longer the entire focus; instead, reading involves moving beyond self to otherness and responsible engagement to the other. Reader responsibility includes

1. being open to what the text could teach with a spirit of acceptance of difference, and
2. acknowledging one's own limited knowledge of the culture presented in a book, while
3. realizing the book is only one book and cannot represent an entire culture, and
4. being open to learning about the situation presented in the narrative.

By granting such a space to the text and the author behind a novel, readers are, by extension, learning to recognize any cultural stance, including their own, as unique and one of many.

In addition, reader responsibility includes recognizing that a reader's concept of cultural authenticity within a particular text may be conditioned by his or her own cultural understandings of the world, which could limit that reader's understanding and acceptance of that text. This stance thus requires being diligent about the biases a reader brings to the text. While working with middle school students who were reading books outside their cultural locations, I found that many questioned the authenticity of the narratives because the characters' stories did not match their own realities. Asking them to research the culture or to ask someone from the cultural location found in the book showed them that, although their experiences helped them become who they were, reading books from another culture helped them expand their knowledge of themselves and their assumptions about the world as well as learn about that culture. Furthermore, by researching the cultures they were reading about, students recognized their own limited knowledge and how the book helped them learn about the wider world as well as withhold judgment simply because the book was different from their lives.

In a classroom situation, becoming socially responsible readers involves students taking turns deciding on a book for a small group, committing themselves to reading it for what they might learn about others who may be different from themselves, and speaking honestly about how their individual values, not necessarily the book's content or who recommended it, created their responses. This type of process strengthens young people's commitment to reading outside their comfort zones and to the idea of "giving the book a chance" so they can appreciate and look for meaning and connection to all types of stories. Furthermore, they come to recognize that what they find appealing may not satisfy another, or what they dismiss may actually be thoroughly enjoyed by another. Additionally, they expand the classroom's book selections and possibilities.

Students are invited to expand their thinking about literature and the world when they are taught to think about themselves as readers, understand that reader responsibility creates an openness that values texts outside an individual's particular experience, and recognize that what is said to peers could limit their friends' enjoyment of a book. This thoughtfulness can lead other readers to embrace a *socially responsible* stance toward global reading by recognizing that, although transactions are subconscious, as readers, they can still closely examine their responses and the social and cultural values that influenced them.

Cultural Authenticity and Accuracy

Issues of cultural authenticity and the insider/outsider dilemma play a role in socially responsible reading. These issues have been debated and remained controversial for years. The discussion has moved beyond who can write and if a narrative may be culturally authentic only if an insider wrote it to more complex issues about authorial location within the writing of the text and issues of authenticity and representation. A gap continues to exist in the definition of cultural authenticity, which for me includes the concept of accuracy—representing the details, language, and nuances of a culture realistically and, in a sense, right.

Fox and Short (2003) note the complexity of this concept, and determined that it cannot adequately be defined, "although 'you know it when you see it' as an insider reading a book about your own culture" (4). Yoo-Lee et al. (2014) blend definitions and assert that "cultural authenticity comprises not only the absence of stereotypes but also the presence of values consistent with a particular culture and the accuracy of cultural details in text and illustrations" (326). Yokota and Bates (2005) contend that an insider perspective can be gained through experience and study, and that there is no guarantee that being born into a particular cultural group will ensure an insider perspective.

Mikkelsen (1998) emphasizes that although some works by outside authors appear authentic and accurate, the distance between the author and the subject of the work can still fail to examine "the bigger picture—the values, beliefs, and world view"(38) of the group represented, which results in a loss of representational accuracy and authenticity beyond the outsider's perspective on that experience. Fernando (2009) asserts that frequently an outside reader imposes or assimilates the narrative to the reader's under-standings of the world even when written by an insider to the culture, unless the reader takes the responsibility to understand the cultural juxtaposition that exists between the text and the reader. Fernando further suggests that a reader should attempt to perceive the validity and value of experiences and people outside the reader's own understand-ings and allow them to be separate from the reader's concepts of them. He asserts that reading is an encounter with another who is independent of the reader, and so asks readers to consider how they assimilate the author's experience to fit into the reader's worldview rather than seeing the narrative as a distinct and noteworthy situation in its own right. To think about global literature in this way can help readers view those nar-ratives as spaces where authentic portrayals of alternative voices are valid even as they are different.

Socially responsible reading includes understanding the issue of cultural authen-ticity as related to texts written from around the globe. All too often, when stories from another part of the world are misunderstood or refer to events that are shocking or in opposition to the reader's experience, the reader is unable to learn from the reading experience or, worse yet, marginalizes the situation within the text by discounting it. Resistance to these narratives can involve seeing them as too foreign, too incredible, too "other." If such a negative reaction is taken, the danger exists of a more ethnocen-tric world whereby readers invalidate the authenticity of such stories, and the divide between readers and the author's created or lived world becomes greater. By attempting to hold off judgment and open themselves to an alternative perspective or experience, readers gain a broader image of the world while simultaneously learning more about themselves in relation to the wider world.

Being open to the other, and through that process, perhaps gaining a broader view of the world does not mean readers must uncritically accept the author's text or opinion. Instead, reading global literature with a sense of social responsibility requires readers to understand and accept that their responses to literature are culturally situated. Critical-ly questioning the text is an aspect of reader responsibility, but the questioning must go beyond the text and include an interrogation of one's own responses.

Critical stances toward literature often include questioning who has power, what is missing from the text, and who is or is not heard. This critical questioning as part of reader responsibility requires individuals to turn such questions upon themselves. This is especially crucial in light of a reader's ability to assimilate the other or to subsume an author's creative work by overriding it without reflecting upon the value judgments readers bring to the text or noting their lack of knowledge about the culture, language, or experiences presented in a story.

Without readers questioning their own cultural position—and through that process, learning more about the situation presented in a book—they will have difficulty determining the authenticity and accuracy of the story, its worldview, or the representation of characters (Enciso 1994). In addition, readers open themselves up to the danger of relativity whereby the only culturally authentic texts are those within their own understanding, and whatever falls outside their understanding is not real or important. This feeds a cycle of cultural separation and a type of agnosia in which readers fail to recognize the validity of a diverse and wider world.

Strategies for Addressing the Reader's Responsibility

Stories empower, restore or repair dignity, and humanize (Adichie 2009), but it takes sensitive authors *and* readers for such transcendence to occur. Accepting reader responsibility also means questioning traditional criteria of what is literary, what is an appropriate response, and what it means to address issues of power in reading literature from international writers (Grobman 2005). Given these goals, educators have developed strategies for exploring global literature with the openness necessary to hear new voices, examine reader responses, and value often-marginalized narratives.

Researchers and teachers have found ways to challenge students' thinking while engaging them with alternative perspectives. Beginning with a positioning of author, text, context, and reader (Sipe 1999) and then finding "reception moments" (Sullivan 2002) or making space for explicit discussions of reader positioning in literature discussions (Wortham 2001), teachers can help students read cross-culturally with a sense of responsibility. Thein and Sloan's (2012) perspective-taking is also promising for viewing literature from alternative cultures.

Because a reader's social responsibility critically engages a text as an author's unique and authentic creation as well as the reader's responses, instruction based on Lawrence Sipe's (1999) responses to literature can support reading interculturally. Sipe divides responses into four categories: (1) the author of the piece of work, (2) the work itself, (3) the reader, and (4) the context of the experience. And although literary critics examine these elements through a particular literary lens (New Criticism, post-structural, and so on), this model of response provides a starting place for older students' acquisition of literary criticism, as well as an effective way to guide younger children in learning about how authors, readers, texts, and contexts work together to create a reading and response event.

Golden Boy (Sullivan 2013) is an adventure story fraught with danger combined with elements of compassion and acceptance. Sipe's (1999) model provides a way into this novel, given its location outside their cultural experience, so that readers do not dismiss it as irrelevant or too incredible to believe. Adolescents miss an authentic read if they do not take the time (and responsibility) to learn about how others are treated in the world. *Golden Boy* takes place in Tanzania, where people with albinism are seen as lucky or frightening. If seen as lucky, albinos can be killed in the smaller villages to bring power to traditional medicines or good luck to the hunt. Habo is such a boy, and must eventually escape to the larger city of Dar es Salaam where the biases and the superstitions about albinos in other parts of his nation are not so prominent.

By addressing each area of response through classroom discussion, young people learn about the traditional practices connected to albinism in Tanzania, the danger Habo faces, the condition of albinism, their own responses and treatment of those with albinism, why the author wrote this story, and the piece of literature itself. Additional strategies as listed in Figure 2.2 would further deepen students' responses, with each category containing strategies for developing their understandings of a reader's social responsibility.

AUTHOR	TEXTS

1. Questioning of the Author's Intention
 	
2. Author's Cultural Location
 	
3. Author's Ideology/Stance:
 	
  • Politics of advocacy—promotion of particular sociocultural practices that reflect differing perspectives and values
 	
  • Politics of assent—representation of societal norms without reflection on issues of power
 	
  • Politics of attack—denouncing particular sociocultural practices
	1. Intertextuality
	
	2. Genre Studies
	
	3. Readerly/Writerly Texts
	
	  • Readerly allows for passive assimilation of content
	
	  • Writerly requires inference to construct deeper meaning
	
	4. Visual Literacy within a picturebook
	
	5. Text as Mirror or Window:
	
	  • Reflection of one's own culture and in what ways there are matches/mismatches with text.
	
	  • Affordances into another culture and what is needed to better understand that culture.

READERS	CONTEXT

1. Individual Reader Responses
2. Reader Resistance and Cultural Relevance
  • How readers accept or reject a book's content based on their values and beliefs
3. Reader Pleasure:
  • Pleasure in seeing one's self as well as one's culture in a text
  • Pleasure in being surprised, shaken, mystified, or delighted by having our assumptions turned upside down
	1. Nested context of an author's text and a reader's response
	2. Environment in which a text is read
	3. Expectations and agenda reader brings to the text (reading for information, pleasure, school, own knowledge, a combination)
	4. External reasons for reading (class assignment) and expectations for a particular report of response
	5. Cultural situatedness of the reader and the text:
	  • What is valued as a good book by culture
	  • Gendered responses
	  • How a narrative is written may differ from culture to culture
	  • The role of popular culture and the reception of the text socially

Figure 2.2 Sipe's (1999) Model of Areas for Response

Sullivan's (2002) strategy of "reception moments" involves periods of time or moments in which a text is "received" and the way in which it is received, thus embracing the notion that any meaning making with a literary text involves a dynamic and collaborative process between author, reader, culture, and language. By helping students understand the interrelationship of language, culture, and history that produced a text, teachers also help them understand how those elements influence readers' responses to and reception of texts. With reception moments, teachers can begin discussions of a piece of global literature by asking students about their responses to the text. This general discussion contextualizes the book and allows students to discuss how responses and "receptions" differ across readers. From this overview, a more specific mini-lesson on the cultural aspects of the text and (perhaps) the literary lens through which the teacher wants to examine the text can be introduced. This is followed by a discussion of how readers and texts are historically and socially embedded, which includes a discussion of how that positioning influences the way readers—and a society—perceive and interpret the text, including the situations and values represented in it.

In *Lost Girl Found* (Bassoff and DeLuca 2014), many adolescents do not understand Poni's desire for an education in war-torn Sudan or her ability to leave her dying mother to catch a plane that is leaving Sudan. Some readers see Poni as callous and self-absorbed rather than understanding that by leaving, Poni has a chance to save her own life and eventually the life of her country. By discussing education as privilege versus right, students garner a better idea of Poni's actions, allowing teachers to address how an interpretation of a text is influenced by societal norms and values and how an individual's cultural location (race/ethnicity, socioeconomics, age, gender, and life experiences) as well as past literary experiences condition the transaction between an individual and any piece of literature. This influence of cultural location and societal norms is especially influential with stories that reside outside a reader's particular culture. Through the process of using "reception moments," teachers ask students to think about how the text has been received throughout its history, but this is also an excellent way to discuss how, as readers interested in becoming socially responsible, we are receptive to particular texts and why, and how that receptivity or openness can shift over time.

As is often the case with global literature, stories that reside outside a reader's particular culture can cause students and teachers to take political and ethical positions in juxtaposition to particular groups and issues from the larger society (Wortham 2001). Recognizing this positioning, which is often unconscious but made explicit by addressing the language readers use in respect to characters or situations within the story, helps readers examine their values and openness to alternative realities and cultural ways of being. In addition, noting that readers' language often positions characters with qualities or intentions that may or may not hold true under scrutiny is equally valuable. Thus, addressing how students discussed Poni and other characters in the book is an instance of using reception moments.

Jordan (1997) finds that students who do not understand the culture reflected in a book often think they understand, but what they have done is replace the authentic voice from that culture with their own. Examining the way they talk about stories, including the language they use, and perhaps even the miscues they employ when reading aloud or interpreting passages from a text, gives readers insights into their own thinking about the other. In examining a picturebook about the slave trade with a colleague, I noticed she miscued when she read aloud a particular passage. The text noted that Africans were "captured" and then delivered to ships for transport to the Americas. My colleague used the word *kidnapped* rather than *captured*. In discussing this miscue, we agreed that *captured* is a word often used with animals, whereas *kidnapped* is always used with people. Through this miscue, we were able to see an aspect of my colleague's values in respect to the slave trade and the human beings enslaved. Examining the language used in respect to the characters and situations found in a book can give insight into readers' thinking.

This discussion fits within Wortham's (2001) assertion that classroom discussions are simultaneous and interconnected activities that include responses to and interpretations of the text along with the political and ethical positions adopted in relation to those responses and interpretations. Perspective-taking asks students to consider alternative perspectives so they can explore the values connected to those perspectives (Thein and Sloan 2012). Perspective-taking includes role-playing a particular character or writing from that character's point of view. Asking students to write alternative texts to the story that highlight views other than those that students constructed through their initial readings is another way of perspective-taking. Shyam's (2014) visual memoir, *The London Jungle Book,* is an excellent example of how cultural understandings create a lens or overlay from which individuals see the world. Shyam discusses his first trip to London from his central village in India. An artist of the Gond tradition, he illustrates how he perceived London. Asking students to consider both Shyam's perception of London and Rudyard Kipling's perceptions of India invites them to see how perceptions work.

Critical questioning allows students to more closely examine the values within a narrative that might be counter to those of a reader or unfamiliar to a reader. Opportunities for students to use a critical stance that questions positions of power within the text and who is silenced or privileged also facilitates perspective-taking. In addition to perspective-taking of another, learning to distance themselves from their own values and biases by naming them allows students to examine their particular perspectives. Creating such distance is difficult, but with practice and discussions of how everyone holds a perspective that is culturally embedded (think about the fish not knowing it lives in water), students can see their unique stance on the texts they read, as well as have a better sense of the uniqueness of the text and the singular perspective from which the author created the text. Such perspective-taking disrupts stereotyping and opens spaces where readers come to recognize their common humanity with those who may inhabit very different cultural locations.

Throughout perspective-taking, students are encouraged to examine their first responses while also considering the multiple and perhaps conflicting views of their responses in relation to others, including critics and book reviewers. Students are encouraged to own their responses, creating more ethical and responsible stances toward global texts and allowing them to reexamine how their initial responses were conditioned by cultural differences.

Each of these strategies creates opportunities for students to remain open to what a story can teach along with the potential for developing a deeper acceptance of difference. In a sense readers have the ability to take ownership and responsibility for their responses to the text (Addridge 1999). In addition, students understand their own limited knowledge of a culture and remember that one story cannot represent an entire culture, because there is always complexity, regardless of the situation presented in a narrative. That complexity extends to the culture and people represented in the story, but this attention to complexity needs to be taught. As these strategies are used with students or within book group discussions, teachers have the opportunity to discuss how our cultural upbringings are one of many, and thus a reading stance that embraces social responsibility means being critically observant of the cultural biases all readers bring to all texts.

Remembering the author (and illustrators) behind each text, and when possible communicating with them or someone from the culture represented, can give insight into the content and situations—or artistic styles—within the book. Working with the same group of second graders, I read *Hope Is a Girl Selling Fruit* (Das 2014), a picturebook with illustrations that include a traditional art form from the author/artist's culture. It is a beautiful story from north India about a young girl garnering hope from seeing another girl who owns her own fruit cart and gains financial freedom. Without understanding the culture from which this text comes, second graders were ready to dismiss the text as incongruous with their own experiences. Discussion about the illustrations, however, helped them expand their knowledge about the world of art and India. It also had them thinking about how powerful it feels to know you can do something for yourself. For older readers, pointing out how beautifully the text and illustrations come together creates a powerful example of art and literature as empowerment as well as raises issues of gender.

By taking the time to learn about art forms and the sociohistorical and political contexts of a book, readers appreciate the text as well as gain new perspectives on the world. Through access to a wide variety of sources via the Internet, students enrich their understandings about a particular story or topic of interest. They then know a bit more about the text, the culture in which it was produced, and how it enhances their knowledge of the world.

Final Reflections

Socially responsible reading is a stance that is especially useful with global literature and for developing intercultural understanding. Readers are asked to connect with the text as a culturally authentic piece of literature that may not adhere to their understandings of the world. Readers are also asked to hold off embracing a text or its characters to appreciate and attempt to understand its unique values and differences from the reader's own experiences. Both stances of holding off and connecting are needed. Readers need to recognize their own current position as a member of a set of cultural groups and recognize that all cultures are parallel—distinct, diverse, and fully equal—to one another (Hamilton 1993). Holding on to this concept of parallel cultures allows readers to approach literature from another culture with the willingness to "give the book a chance"—a chance to see what can be learned, what is unique and distinctive, and what value and values that story holds for members of a particular culture. And although some cultures may hold dominant positions within the world or community, such positioning does not allow readers to invalidate or diminish the stories from other cultural groups.

Global literature can expand students' thinking, their ideas of the world, their sense of self, and their recognition of those with whom they share the planet. Through this expansive thinking—a responsibility to take seriously the literature of others—readers can gain a type of paradise of knowing and accepting one another across cultural situations. A social responsibility of reading embraces authentic narratives from every culture as stories to honor that deserve readers' sincere attention and intention for learning.

Recommended Books That Invite Global Perspectives

Arnaldo, Monica. 2014. *Arto's Big Move*. Toronto, ON: Owlkids.
Arto, a young Canadian boy, resists his family's move to the US Southwest for a year so his parents can work at a local university. Eventually, Arto's resistance is tempered by a new friend, who has also moved to the Southwest.

Bassoff, Leah, and Laura DeLuca. 2014. *Lost Girl Found.* **Toronto, ON: Groundwood.**

In her village in Sudan, Poni had decided that staying in school is the most important decision she'll ever make. But then war comes, and Poni is faced with heartbreaking decisions about her future, one of which is to flee her village in order to survive.

Das, Amrita. 2014. *Hope Is a Girl Selling Fruit.* **London: Tara Books.**

Through stunning Mithila folk art, the author re-creates a childhood memory of a train journey. She discovers the possibility of personal and financial freedom for poor girls through the ordinary sight of a girl owning her own cart from which to sell fruit near the train station in India.

Shyam, Bhajju. 2014. *The London Jungle Book.* **London: Tara Books.**

The author/artist uses his distinctive style to show how humans connect and accommodate differing cultures. Through an overlay of London, the city is transformed into a jungle inhabited by a host of wondrous creatures that reflect his own cultural understanding as a visitor from India.

Sullivan, Tara. 2013. *Golden Boy.* **New York: G. P. Putnam's Sons.**

Living with albinism in a small village in Tanzania, Habo becomes a target for hunters and traditional medicine men, who believe killing him will bring them luck. Habo sets out to Dar es Salaam to find a better way of living without biases against his skin color.

References

Adichie, Chimamanda. 2009. "The Danger of a Single Story." TED Talk. http://www.ted.com/talks/chimamanda_adichie_the_danger_of_a_single_story/.

Attridge, Derek. 1999. "Innovation, Literature, Ethics: Relating to the Other." *PMLA* 114 (1): 20–31.

Booth, Wayne. 1988. *The Company We Keep: An Ethics of Fiction.* Berkeley: University of California Press.

Cocks, Neil. 2004. "The Implied Reader. Response and Responsibility." In *Children's Literature: New Approaches*, ed. Karin Lesnick-Oberstein, 93–117. New York: Palgrave.

Enciso, Patricia. 1994. "Cultural Identity and Response to Literature: Running Lessons from *Maniac Magee.*" *Language Arts* 71 (7): 524–533.

Fernando, Jeremy. 2009. *Reading Blindly: Literature, Otherness, and the Possibility of an Ethical Reading.* London: Cambria.

Fox, Dana, and Kathy G. Short, eds. 2003. *Stories Matter: The Complexity of Cultural Authenticity in Children's Literature.* Urbana, IL: National Council of Teachers of English.

Freire, Paulo. 1970. *Pedagogy of the Oppressed.* New York: Continuum.

Grobman, Laurie. 2005. "Mediating Politics and Aesthetics in Multiethnic Literary Pedagogy." *MELUS* 30 (2): 139–155.

Hamilton, Virginia. 1993. "Everything of Value: Moral Realism in the Literature for Children." May Hill Arbuthnot Lecture. Virginia Center for the Book, Richmond, VA.

Harris, Violet J. 2003. "The Complexity of Debates About Multicultural Literature." In *Stories Matter: The Complexity of Cultural Authenticity in Children's Literature*, ed. Dana Fox and Kathy G. Short, 116–134. Urbana, IL: National Council of Teachers of English.

Hull, Glynda, Amy Stornaiuolo, and Laura Sterponi. 2013. "Imagined Readers and Hospitable Texts: Global Youth Connect Online." In *Theoretical Models and Processes of Reading,* ed. Donna Alvermann, Norman Unrau, and Robert Ruddell, 1208–1240. Newark, DE: International Reading Association.

Jollimore, Troy, and Sharon Barrios. 2006. "Creating Cosmopolitans: The Case for Literature." *Studies in the Philosophy of Education* 25:363–383.

Jordan, Sarah. 1997. "Student Responses to Culturally Diverse Texts." In *Beyond the Cultural Tours: Studies in Teaching and Learning with Culturally Diverse Texts*, ed. Gladys Cruz, Sarah Jordan, José Meléndez, Steven Ostrowski, and Alan C. Purves, 9–34. Mahwah, NJ: Erlbaum.

Larrick, Nancy. 1965. "The All-White World of Children's Books." *Saturday Review* 48:63–65.

Mikkelsen, Nina. 1998. "Insiders, Outsiders, and the Question of Authenticity: Who Shall Write for African American Children?" *African American Review* 32 (1): 33–49.

Rizvi, Fazal. 2009. "Global Mobility and the Challenges of Educational Research and Policy." *Yearbook of the National Society for the Study of Education* 108 (2): 268–289.

Rosenblatt, Louise. 1938. *Literature as Exploration*. New York: Modern Language Association.

———. 1978. *The Reader, the Text, the Poem*. Carbondale, IL: Southern Illinois University Press.

Sipe, Lawrence. 1999. "Children's Response to Literature: Author, Text, Reader, Context." *Theory into Practice* 38 (3): 120–129.

St. Pierre, Elizabeth. 1996. "The Responsibilities of Readers: Towards an Ethics of Responses." *Qualitative Sociology* 19 (4): 533–537.

Sullivan, Patrick. 2002. "'Reception Moments': Modern Literary Theory, and the Teaching of Literature." *Journal of Adolescent & Adult Literacy* 45 (7): 568–577.

Taxel, Joel. 2002. "Children's Literature at the Turn of the Century: Toward a Political Economy of the Publishing Industry." *Research in the Teaching of English* 37 (2): 145–197.

Thein, Amanda, and DeAnn Sloan. 2012. "Towards an Ethical Approach to Perspective-Taking and the Teaching of Multicultural Texts." *Changing English: Studies in Culture and Education* 19 (3): 313–324.

Wortham, Stanton. 2001. "Teachers and Students as Novelists: Ethical Positioning in Literature Discussions." *Journal of Adolescent & Adult Literacy* 45 (2): 126–137.

Yokota, Junko, and Ann Bates. 2005. "Asian American Literature: Voices and Images of Authenticity." In *Exploring Culturally Diverse Literature for Children and Adolescents: Learning to Listen in New Ways*, ed. Darwin Henderson and Jill May, 323–335. Boston: Pearson

Yoo-Lee, EunYoung, Lauren Fowler, Denice Adkins, Kyung-Sun Kim, and Halima Davis. 2014. "Evaluating Cultural Authenticity in Multicultural Picture Books: A Collaborative Analysis for Diversity Education." *The Library Quarterly* 84 (3): 324–347.

Children's Books Cited

Arnaldo, Monica. 2014. *Arto's Big Move*. Toronto, ON: Owlkids.

Bassoff, Leah, and Laura DeLuca. 2014. *Lost Girl Found*. Toronto, ON: Groundwood.

Das, Amrita. 2014. *Hope Is a Girl Selling Fruit*. London: Tara Books.

Shyam, Bhajju. 2014. *The London Jungle Book*. London: Tara Books.

Sullivan, Tara. 2013. *Golden Boy*. New York: G. P. Putnam's Sons.

PART 2

Personal Cultural
Identities

Chapter 3

Young Children's Explorations of Their Cultural Identities

Ray Martens and Prisca Martens with Michelle Hassay Doyle, Jenna Loomis, Laura Fuhrman, Elizabeth Soper, Robbie Stout, and Christie Furnari

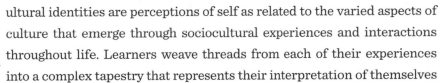

Cultural identities are perceptions of self as related to the varied aspects of culture that emerge through sociocultural experiences and interactions throughout life. Learners weave threads from each of their experiences into a complex tapestry that represents their interpretation of themselves in relationship to their world, based on what they have experienced as well as the experiences they imagine in the future (Sumara 1996). Cultural identities are never simple or fixed. They are multifaceted and complex, changing to reflect the ebb and flow of new experiences in new contexts. With cultural identities that include assuredness, openness to change, and willingness to accept and learn from others, learners are prepared to be valuable and resourceful citizens of their global world (Banks 2011; Snowball 2009).

Global literature provides rich opportunities for children to explore and develop their cultural identities. Stories are how humans make sense of their lives and the world (Rosen 1985; Short 2012). As children read stories, they live through new experiences. Their unique "personality traits, memories of past events, present needs and preoccupations, particular mood of the moment, and particular physical condition" (Rosenblatt 1978, 30) determine their responses to the story and influence their cultural identities. Stories help children understand who they are, their place in our intercultural and global world, and their connections to others (Bishop 1990).

Cultural identities are at the core of creating a curriculum that is intercultural, and in this chapter we share how we helped prekindergarten, kindergarten, and first-grade children explore their cultural identities from a critical stance. Global literature encouraged children to go beyond superficial aspects (i.e., likes/dislikes) of who they are to critically consider influences on their identities (i.e., family, culture, gender, race, class). Through experiences with global literature, young children developed deeper understandings of themselves as cultural beings.

Learning and making meaning through art is an important part of our work. Although schools and society value language/linguistics as the central mode of communication, modes such as art, music, and drama are equally valid (Kress and Jewitt 2008). We emphasize art as a means of representing meaning and help children learn the language of art so they can read and communicate meanings through art. When reading picturebooks, we talk about the ways the artist represents meaning through the use of color, line, shapes, media, and so on, and children think about how to represent their own meanings in art.

Setting the Context for Our Work

We have been a literacy community with six public school teachers in two schools in the Baltimore, Maryland, metropolitan area for several years (Martens 2011, 2013a, 2013b). One school is close to the city, and the other is in a more rural area.

The Baltimore metropolitan area school:

- Five teachers: Christie Furnari taught prekindergarten, Liz (Elizabeth) Soper and Robbie Stout kindergarten, and Laura Fuhrman and Michelle Doyle first grade.
- Student population: 38 percent European American, 27 percent African American, 16 percent Hispanic/Latino, 14 percent Asian; 5 percent two or more races; 41 percent free/reduced meals

The rural school (twenty miles away):

- One teacher: Jenna Loomis taught first grade.
- Student population: 88 percent European American, 2 percent African American, 4 percent Hispanic/Latino, 2 percent Asian; 4 percent two or more races; 11 percent free/reduced meals

We are teacher educators in literacy (Prisca) and art education (Ray) at a nearby university and facilitate our group. As a literacy community we focus our work on global literature and art (i.e., Martens, Martens, Doyle, Loomis, and Aghalarov 2012/2013, 2013; Martens, Martens, Doyle, and Loomis 2013; Martens et al. 2015).

We meet monthly as a community to discuss readings on global literature, share happenings in classrooms, examine children's writings and art, and brainstorm possible engagements around global literature, including art concepts to explore. As facilitators, our role is to locate global literature and other materials to meet teachers' needs. We also visit classrooms to read and discuss literature and art with children.

Teachers support children in critically exploring their personal cultural identities by examining some of the intricate interwoven threads that make them each special. Though the children are young, developing their awareness of these complexities over time helps them consider and appreciate who they are in the world. We begin with children's explorations of their families, since families are central to the individual identities of young children. Traditions, religious beliefs, family histories, and experiences influence children's values and perspectives of themselves, each other, and the world.

Exploring Cultural Identities

The cultural identity text set we created included fiction and nonfiction global literature (primarily picturebooks, since we worked with young children) that invited children to think about themselves as cultural beings. Bates (2000) contends that children learn from the inside out, and we selected books for our text set that helped children consider what made them unique as well as the commonalities they shared with others. To help children understand the complexities and reflect on the multifaceted aspects of their personal identities, we included books related to such themes as family, unique individualities, feelings and emotions, and decision making. A sampling of the books in the text set along with aspects of art we highlight is found in Figure 3.1. Additional books are included in our discussion of the following cultural identity themes.

Learning About Families

To begin our exploration of families we surveyed parents to learn aspects of their cultural backgrounds, including their country/countries of origin, where their child was born, languages they spoke at home, holidays they celebrated, how and why the child received his or her name, and what the name meant. The surveys were rich with information. We learned that families originated in places like Mongolia, Ireland, Jamaica, and Saudi Arabia and spoke languages such as Tagalog (Filipino), Korean, Napali, and Talugu.

TITLE (AUTHOR/DATE) (CULTURAL SETTING) (TEXT SET THEME)	CONNECTION TO IDENTITY	ART
You Be Me, I'll Be You (Mandelbaum 1990) (France) (Family/Biracial)	Family/Biracial; accept and be proud of who you are; don't judge yourself or others by outer appearances.	• Contrasts (value, color, shape, texture) parallel contrasts in family members • Emotions shown through body positioning, facial expressions
Guji Guji (Chen 2004) (Taiwan) (Family/Adoption)	Family/Adoption; be yourself; stand up for what you believe.	• Warm colors/rounded shapes for Guji Guji • Cool colors/pointed shapes for the mean crocodiles • Movement shown with repeated lines and shapes
Unique Monique (Rousaki 2003) (Greece) (Unique Individualities)	Be proud of who you are and let your individuality shine.	• Red is Monique's unique color; symbolizes "stop," love • Facial features exaggerated to emphasize uniqueness • Confidence shown through body language, facial expressions
Suki's Kimono (Chieri Uegaki 2005) (Japan/Canada) (Unique Individualities)	Be yourself despite what others think, and stand up for what you believe.	• Primary colors, emphasis on red (cultural) • Movement shown with repeated lines, shapes • Confidence shown through body language, facial features
Sam and the Lucky Money (Chinn 1997) (Chinese Americans) (Making Decisions)	Be confident in who you are; put others first.	• Depth shown through saturated colors and detailed painting in the foreground and more neutral colors and less detail in the background • Red, as primary color in China, is highlighted in the art.
Four Feet, Two Sandals (Williams and Mohammed 2007) (Pakistan) (Making Decisions)	Be a friend who shares; put others first.	• Muted earth tones for camp parallel the dullness of the girls' lives. • Lack of detail reflects simple life in a refugee camp. • Brightly colored clothing highlights girls' humanness and their hope

Figure 3.1 **A Sampling of the Books in the Cultural Identity Text Set**

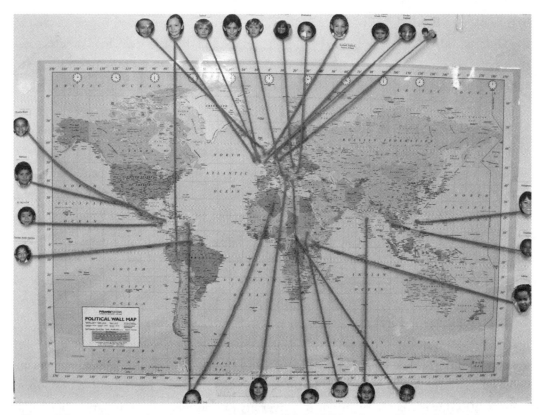

Figure 3.2 World Map Showing Countries from Which Children's Families Originated

Teachers plotted the countries of origin on a world map (approximately 2 by 3 feet) that remained in the classrooms all year. The map was laminated and mounted on foam core so that it was easily accessible for close-up work and could be easily moved, depending on the teaching situation. Children's photographs were placed around the outer border of the map, with yarn connecting each photo to that child's country of origin using multiple strings when needed (see Figure 3.2). Although conceptually it was difficult for some children to understand that their ancestors lived in another country, conversations helped them begin to comprehend, appreciate the cultural histories of their families, and develop global awareness.

Reading global literature also facilitated this developing understanding for children. *My Name Is Sangoel* (Williams and Mohammed 2009) is a favorite book. In the story, Sangoel moves from Sudan to the United States because of a war. Plotting where Sangoel lived before moving helped children conceptualize that their families once lived in different cultures globally and, because of hardships and/or opportunities, moved to the United States. The maps helped children understand that their world is much larger than what they see each day in their communities, including where they live, play, go to school, and shop with their parents. They took pride in putting up their piece of yarn and naming their country.

First-grade teachers highlighted families through a focus on traditions in different fall and winter celebrations, including Diwali, Las Posadas, Christmas, Hanukkah, and Kwanza. They sent large baggies with a note to parents, asking about family and cultural traditions. Parents responded positively and returned the baggies filled with pictures of food, clothing, festivities, and so on. Some children also brought artifacts. Leela brought items and background information for the Indian celebration Diwali, and Malick brought in his prayer rug from Senegal. Reading and discussing books like *Hanukkah!* (Schotter 1990), *Diwali* (Gardeski 2001), *Bringing in the New Year* (Lin 2008), and *Celebrate! Connections Among Cultures* (Reynolds 2006) provided contextualizing information that deepened children's understandings and appreciation of family cultural traditions and celebrations.

In prekindergarten, Christie Furnari (2013b) read and discussed books such as *Families* (Easterling 2007*), Homes* (Mayer 2007), and *Loving* (Morris 1990) to help students think about families. *You and Me Together: Moms, Dads, and Kids Around the World* (Kerley 2005) was read to highlight the diversity of families. This nonfiction book displays color photos with brief phrase descriptions of parents and children around the world involved in everyday activities. The book generated lots of conversations about families that helped children see the unique aspects of their own and others' families. In first grade, when Michelle Doyle (2011) engaged her class in a discussion related to one of the photographs, Brendan commented, "My mom takes care of the family, and my dad makes the money" to which Tate quickly responded, "That's *not* how it is in my family!" Other discussions related to such aspects as families working together, eating different foods, wearing different clothes and jewelry, and different religious customs. Through books like this, children understood that families are unique in how members relate to each other and the roles they take on in the family.

In kindergarten, after Liz Soper (2013) read this book, Charlotte suggested, "Why don't we make a book like that about us?" Liz couldn't resist and invited parents to send a photograph that showed their child doing something with a family member or members. She compiled the photographs into a class book that included the families' origins and children's comments about the photographs. Deyana's (Iran) picture showed her on equipment at gymnastics, and she said, "I am trying to practice and not give up." The children loved seeing themselves and their classmates and the different ways families are special as Liz read and reread their book. (Read the book at http://wowlit.org/wp-content/media/PreK-K_4_PowerPoint.pdf.)

Teachers invited children to respond to literature in different ways to explore children's understandings and how they were connecting to books. Children drew and wrote stories about their families and created heart maps. Their heart maps were large heart shapes the children filled and surrounded with images and writing about what they loved and considered special about their families (Doyle 2011). These maps included names of family members, places their families went (such as the beach or amusement park), things they did together (for example, play board games or sports, watch television), favorite foods they ate (for example, pizza, chicken), and religious places they attended together (such as a church, synagogue, or temple). On his heart map Brendan included things his family did together, such as vacation, taking care of the pets, and eating. Around the outside he wrote, "I love my dad. I love my mom. I love Lexi [sister]."

Discovering Unique Individualities

Our cultural identity text set also included books that helped children appreciate how unique they were as individuals. We wanted them to know that their physical features, ways of thinking and learning, and ideas were unique to them, and to celebrate their own and others' distinctive qualities.

Christie Furnari (2013a) read books such as *I Like Me!* (Carlson 2009), *Whoever You Are* (Fox 2006), and *Spoon* (Rosenthal 2009) to help prekindergarten children know and appreciate themselves. In *Marvelous Me* (Bullard 2003), young Alex is like other children in some ways (imaginative, sometimes sad, sometimes happy) but in other ways he is special and unique (for example, his smile, his hug). Children created large faces of themselves that were attached to a lunch bag to create Marvelous Me bags. They took the bags home to fill with marvelous things about themselves that they shared with their classmates. Christie also had children draw how they were marvelous and interviewed them about their drawings. Children's drawings and verbal responses in the interview helped Christie see the differing ways in which they thought they were marvelous. Carmelita, a second language learner, responded with such things as "I like to play my bicycle in my house. I like to play with my jump rope in my house. I like to eat too much fruit."

In first grade, teachers read *Marisol McDonald Doesn't Match,* written by Monica

Brown (2011) and illustrated by Sara Palacios, to invite children to think about what made them special. Marisol, a biracial girl, is seen by others as a mismatch: she has red hair and brown skin, likes to wear polka dots and stripes, and eats peanut butter and jelly burritos. Though Marisol likes who she is, one day she decides to try to "match" and please everyone else. By the end of the day, she realizes she needs and wants to be her unique self and announces to her family, "My name is Marisol McDonald and I don't match because . . . I don't want to!" Palacios uses mixed media for the art (acrylics, cutout/glued-on and colored newspaper shapes), which create a unique cohesive story that "matches" Marisol's uniqueness.

Michelle read the story and helped the children look closely at the art. They noticed the newspaper shapes and textures, how Palacios filled each page with color, and that the colorful and cheerful art was like Marisol. When looking at the page showing Marisol sitting at the table with her family, Leslie commented how Marisol's family was like Anna's family in *You Be Me, I'll Be You* (Mandelbaum 1990) because her parents have different skin tones. Tyra connected Marisol to Maya in *Each Kindness* (Woodson 2012) "because she dressed differently" from others. Throughout the reading, Michelle helped children think about the ways in which Marisol was unique and special and the ways Palacios created unique pictures.

After the reading, Michelle encouraged children to think about what made them "one of a kind." She provided a range of materials, including magazine clippings, newspaper, and other paper, and invited them to create a picture that highlighted something special and unique about them. Mateo drew his mom, dad, and himself feeling very happy. He cut and glued a sun, a heart to represent the love his family shares, and his mother's purple shirt to show that she's a fan of the Baltimore Ravens. He wrote, "My name in Spanish is Mateo. I am unique because my name is popular and I like to play. Walking my black Lab and Race for Education and school are fun." Marcy drew herself doing a hula dance and cut and glued two sea creatures and a starfish into her picture. She wrote, "My name is Marcy. I'm unique because nobody [in my class] has done a hula dance before. I can read a nine chapter Blue Blue [leveled book] book and I do the best ballet ever."

Examining Feelings and Emotions

Identity includes understanding one's personal feelings and emotions and what influences them, and one's way of responding. Over time, teachers read books and discussed the range of emotions children feel, including anger, loneliness, pride, and confidence.

Exploring Anger

One picturebook that addresses emotions, especially anger, is *The Day Leo Said I Hate You!* written by Robbie Harris (2008) and illustrated by Molly Bang. Leo's anger escalates when his mother continually responds with "no" to his actions one day. Finally, he screams, "I HATE YOU!" to her. Mother and Leo talk and reestablish their relationship.

Bang's use of color and facial expressions shows the range of emotions in the book. When Leo yells, "I HATE YOU!" his face is red, his hair is spiked in pointed triangles, his eyebrows and eyes show deep anger, his mouth is large, and his head is enormous compared with his small body. The words *I HATE YOU* are in oversized print, bursting from his mouth with bright red and yellow lines running through each letter. Lines in the background are sharp to convey anger. Other emotions, such as sadness, happiness, and regret, are shown in illustrations, even in Leo's toy animals. All of these features in Bang's illustrations helped children understand how an artist can express anger.

Figure 3.3 Teddy's Picture of Himself Feeling Angry

After talking about the story and art, children drew a picture in Molly Bang's style about something that makes them angry and wrote about it. Teddy's drawing in Figure 3.3 shows how he made his face red, enlarged his head and drew his body smaller, used diagonal lines for his eyebrows so he looked angry, and gave himself spiky hair and pointed teeth. He also made fire in the speech bubble coming from his mouth. Teddy wrote, "I am mad because my brother took my books and toys." The book generated lots of discussion, opening opportunities to talk about relationships with family and friends, emotions in different situations, and appropriate ways of responding to others. As the discussion continued, children explored the complexities of emotions and the multiple ways in which they can respond to a particular event, especially when angry.

Exploring Loneliness and Feeling Left Out

Teachers also read books that helped children think about times they felt alone and ignored. *The Invisible Boy,* written by Trudy Ludwig (2013) and illustrated by Patrice Barton, is the story of young Brian, who feels invisible at school. No one talks to him or invites him to play, so he keeps to himself and draws. Then Justin joins their class. When children laugh at Justin for eating his Korean lunch with chopsticks, Brian and Justin become friends. Barton highlights Brian's feeling of invisibility on the beginning pages of the story by drawing Brian in pencil and everything else in color. As Justin and Brian become friends, Brian gradually gains color until he is drawn in full color at the end. Through the contrast of pencil and color, Barton powerfully conveys feelings of loneliness and acceptance, inviting children to reflect on times they've felt invisible and longed to be with friends.

After discussing the story, first graders drew and wrote about a time they felt invisible, contrasting color and pencil as Barton did. We weren't sure if they would be able to relate to feeling "invisible," but they had no problems doing so. Carmen's picture (see Figure 3.4) recounts the time she invited her friend Emily over to play but Carmen's older sister Laura took Emily so the two of them could play without Carmen. Carmen drew herself small and in pencil in the background, calling "Emily." Emily and Laura are drawn in center front and in color, along with the rest of the picture. Emily is responding, "No" to Carmen while Laura says, "She's mine." Carmen's pain of feeling "invisible" in this incident is evident. Books like this invited children to reflect on their feelings, on how their actions affect others, and ultimately on their identity as a friend.

Figure 3.4 Carmen's Picture of Her Feeling Invisible

Exploring Confidence and Pride

Sebastian's Roller Skates, written by Joan de Deu Prats (2005) and illustrated by Francesc Rovira, invites children to think about times they've been afraid to try something new but how proud and confident they felt when they took the risk and accomplished something successfully. Young, shy Sebastian doesn't speak much, even though he has a lot to say. One day he finds a pair of roller skates in the park and decides to try them on. He falls down, but over the next several days, he continues to try to skate until he is successful. Sebastian uses the courage he gains from learning to skate to confidently share his thoughts with those around him, including Ester, whom he likes but was too shy to speak to before. Rovira's art shows Sebastian's growing confidence. On the beginning pages, when Sebastian is shy, the large thought bubbles are created with a collage of black-and-white newspaper scraps. Once he gains confidence, Sebastian's speech bubbles are a bright collage of colors as he shares all he has to say.

Discussions of taking risks to overcome fears included how Rovira represented those meanings in the art and how his collages enhanced understandings of Sebastian's fears and eventual pride in his accomplishment and the joy that came with it. Children reflected on times they were nervous or afraid to do something or times they wanted to learn something but hadn't yet. They created collages, following Rovira's style.

Figure 3.5 **Ryan's Collages Showing His Confidence and Pride in Riding His Bike**

First grader Ryan made two collages ("Then" and "Now") about learning to ride his bike (see Figure 3.5). On the left ("Then") when he was sad because he couldn't ride, his speech bubble is in newspaper. On the right ("Now") his speech bubble is in bright colors because he can ride. Ryan wrote, "One day I got a new bike. I tried to ride it. I fell off. Mom told me how to ride my bike. It took a long, long time! In a couple weeks I learned how to ride my bike! I was so happy! The End."

Clarisse, a first grader, created a collage showing her hope to do figure eights when ice skating, using bright pink, blue, green, orange, and yellow hearts and other shapes. Clarisse wrote, "I am ice skating! I am joyful because I am 'figeratating' [sic]! I showed that I did a 'figerate' [sic] because I showed the shape of the 'figerate' [sic]. I put lines around me to show that I am moving. In my speech bubble I put hearts because I've never really done a 'figerate' [sic] and that would be special to me if I did." Sebastian encouraged children to set goals, take risks, feel proud of their accomplishments, and be hopeful about future successes.

Making Decisions

Children were also immersed in global literature and experiences that helped them reflect on who they were as individuals and the type of person they wanted to be. We read books that dealt with cultural conflicts and real-life issues that pushed children to consider the decisions they made (or would make) and why, their relationships with others, and what was important to them.

In first grade, Laura Fuhrman (2013) read *Pedrito's Day* (Garay 1997), the story of young Pedrito, who lives in Nicaragua and is saving the money he earns shining shoes to buy a bicycle. While running errands for his *tia*, he stops to play with friends and loses her money, leaving him with the decision of what to do. Pedrito decides to give his bike money to his tia.

Children created a sketch to stretch (Short, Harste and Burke 1996) of the story's meaning. Jason's sketch to stretch showed Pedrito giving Tia Blanca his bicycle money. Jason wrote, "[Pedrito] did what he had to do. He replaced the money [with] the money he was using for the bike." Avery wrote, "[Pedrito] was brave. He told the truth." As the children shared their sketches, the class discussed Pedrito, his decision, and what they would do, pushing them to think about the type of person they wanted to be.

Michelle read *First Come the Zebra* (Barasch 2009) with first graders. This book tells the story of two African boys, one each from neighboring rivaling tribes in Kenya that had long quarreled over the grasslands for their livelihood. When the boys see a baby facing danger from three warthogs, they work together to save the toddler's life.

Michelle asked children to make a sketch to stretch. Christina thought the story was about sharing, that the boys and their tribes should decide to share the grasslands rather than fight over it. In her sketch to stretch she drew two children sharing a ball and wrote, "Share everything because it would be nice to share things." During the class discussion about their sketches, Christina said, "We should treat others the way we want to be treated, and we should be nice to each other and share." Alex added, "That's our golden rule: to treat others and the environment the way we wish to be treated."

Figure 3.6 Kayla's Collage for Her Friendship Story

In prekindergarten, Christie Furnari (2013b) liked to read *Taking Kindness with Me* (Chappell 2007) to help children understand what it means to be kind. In kindergarten Robbie Stout and Liz Soper (2013) read *Listen to the Wind: The Story of Dr. Greg and Three Cups of Tea* (Mortenson and Roth 2009) and talked about the ways Dr. Greg was a friend to people in a Himalayan village and made the decision to build a school and help people who were sick. In art class the children made collage pictures similar to Susan Roth's illustrations in the book. Back in their classrooms, they wrote stories about decisions they've made about being a friend. Kayla's collage in Figure 3.6 is about finding a flower and deciding to share with her family, showing friendship in her family.

Books like these challenged children's thinking and encouraged them to reflect on difficult decisions and relationships and the types of actions they could take in these situations. By helping them wrestle with possibilities through story, our hope was that they would develop their "critical, ethical, and reflective capacities so that they may have a deeper understanding of the human in both the universal and the particular" (Choo 2013, 110).

Visualizing Cultural Identities through Cultural X-Rays

The complexity of cultural identities becomes more evident through cultural x-rays, a "gingerbread" figure outline on which physical/visible characteristics are written around the outside (such as age, skin color) and important things the person values (for example, family, things they care about) are written inside the heart. Creating cultural x-rays helps children visualize the different aspects of culture and the complexity of their cultural identities.

Jenna, Michelle, and Laura introduced first graders to cultural x-rays and what they represent at the beginning of the year. Periodically, after reading global literature, they created cultural x-rays of characters as a class. After reading *Guji Guji* (Chen 2004) children wrote something they knew about Guji Guji on a sticky note and placed it around the outside of a large drawing of Guji Guji if it dealt with a visible physical feature or characteristic (for example, he's a crocodile, he walks on two legs) and inside the heart if it was something Guji Guji valued (for example, he loves his family, he is brave). Over time the children created x-rays about story characters in small groups or with partners. Eventually, they created x-rays independently about themselves. The children's personal cultural x-rays offered a window for teachers into children's understandings of their cultural identities.

Figure 3.7 shows Marcus's and Harun's cultural x-rays. Around the outside of his x-ray, Marcus wrote, "brownish black hair, black eyes, brown lips, white teeth, a brown nose, a shaky tooth, dark brown neck, brown-dark skin, green shoes, and sometimes smiles." At the bottom he wrote, "I am very helpful person." Inside his heart he included "very helpful, friendly, love God, family, everyone," adding a heart to emphasize his love.

Around the outside of his x-ray, Harun wrote, "I have one sister, born in Egypt, curly hair, neck, enjoy playing soccer, I am 6, legs, playing soccer, feet, didn't lose teeth, quiet, belly, light skin, black hair, no back yard [sic], so awkward, and brown eyes." When asked what he meant by *awkward*, Harun said, "When I have a bad dream, I go to my sister and say, 'Please, can I come sleep next to you?'" "No backyard," he explained, meant that he lives in an apartment and doesn't have a backyard in which to play. Inside his heart, Harun wrote, "brave, strong, cool, practice, and caring." He clarified that *practice* referred to his liking to "practice doing stuff." He circled the word *caring* in red because, "I care about my mom and dad and sister . . . and I wanted it to stand out like it's important to me."

Figure 3.7 Marcus's (left) and Harun's (right) Cultural X-Rays

Cultural x-rays supported children's developing understandings of the complexity of cultural identities and of culture as far more than the color of their skin. Culture included information about their beliefs, values, families, language, heritage, gender, and a range of other factors that made them who they were. (For examples of how Christie created cultural x-rays with prekindergarten children, see Chapter 15.)

Negotiating School Mandates

The experiences with global literature described in this chapter occurred just before the implementation of the Common Core State Standards in our state. Teachers were required to follow the district curriculum based on the state standards. The curriculum included some global literature in the anthologies, but the content was sequenced and controlled, and focused on teaching skills. Global literature for developing intercultural understandings, a critical stance and thinking, and inquiry that built on the knowledge and needs of children were missing.

Teachers had some flexibility to reframe their curriculum, with the support of their administrators, and addressed the expectations and skills and standards in their district curriculum with global literature. In many instances, they used global literature in literacy for read-alouds and comprehension instruction. At other times, they followed the district curriculum, particularly to ensure that children understood terminology, questions, formats, and so on that they would encounter on district assessments. The focus on families, their originations on the maps, culture, and traditions aligned with the social studies curriculum.

In recent years the climate has changed and teachers have less flexibility. Knowing the richness of global literature and having observed children's learning and growth through reading, discussing, and responding to global literature, teachers are not willing to give up those experiences and have found ways to continue to bring these books into the curriculum. They seize any opportunity, such as read-alouds of global literature, making global books available during silent reading or partner time, and substituting global literature within appropriate literacy lessons. Time for writing is expected but with no formal curriculum, and teachers use global literature for mini-lessons and to inspire children's writing and art. Although they sometimes feel frustrated, they are mindful of Kozol's (2007) advice that the teacher's role with mandated curriculum is "to navigate the contradictions without entirely forfeiting one's personality or undermining the ideals that make our work with children a 'vocation' in the truest sense rather than a slotted role within a spiritless career" (203).

Final Reflections

Immersion in the range of global literature stories in our text set challenged children to think deeply and critically about their cultural identities. The books and experiences built on each other in ways that encouraged children to weave together threads from different aspects of and experiences in their lives. Taken together, they helped children understand the range of complexities that make them unique and special. The art experiences invited them to reflect and linger in their thoughts as they expressed their meanings and understandings. Because these children were young, they were only beginning their lifelong tapestry weavings that will certainly change to reflect their new knowledge, learning, and experiences in an array of diverse contexts.

Our experiences with exploring cultural identities convinced us of the importance of knowing oneself and one's place in the family, community, and world. These understandings are foundational to life, learning, and relationships and necessary to appreciate and understand others and the importance of culture in our lives. Time and space to think, reflect, and respond to global literature provided children with opportunities to weave the ever-changing, dynamic tapestries of their cultural identities and grow as respected and creative citizens in their global world.

Recommended Books That Invite Global Perspectives

Chen, Chih-Yuan. 2004. *Guji Guji.* **La Jolla, CA: Kane/Miller.**
In this picturebook from Taiwan, Mother Duck doesn't notice when a crocodile egg rolls into her nest, and she loves and raises three ducklings and a crocodile. Other crocodiles try to persuade Guji Guji to make the ducks their dinner, but he makes a different choice.

Mandelbaum, Pili. 1990. *You Be Me, I'll Be You.* **La Jolla, CA: Kane/Miller.**
Anna is the child of a biracial couple in Belgium and worries that she does not look like either of her parents. She comes to realize that her skin color is like the coffee-milk her father makes and that physical appearances don't define her identity.

Mortenson, Greg, and Susan Roth. 2009. *Listen to the Wind: The Story of Dr. Greg and* **Three Cups of Tea. Illus. Susan Roth. New York: Dial.**
Dr. Greg gets lost while climbing in the mountains of Pakistan and stumbles into a village. While he recovers, he takes care of the sick and helps teach the children. To repay the villagers for their kindness, Dr. Greg returns to build a much-needed school.

Woodson, Jacqueline. 2012. *Each Kindness.* **Illus. E. B. Lewis. New York: Penguin.**
Chloe and her friends do not welcome Maya, a new student in their class. They make unkind remarks and deliberately exclude her from their activities. When their teacher compares acts of kindness with the ripples that radiate from a pebble tossed in water, Chloe rethinks her behavior.

References

Banks, James. 2011. "Educating Citizens in Diverse Societies." *Intercultural Education* 22 (4): 243–251.

Bates, Jane. 2000. *Becoming an Art Teacher*. Belmont, CA: Wadsworth.

Bishop, Rudine Sims. 1990. "Mirrors, Windows, and Sliding Glass Doors." *Perspectives: Choosing and Using Books for the Classroom* 6 (3): ix–xi.

Choo, Suzanne. 2013. *Reading the World, the Globe, the Cosmos: Approaches to Teaching Literature for the Twenty-First Century*. New York: Peter Lang.

Doyle, Michelle Hassay. 2011. "'That's NOT How It Is in My Family!' Children Develop Intercultural Understandings of Themselves and Others." *WOW Stories* 4: (1). http://wowlit.org/on-line-publications/stories/storiesiv1/4/.

Fuhrman, Laura. 2013. "Getting to Know Ourselves Through Global Literature." *WOW Stories* 4: (5). http://wowlit.org/on-line-publications/stories/iv5/5/.

Furnari, Christie. 2013a. "A New Focus: Understanding Ourselves Through Global Picturebooks." *WOW Stories* 4: (5). http://wowlit.org/on-line-publications/stories/iv5/4/#1.

_____. 2013b. "Everybody Has a Story: Telling Our Stories in Pre-Kindergarten." *WOW Stories* 4: (7a). http://wowlit.org/on-line publications/stories/storiesiv7a/4/.

Kozol, Jonathan. 2007. *Letters to a Young Teacher*. New York: Crown.

Kress, Gunther, and Carey Jewitt, eds. 2008. *Multimodal Literacy*. New York: Peter Lang.

Martens, Prisca, and Ray Martens. 2011. "Building Intercultural Connections Through Literacy: Community Explorations of Global and Multicultural Literature." *WOW Stories* 4: (1). http://wowlit.org/on-line publications/stories/storiesiv1/.

_____. 2013a. "Learning About Ourselves and Others Through Global Literature." *WOW Stories* 4: (5). http//wowlit.org/on-line-publications/stories/iv5/.

_____. 2013b. "Artists Reading and Thinking: Developing Intercultural Understandings Through Global Literature." *WOW Stories* 4: (7a). http://wowlit.org/on-line-publications/stories/storiesiv7a/.

Martens, Prisca, Ray Martens, Michelle Hassay Doyle, and Jenna Loomis. 2013. "Writing Pictures, Drawing Stories: Reclaiming Multimodal Composing in First Grade." In *Reclaiming Writing*, ed. Richard Meyer and Kathryn Whitmore, 119–130. New York: Taylor and Francis/Routledge.

Martens, Prisca, Ray Martens, Michelle Hassay Doyle, Jenna Loomis, and Stacy Aghalarov. 2012/2013. "Reading Picturebooks Multimodally in First Grade." *The Reading Teacher* 66 (4): 285–294.

_____ . 2013. "'Now It's Getting Happier Because It's More Colorful': Reading the Art in Picturebooks." *The Dragon Lode* 31 (2): 3–12.

Martens, Prisca, Ray Martens, Michelle Hassay Doyle, Jenna Loomis, Laura Fuhrman, Christie Furnari, Elizabeth Soper, and Robbie Stout. 2015. "Building Intercultural Understandings Through Global Literature." *The Reading Teacher* 68 (8): 609–617.

Rosen, Harold. 1985. *Stories and Meanings*. Sheffield, UK: NATE.

Rosenblatt, Louise. 1978. *The Reader, the Text, the Poem*. Carbondale, IL: Southern Illinois University Press.

Short, Kathy G. 2012. "Story as World Making." *Language Arts* 90 (1): 9–17.

Short, Kathy G., and Jerome Harste, with Carolyn Burke. 1996. *Creating Classrooms for Authors and Inquirers*. Portsmouth, NH: Heinemann.

Snowball, Lesley. 2009. "International Education: A Bridge to Intercultural Understanding. Teachers as Bridge Builders." *International Schools Journal* 28 (2): 16–23.

Soper, Elizabeth. 2013. "Celebrating Our Families." *WOW Stories* 4: (5). http://wowlit.org/on-line-publications/stories/iv5/4/#2.

Stout, Robbie, and Elizabeth Soper. 2013. "Developing Art, Language, and Writing Through Discussions of Friendship and Culture in Kindergarten." *WOW Stories* 4: (7a). http://wowlit.org/on-line-publications/stories/storiesiv7a/5/.

Sumara, Dennis. 1996. *Private Readings in Public: Schooling the Literary Imagination*. New York: Peter Lang.

Children's Books Cited

Barasch, Lynne. 2009. *First Come the Zebra*. New York: Lee and Low.

Brown, Monica. 2011. *Marisol McDonald Doesn't Match/Marisol McDonald no combina*. Illus. Sara Palacios. New York: Children's Book Press.

Bullard, Lisa. 2003. *Marvelous Me: Inside and Out*. Illus. Brandon Reibeling. Mankato, MN: Picture Window Books.

Carlson, Nancy. 2009. *I Like Me!* New York: Puffin.

Chappell, Jackie. 2007. *Taking Kindness with Me*. Vero Beach, FL: Rourke.

Chen, Chih-Yuan. 2004. *Guji Guji*. La Jolla, CA: Kane/Miller.

Chinn, Karen. 1997. *Sam and the Lucky Money*. Illus. Cornelius Van Wright. New York: Lee and Low.

de Deu Prats, Joan. 2005. *Sebastian's Roller Skates*. Illus. Francesc Rovira. La Jolla, CA: Kane/Miller.

Easterling, Lisa. 2007. *Families*. Portsmouth, NH: Heinemann.

Fox, Mem. 2006. *Whoever You Are.* Illus. Leslie Staub. New York: Houghton Mifflin Harcourt.

Garay, Luis. 1997. *Pedrito's Day.* New York: Orchard Books.

Gardeski, Christina. 2001. *Diwali.* New York: Children's Press.

Harris, Robbie. 2008. *The Day Leo Said I Hate You!* Illus. Molly Bang. New York: Little, Brown.

Kerley, Barbara. 2005. *You and Me Together: Moms, Dads, and Kids Around the World.* Washington, DC: National Geographic.

Lin, Grace. 2008. *Bringing in the New Year.* New York: Knopf.

Ludwig, Trudy. 2013. *The Invisible Boy.* Illus. Patrice Barton. New York: Knopf.

Mandelbaum, Pili. 1990. *You Be Me, I'll Be You.* La Jolla, CA: Kane/Miller.

Mayer, Cassie. 2007. *Homes.* Portsmouth, NH: Heinemann.

Morris, Ann. 1990. *Loving.* Illus. Ken Heyman. New York: HarperCollins.

Mortenson, Greg, and Susan Roth. 2009. *Listen to the Wind: The Story of Dr. Greg and* Three Cups of Tea. New York: Dial.

Reynolds, Jan. 2006. *Celebrate! Connections Among Cultures.* New York: Lee and Low.

Rosenthal, Amy Krouse. 2009. *Spoon.* Illus. Scott Magoon. New York: Scholastic.

Rousaki, Maria. 2003. *Unique Monique.* Illus. Polina Papanikolaou. La Jolla, CA: Kane/Miller.

Schotter, Roni. 1990. *Hanukkah!* Illus. Marylin Hafner. New York: Scholastic.

Uegaki, Chieri. 2005. *Suki's Kimono.* Illus. Stephane Jorisch. Tonawanda, NY: Kids Can Press.

Williams, Karen Lynn, and Khadra Mohammed. 2007. *Four Feet, Two Sandals.* Illus. Doug Chayka. Grand Rapids, MI: Eerdmans.

———. 2009. *My Name Is Sangoel.* Illus. Catherine Stock. Grand Rapids, MI: Eerdmans.

Woodson, Jacqueline. 2012. *Each Kindness.* Illus. E. B. Lewis. New York: Penguin.

Chapter 4

Connecting and Extending Children's Identities Through Inquiry

Sandy Kaser

Several weeks ago, a friend and I went to a movie about a teacher who took a job in California working with students in a community of migrant farmworkers. His students worked in the fields before and after school, and their lives were characterized by poverty, frustration, and hard work. Living in Arizona, I was familiar with families who work the farms picking fruit, lettuce, and chili peppers, but my friend was not. She looked at me and said, "I have traveled through that area of California. I can't believe I thought it was picturesque, looking out at the people working in the fields." After only two hours in a movie theater, my friend had a different perspective about the lives of migrant farmworkers, realizing that the people she saw standing in the fields were doing difficult work for little pay and poor living conditions.

Our students also come to us with certain notions about the world in which they live and with fragile identities that are forming through their perceptions of the world as young people. I believe that those of us who teach have a responsibility to recognize and value the personal cultural identities and perspectives within our classrooms and to encourage students to examine those perspectives. Our students bring life experiences to school, and therefore, for school to be relevant, we need to develop curriculum that acknowledges and builds on those experiences to generate new understandings about themselves and others. Mike Rose (1989) reflects on how America's educational system can fail students, suggesting that students often have knowledge and resources within them that cannot be retrieved through standard school methods. He notes that every day in schools, "young people confront reading and writing tasks that seem hard or unusual, that confuse them, that they fail. But if you get close enough to them, you will find knowledge that the assignment didn't tap and find clues to the complex ties between literacy and culture" (8).

My challenge was how to create a reading and writing curriculum that would tap into the knowledge students bring to school and find a connection between literacy and culture. I considered my own classroom of students, many of whom were born in Mexico or born in the United States to Mexican parents. Although the school participated in celebrations of culture, these events often did not seem effective in broadening cultural understandings and often did not even seem of interest to the very students they were meant to serve. Nieto (2011), who has written extensively about culture, identity, and education, holds that a true valuing of culture begins with self, and suggests that students need experiences that not only support their developing identities but also encourage them to ask questions. These experiences begin with educators who develop their own self-awareness, such as my friend did, and show a willingness to develop curriculum that will support students' cultural identities. This is not an easy task, especially when one wants to go beyond holidays and celebrations to an orientation toward cultural identity that encourages a critical, reflective stance (Banks 2013).

In this chapter, I share my experiences bringing together literacy and personal cultural identity by reading *Esperanza Rising* (Ryan 2000) with my fifth-grade class as well as reading the biographical stories by Francisco Jiménez in *The Circuit* (1997). An inquiry study based on student questions and comments followed the reading of these books. The connections to students' own personal cultural identities led to a powerful study of Francisco Jiménez and his books, and a critical look at issues related to our lives on the Mexico–United States border.

Making Connections to *Esperanza Rising*

I teach in southern Arizona, the land of cactus, lizards, rattlesnakes, and beautiful sunsets, at an elementary school approximately seventy-five miles from the Mexico border. Most students speak Spanish as a first language but are also English speakers. Many have direct ties to Mexico, either having been born there or with extended family members there. Some have a parent living and working in Mexico. Almost all take trips to Mexico for one reason or another.

I do not speak Spanish and have no connections to Mexico other than my students and their families, so I was concerned about how to support their cultural identities in authentic ways. I made the choice to start the year with *Esperanza Rising* (Ryan 2000), a story based loosely on the life of the author's grandmother. Esperanza lives a life of luxury and privilege in Mexico on El Rancho de las Rosas until her father is killed. Fearing for their lives, Esperanza and her mother leave Mexico. Living among migrant farmworkers in California, Esperanza learns about manual labor, but she also learns about herself. I was hopeful the book would help us build community and signal my interest in my students' lives and connections to Mexico.

We made the book visual by creating a chapter-by-chapter outline on which to record our thinking. Students identified with the Mexican culture within the book and were eager to write their connections on the outline, using it to validate their thinking. Students also found it interesting that Esperanza had left a life of luxury and become a migrant farmworker. Some had family or knew of those who "worked the crops" either in Arizona or California, were concerned about the living conditions described in the book, and wanted to know more. One character in the book is trying to get the families in the story to go on strike for better wages and working conditions. The class wondered if her efforts brought about any change or if the terrible conditions still remain today.

When we finished the book, their comments and questions from the time line were organized into categories. We went to the library to look for fiction and nonfiction picturebooks to form text sets for further exploration and discussion on family, Mexico, Mexican traditions, and Cesar Chavez (see Figure 4.1). The text sets and subsequent response projects were crucial in supporting their personal cultural identities. Some students wanted to put together a small dictionary of common Spanish words, beginning with the ones used in the book. They led the class in a critical discussion of how difficult a language barrier can be and shared their opinions about not being allowed to speak Spanish in school.

One of the most significant learning engagements occurred when we followed the lead of a group who mapped the journey Esperanza took and included the changes in her character as she lived through the experiences in her life. This led us to mapping our life journeys and considering how our experiences have changed us. Some students' journeys were longer than mine as they shared events in their lives that were of significance. As each student discussed his or her journey with others in a small group, it became clear that many had experienced special challenges because of their Mexican identity.

CHILDREN'S BOOKS WITH THEMES OF MEXICAN IDENTITY

Brown, Monica. 2009. *Side by Side: The Story of Dolores Huerta and Cesar Chavez/Lado a lado: Historia de Dolores Huerta and Cesar Chavez.* Illus. Joe Cepeda. New York: HarperCollins.

Lainez, Rene C. 2004. *Waiting for Papa/Esperando a Papa.* Illus. Anthony Accardo. Houston: Pinata Books.

Lowery, Linda. 2009. *Truth and Salsa.* Atlanta, GA: Peachtree.

Peréz, Amad I. 2013. *My Diary from Here to There/Mi diara e aqui hasta alla.* Illus. Maya Christina Gonzalez. New York: Children's Book Press.

Tonatiuh, Duncan. 2013. *Pancho Rabbit and the Coyote: A Migrant's Tale.* New York: Abrams.

Figure 4.1 Text Set of Children's Books Exploring Mexican Identity

One group continued to be interested in Mexican migrant farmworkers. Among other crops in our area of Arizona are chili-pepper farms, and students were aware that people came from Mexico to harvest chili peppers. They had many questions related to the farmworkers in Arizona. Did people stay migrant farmworkers their whole lives? Did the children ever get to go to school? Did workers have "papers"? These questions led to more questions about living on the border, and the sharing of many comments and opinions about being Mexican American. The questions from this group were a beginning move from looking at themselves and their own connections to thinking about the Mexican American experience more broadly. I was eager to see how all the small-group inquiries would be meaningful to the rest of the class.

I brought in a newspaper each day so students could read it and look for articles related to the border. In our city, hardly a day goes by without an article about border issues. We created a bulletin board and later a scrapbook to house these articles. It was our version of "current events," and reading all or part of the articles led to more dialogue. Gradually the text-set groups finished their work and interest in the topics waned, but reading articles kept us interested in and discussing border issues on a regular basis.

The stories and conversations that grew out of *Esperanza* showed how strongly students identified with the book, text sets, and newspaper articles. I was hopeful that these experiences were bringing together literacy and culture effectively. But we needed to go further in our knowledge and exploration and in critically examining our perspectives. It seemed we were often just repeating the same ideas and attitudes and needed to look closely at our thinking and expand on it. While attending a fall conference, I came across books written by Francisco Jiménez. Since interest in the fate of migrant farmworkers still seemed to be hanging on after we'd finished with *Esperanza*, I bought the books.

Reading the Work of Francisco Jiménez

The books by Francisco Jiménez, starting with *The Circuit* (1997), are memoirs that chronicle his life with his family after they emigrated from Tlaquepaque, Mexico, and as they moved through migrant camps harvesting various crops throughout the year. Three books follow *The Circuit,* taking him through elementary school, middle and high school, and college. He lives in Santa Clara, California, where he is chairman of the Modern Languages and Literatures Department at Santa Clara University. I chose these books because I thought they would support Mexican identities in the class, as well as help us understand the role of migrant farmworkers in the United States. I also thought the short vignettes that make up the chapters could be a model for students in writing their own stories from their life journey maps. I began by reading *The Circuit* aloud. The work with *Esperanza* was the foundation for what became an exceptionally meaningful literature engagement with fifth-grade students that took us not only through *The Circuit*, but into his next two books, *Breaking Through* (2002) and *Reaching Out* (2009), before our year ended.

Encouraging dialogue is important to me as a teacher. Students are always thinking about things, and need an environment where they can share that thinking and make sense of it. Dialogue is crucial to adults in forming the society in which we live, but often we do not value that same kind of dialogue with children. Wells (2009) argues that "dialogue within a classroom helps to create community while simultaneously building a bridge between individuals and the society of which they are members. Class discussion both enacts societal values and creates a forum in which those values can be considered, evaluated, revised, or rejected" (300).

Sometimes the time spent "talking" can be seen as wasted. I valued listening and talk, but getting real dialogue started often evaded me. The dialogue that began with the reading of *Esperanza,* however, continued and grew more critical with the reading of Francisco Jiménez. We were building bridges of understanding as we read and talked together. We felt we had a dialogue *with* Jiménez through his books and online interviews. His words and his faith in the Mexican people connected strongly to students' identities and not only brought us closer together as a community of learners but supported us as we reflected on current issues and values related to border living in Arizona.

In an interview retrieved from the website www.teachingbooks.net, Jiménez told about his older brother questioning the personal nature of his stories. Jiménez replied, "Well, you know, I don't think about these stories as only our family's stories. They are the stories of many families." He says his brother then saw that publishing the stories was the right thing to do. His books reflected some of the family stories we had already been sharing and took us further. The books had a powerful influence on our thinking because students connected strongly to him as a person, an author, and a Mexican.

Identifying with Two Cultures

Throughout *The Circuit* as well as his other books, Jiménez often writes about moving between and through two cultures. When interviewed by Carlile (2004), he talks about the struggle of trying to reconcile two cultures, a Mexican culture and an American culture, and attempting to blend the two by taking the best from each one.

The necessity for students to incorporate both American and Mexican cultures in their identities was at the heart of our dialogue during this part of the reading. We created a chart, and students listed what they felt were traits of Mexican culture in their lives and what traits were unique to American culture. This was difficult, as students often combined these identities, which seemed to truly define the term *Mexican American*.

First on the list was the language difference experienced by their families. Jiménez writes from a child's perspective about the difficulties in learning to speak English and wanting to be successful in school, a struggle with which many students could identify. In an interview with Day (2006), Jiménez says, "I had to relive many painful experiences. I emotionally got caught up in my writing, and that kept me awake at night. Often I would break down with some of the stories like 'Inside Out' where I tell about the experience I had going to school, not knowing a word of English, flunking first grade, and feeling the frustration of trying to understand the teacher. I felt alienated and disconnected" (268).

Students struggled to convey their feeling that Mexican culture was "more real" for them. They talked about differences in holiday celebrations, such as Halloween and the Mexican tradition of the Day of the Dead, which are close together on the calendar. In school, the Day of the Dead seemed to be something interesting to read about or a chance to create related crafts such as sugar skulls, but for children from Mexico it was an important tradition in which altars were made to the dead and families visited grave sites, even making trips to Mexico to do so. Halloween was a fun dress-up and candy day that appealed to everyone but had little significance otherwise. This is but one of many examples of students attempting to identify with both cultures. The struggle to blend the two cultures is evident in all of Jiménez's books and struck a strong chord with students. In an interview related to social justice, Jiménez makes this statement about bringing together Mexican and American culture:

> I think overall cultural and human understanding between the United States and Mexico has improved. In the recent years, I have felt discouraged; but overall I think it has improved, especially in education. I think our society as a whole is much more receptive to cultural and linguistic differences than they were many years ago. My hope is that through my teaching, writing, and my public speaking, I can serve as a bridge for cultural understanding... that I might make a difference in our society. (Carlile 2004, 45)

Jiménez also speaks frankly about his experiences of racism and the kind of stereotypical attitudes toward Mexicans that students were familiar with. He shares how he came into the United States without documents the first time and lived in fear that he would be found out. He was taken out of a middle school classroom and sent back to Mexico, but eventually came back legally. The importance of his family and his faith are woven throughout his books, and students shared those values as well as his belief in the importance of education. "That is why many of us come to the US," said one of my students—"to go to school."

The stories from Jiménez are believable and easy to understand, and strike at the heart of how daily events serve to mold and create our identities. The dialogue surrounding the readings led to more entries in student journals as journal writing became a time to write personal narratives that explored their experiences of racism and of family members crossing the border without documents. They made life connections to Jiménez's experiences in a way that took them outside themselves to take a look at their lives and society.

Students connected to Jiménez and developed a growing interest in him that eventually led to research during their computer time. I remember vividly when one student rushed up to me, grabbed my arm, and said, "I found him on the Internet. He is talking. Come and see!" An author of a book became a living person and our friend.

Returning to the Lives of the Farmworkers

Central to *The Circuit* was Jiménez's life as a migrant farmworker. He shares a description of the kind of housing in which his family lived and their numerous struggles.

I wrote *The Circuit* and *Breaking Through* to chronicle part of my family's history, but more importantly to voice the experiences of an important sector of our society that has been largely ignored. Through my writing I hope to give readers an insight into the lives of migrant farm worker families and their children, whose back breaking labor puts food on our tables. Their courage, struggles, hopes and dreams for a better life for their children and children's children give meaning to the term "the American dream." Their story is the American story. (interview retrieved from www.scholastic.com)

Reading and listening to the words of Jiménez in both his books and interviews gave us a sense of the voices of migrant workers. Although his experiences took place in California, it was evident from our knowledge of the farms in Arizona that similar problems existed and that people die in the desert while attempting to come across the border. But now we began to understand on a deeper and more personal level why people chose to come to the United States from Mexico and their fears in crossing the border or living in America without documentation. We could sense the toll on their bodies from harvesting lettuce and grapes. We were hurt by their mistreatment and impoverished conditions. We began to not only know but to care.

Getting Support from Outside the Classroom

We needed to talk to people from outside our classroom to continue our dialogue and further our understandings. A woman who was serving on our city council grew up in a migrant farmworker family. One of the things that made *The Circuit* powerful for us was that we knew the end of the story. That same feeling was present with the visit of the council member. We had an extended conversation with her. She picked lettuce and told us in detail how hard it was and about the quotas they had to fill. She spoke of the lack of medical care. She was badly cut one day and still carries the scar because her family could not afford to take her to the hospital for stitches. Like Jiménez, she shared how she found a way to get an education and about her involvement in border and immigration issues that face our city council. She shared some of the council's goals for our city. Her visit made the stories from Jiménez even more authentic, and students asked interesting questions, most of which related to their knowledge of the fence being built along our border, the role of the Border Patrol, and the plight of undocumented workers. Since the purpose of her visit was to discuss her childhood and education, we invited additional experts to visit our classroom and continue the conversation. This led us to the office of immigration lawyers.

We had read in the newspapers and heard news reports about people coming across the border without documentation, or "papers" as students referred to it. Yet many students did not really understand why people did or did not get papers and why they paid money to "coyotes" to get them across the border. There was a possibility that some students were from families who did not have legal paperwork to be in the United States and so were familiar with these topics that related closely to their own identity. Other students were beginning to see that these issues were connected not only to their personal cultural identities, but also to the broader cultural identities of Mexicans within Arizona's borders, and maybe even a growing global perspective. Whispers of these perspectives began when the city council member visited, but grew stronger as we listened to our next guest.

The immigration lawyers in our city are willing to send a retired lawyer from their group into classrooms. The lawyer who came to visit us was patient and spent all morning explaining the immigration laws, specifically as they relate to people coming from Mexico. He told us what Mexicans have to do to be documented. He helped us understand the need for certain literacy skills along with money to pay fees. He also explained that there are quotas and that only a certain number of people can be admitted in any one year. He said that there are issues that move some people ahead of others in the application line for coming to the United States. His comments helped students understand the frustration that could occur and why it might seem easier to come across the border under cover of darkness. People place their confidence in "coyotes," or men who know the desert and promise to direct them across it safely. He made us aware of the humanitarian efforts to help people who want to come into the United States legally, such as lawyers who volunteer their time and organizations that provide funding. As I listened and looked at students' faces, I thought about how relevant this discussion was for all of us. Finally, he told us that in Arizona, it is now illegal to hire people who do not have appropriate documentation and that this is causing a problem for Arizona farmers.

It seemed logical to ask an Arizona farmer to speak to us. We found a man who had been written about in the newspaper. He farmed chili peppers but was also involved with the university in the research and development of chili peppers and new ways of farming. He was happy to talk about what he does, and especially about the law requiring farmers to "turn in" workers who are undocumented. Many of the farmworkers have been in the

United States for some time, following the harvest season to various areas. He thought that some of the people who harvested his chili peppers in the past were undocumented, but many were families who came every year and had become friends. He felt a personal responsibility to help them get the appropriate papers, but not all were able to do so, resulting in difficulty finding people to work in his fields. In response to the question "Do undocumented workers take jobs away from people in the US?" he said he did not think many people really want to work in the fields if they have other options. He told us that harvesting is considered one of the nation's ten most dangerous jobs because high temperatures lead to heat exhaustion and heatstroke. He explained that the laborers work long days because growers have a limited window to pick, adding quietly, "And the pay is not that much."

The students asked more questions. They were interested in his living facilities for workers, as Esperanza and Jiménez had lived in terrible circumstances. They wanted to know what he did if he found someone without documents. He answered the questions as best he could, and it was clear he worked hard and had a great deal of respect for the people who worked his farm. One student pointed out, however, that probably not all farmers were like him. Clearly we had come to care deeply about this issue.

Our final visitor was an agent from the Border Patrol. The students were nervous about his visit, but he quickly explained that he was there to talk about his job and not to talk to any of them personally. He spoke to us about the people who brought drugs into the state, but was also sympathetic to people coming into Arizona looking for a better life. He told us that Border Patrol officers do often have to pick up people in the desert who are crossing into the state illegally, but that they keep food and clothing on hand to help them, stressing the dangerous aspects of the journey. He also explained who "coyotes" are and how they often abandon the people they are entrusted to lead and steal their money. Students had read an article in the newspaper about a Tucson doctor who spent his days trying to identify the remains of people found in the desert so their relatives could be notified. They asked the agent about this, and he said yes, they bring all the bodies into the medical examiner's office. His visit took a long time, as the students asked many questions. He showed them on a map of Arizona the places where people tend to come across and told them how barren and dangerous it is. He explained the perspectives of people who are for and against the water stations set up by humanitarians. He said he knew the water was helpful, but that it might give crossers a false sense that they would find water when they needed it.

The guest speakers were helpful in pulling together current, critical perspectives toward what we were reading and thinking about. The issues were important to students' perspectives and growing cultural identities.

Writing Letters

By this time our school year was nearing its end, and we each felt like Jiménez was a member of our family—or we were a member of his. Students wanted to *call* him, so I encouraged letter writing instead. The letters took the form of e-mails, and they illustrate how students identified with this author and his culture and experiences. The following excerpts (the students' names are pseudonyms) from the e-mails illustrate these connections:

- **Roberto:** It made me disappointed how some of the people treated you and your family. Like when your girlfriend took you home to meet her parents and they were angry because you were a Mexican. You were brave and devoted and kept going after someone insulted you or put you down. I loved your books.
- **Salina:** The St. Christopher medallion that your father gave you reminds me of the Santa Nino De Atocha medallion that was given to me while I was in the hospital. I never leave the house without it. I recall that Santa Nino is the saint that saved your brother Trampita. You had to have been really scared then. I am alive today because of the Santa Nino.
- **Andres:** I admire you for working out in the fields and following your dream ever since you were a little kid. I myself am Mexican. I did not have to go through learning English. That must have been hard but it needed to be done. When your dad told you that you wouldn't be a teacher because only rich people went to college, you never let that stop you. You really inspired me.
- **Luis:** We read about the work of Cesar Chavez and we are glad you were a part of that.
- **Trinidad:** You had a tough childhood. I did, too. We did not find work. At school I was bullied a lot, got bad grades, no one liked me. But I found a way. I got math books and I studied hard and I got help. I like the way you made it to college, man. Don't stop writing.

It was not long before we had a response. There was a total silence of expectation when I told the class that Jiménez had replied to our e-mails. I read them his e-mail, and a student's voice broke the silence. "Mrs. Kaser, we read his books, and those were his words in his books, but the words in his letter are his words to *us*." How personal, how powerful. Here are some of his words to us:

> You cannot imagine how pleased I was to receive your wonderful letters in which you let me know that you enjoyed reading all three of my books. I thoroughly enjoyed reading your comments and sharing them with my family. Thank you, Mrs. Kaser, for introducing *The Circuit*, *Breaking Through*, and *Reaching Out* to your students. And thank you, students, for your positive reaction to my books. As you know, these stories are autobiographical. However, the experiences I describe in the book are the experiences of many migrant families of yesterday and today. Unfortunately, many families in our country continue to harvest our crops at very low wages and to work in the fields under terrible conditions. Their hard and noble work is the foundation of our agricultural economy and their experiences are an important part of the story of our nation.

Jiménez moved on to a career working on many projects related to education and issues of social justice. Carlile (2004) sums up her review of Jiménez's work with these words:

> Rather than feeling alienated as a result of his personal confrontations with racism and poverty, Jiménez has embraced his experiences and used them for the benefit of his students, readers, and community. He has created a rich, meaningful life—one steeped in service and art . . . a life he considers full of great rewards. (49)

But Jiménez would want us to know that his life of great rewards began with his experiences in the fields of California and the struggles he encountered there. Clearly it was difficult. The letters we exchanged made real the personal and cultural connections we experienced throughout this study.

Negotiating School Mandates

There are many factors to consider as we make decisions about how and what we are going to teach. The art of teaching means that we think about how to fulfill the curricular mandates in a way that also builds on students' strengths and cultural identities. Nieto (1999) encourages teachers to reflect an understanding that all students have talents and strengths that can enhance their education and that they can and should be active, and engaged, and co-constructors of learning (170–171).

Bringing together literacy with issues of personal cultural identity builds a strong foundation for relevant reading and writing. It is easier and more effective to create a foundation for literacy so that students read what is meaningful to them than to teach in the artificial way that so much curriculum demands. I found that reading comprehension and other literacy skills grew in a dynamic way, and the knowledge gained stayed with students. As we lived through the many learning engagements in this study, I taught various skills when they seemed necessary. It is also important to mention that this study did not take over the entire day. There was still time for many other learning experiences. But the energy that this study created carried us through all of our work as a community of learners.

Then there is social studies. Bringing literacy and social studies together is a wonderful way to teach both successfully. The Arizona Curriculum Standards (www.azed.gov/azccrs/) say that the primary purpose of social studies is to help young people make "informed and reasoned decisions for the public good as citizens of a culturally diverse, democratic society for an interdependent world." To encourage this goal, students should

- develop and use knowledge about their community, nation, and world; and
- apply inquiry processes to the past and present.

Our study of migrant farmworkers supports this statement of purpose. In addition to these broad statements, our time together in the study of *Esperanza Rising, The Circuit*, text sets, and Jiménez incorporated standards in reading, writing, and research such as these:

- To read short connected texts reflective of a multicultural perspective
- To read to address a topic, problem, or issue
- To conduct discussion and analyze content
- To provide opportunities for reflection, including quick writes, logs, and journals
- To describe the difference between primary and secondary sources
- To describe current events using information from class discussion and various resources such as newspapers, magazines, books, television, and the Internet
- To draw evidence from literary or informational texts to support analysis, reflection, and research

Finally, two curricular mandates important to me were met through our study:

- Students should engage effectively in a range of collaborative discussions,
- and be able to describe character traits such as respect, responsibility, fairness, and involvement, that are important to the preservation and improvement of democracy.

Since the standards focus on results rather than means, they leave room for the teacher to determine how these goals should be reached (www.azed.gov/azccrs/). When we are given room to use our professional judgment, we should use that judgment to incorporate genuine communication and inquiry about issues of cultural identity and global understandings.

Final Reflections

Luis Moll's concept of funds of knowledge is based on the premise that students have cultural knowledge and resources that come from their life experiences, households, and family practices and that using this knowledge can have a powerful effect on classroom instruction. Moll (1992) believes that teachers are "ultimately the bridge between the students' world, their family's fund of knowledge, and the classroom experience" (137). Building such a bridge means we know the child as a whole person and not only as a student represented by performance. He notes that the addition of community resources can also bridge the gap between the community and the isolation of the classroom.

Using global literature was the key to enabling students to share their knowledge—both students who were from Mexico and those who were not—and the books led us to involve the broader community in our inquiry. Students were able to look at their identity construction, see beyond stereotypes, and understand the ways in which living near the border or coming across the border played a role in forming their attitudes and perspectives. When you learn something new, you do not just open up the top of your head and let it sit there. The new knowledge winds its way around and alters all of your thinking in one way or another. Each experience we have, each person we meet, alters our view of the world.

Although I began the year with Mexican American students in mind, in the end all students, regardless of heritage, connected to this literature and found a way to examine their responses to the plight of a group of people. They came to think more broadly about how to improve conditions of inequity in their lives, neighborhoods, and world. This is the kind of classroom work that makes teaching a joy and a profession worthy of one's lifetime.

Recommended Books That Invite Global Perspectives

Jiménez, Francisco. 1997. *The Circuit: Stories from the Life of a Migrant Child.* **Albuquerque: University of New Mexico Press.**
Jiménez writes short stories about his early years traveling from place to place to harvest crops as a Mexican farmworker. The circuit begins again every year as the family follows the crops and deals with their status as undocumented workers.

Jiménez, Francisco. 2002. *Breaking Through.* **New York: Houghton Mifflin.**
In this sequel, Jiménez continues the story of his youth with another collection of vignettes. While attending middle school, he is summoned by the Border Patrol and returned to Mexico with his family, but is eventually able to return to the United States.

Jiménez, Francisco. 2009. *Reaching Out.* **New York: Houghton Mifflin.**
The stories in this sequel follow Jiménez as he heads to college. He worries that he should be helping his family by working instead of going to school. College is a major adjustment, and he wonders if he can be successful.

Ryan, Pam Muñoz. 2000. *Esperanza Rising.* **New York: Scholastic.**
Esperanza lives a privileged life in Mexico until her father is killed in an accident and she and her mother must escape to California, where they live in a community of Mexican migrant farmworkers.

References

Banks, James A. 2001. *Cultural Diversity and Education: Foundations, Curriculum, and Teaching.* Boston: Allyn and Bacon.

_____. 2013. *An Introduction to Multicultural Education.* 5th ed. New York: Pearson.

Carlile, Susan. 2004. "Challenges Give Meaning to Our Lives: Francisco Jiménez and Social Justice." *Alan Review* 32 (1): 41–49.

Day, Deanna. 2006. "Persevering with Hope: Francisco Jiménez." *Language Arts* 83 (2): 266–271.

Francisco Jiménez Interview Transcript. Retrieved from www.scholastic.com.

Moll, Luis. 1992. "Funds of Knowledge for Teaching." *Theory into Practice* 31 (2): 132–141.

Nieto, Sonia. 1999. *The Light in Their Eyes.* New York: Teachers College Press.

_____. 2011. *Affirming Diversity: The Sociopolitical Context of Multicultural Education.* New York: Pearson.

Rose, Michael. 1989. *Lives on the Boundary.* New York: Penguin Books.

Short, Kathy G., and Jerome Harste, with Carolyn Burke. 1996. *Creating Classrooms for Authors and Inquirers.* Portsmouth, NH: Heinemann.

Wells, Gordon. 2009. Research Directions: Community Dialogue. *Language Arts* 86(4): 290–300.

Electronic Sources

K–12 Academic Standards—Arizona Department of Education. Approved May 2015. www.azed.gov/standards-practices/.

Teaching Books. *Meet-the-Author Movie with Francisco Jiménez.* www.teachingbooks.net (Several videos are available featuring Francisco Jiménez.)

Children's Books Cited

Jiménez, Francisco. 1997. *The Circuit.* Albuquerque: University of New Mexico Press.

_____. 2002. *Breaking Through.* New York: Houghton Mifflin.

_____. 2009. *Reaching Out.* New York: Houghton Mifflin.

Ryan, Pam Muñoz. 2000. *Esperanza Rising.* New York: Scholastic.

Chapter 5

Explorations of Identity with Latina Mothers

Julia López-Robertson

One Friday afternoon the small group of Latina mothers with whom I spend time weekly were engaged in a discussion about *I Know the River Loves Me/Yo sé que el río me ama* (González 2013a). This story of a little girl, Maya, and her best friend, the river, focuses on relationships, showing how the river is always there for Maya as a place to play and Maya is always there to take care of the river. The mothers shared stories of growing up near rivers and even told their own versions of *La Llorona* (the Weeping Woman), a widely popular Latin American traditional story. They also reminisced about their school days in Mexico, sharing stories of recess games and talking about the books they read. Marissa (all names of people and places are pseudonyms) made the following comment in regard to the types of books that were available in Mexico:

> *Es muy importante poder verse en un libro en la escuela. Eso es lo que yo quiero para mis niños. Cuando yo era niña, pues allá en México, claro que habían libros y en español, pero eran solo para enseñar, no para divertirse. Y aunque eran en español, de veras que no eran nunca de mí; yo nací en el campo, y los libros eran de chicas de DF. Ya veo después de leer estos, que es importante para que mi niña vea a quienes se parecen a ella.* [It is very important to be able to see yourself in a book in school; that is what I want for my children. When I was a little girl, in Mexico, of course there were books in Spanish, but they were only

for teaching, not for entertainment. Although they were in Spanish, they were never about me; I was born in the country, and the books were about girls from DF—México City. Now I see, after having read these books, that it is important for my daughter to see others who look like her in books.]

Marissa's personal connections serve as an example of the importance of finding oneself in a book and feeling a sense of validation, which is particularly important for children and families who have been marginalized and made to feel deficient about their identities, language, and culture. Many Latino children do not have the opportunity to see themselves reflected in the curriculum and in books. They do not see examples of people who look and sound like them in leadership positions or positions of power, other than an occasional outlier during "Hispanic Heritage" month. This absence makes it hard for children to gather or maintain momentum toward academic success. Marissa realizes that pieces of her personal story can disprove the notion that her child can't be successful and that she can support the growth of an identity that views success as an expectation and not an accident. Because mothers "play key roles in their children's development, socialization, and earliest school experiences" (Durand 2011, 258), a mother's sense of identity affects the way her children view their own identity, language, and culture, which in turn affects their school success.

A positive sense of self allows Latino children to realize that

- they are a part of society's larger narrative;
- they have positive contributions to make to society;
- they are not isolated—there are others who share similar language, culture, and experiences; and
- the life they see reflected in their everyday existence has value for themselves and for others outside their communities.

The enrollment of school-aged Latino children in American public schools is projected to increase to 15.5 million by 2024 and to represent 29 percent of total enrollment in 2024. Latino children and their families bring a variety of life experiences to school; however, because their ways of making meaning of the world are often not what are expected by schools, children and their families feel disregarded (Freire and Macedo 1987). We must explore ways to actively engage Latino children and their families in our school communities if we are to justly serve all of the children in our classrooms. One way to do so is to engage them in meaningful literacy experiences that draw from their "rich repositories of knowledge" (González 2005, 71).

My concern about the lives of Latino children led to an inquiry about ways of actively engaging Latina mothers, with Latino children's literature as a means to explore their cultural identity and build links to their children's school learning. Because a mother's sense of cultural identity heavily influences a child's cultural identity and success in school, I wanted to explore how to include mothers and their ways of making meaning.

Uncovering Ways of Knowing and Learning

Funds of knowledge, the personal and cultural ways of knowing and making meaning that are a part of everyone's life, are acquired through daily and cultural interactions with family, both immediate and extended, and are essential for thriving within one's community (Gonzalez, Moll, and Amanti 2005). Tenery (2005) suggests that "immigrant households typically contain transnational domains of knowledge" (124). Spanish language and literacy are examples of these domains of knowledge that are often undervalued in schools. My goal in examining the mothers' funds of knowledge was to help them explore their cultural identities and to recognize the unique contributions that their identities make to their children's literacy learning. I chose to focus on Latino children and Latina mothers to dispel the often prevalent deficit views of Latinos by some educators. Additionally, as a Latina student in American schools, I was viewed through a deficit lens and do not wish that for any child or family.

Growing up in Boston with two immigrant parents, I share some of the struggles of the families with whom I work; for example, my parents were gaining proficiency in English and were unfamiliar with the American educational system. This unfamiliarity complicated my family's participation in school and proved challenging as my siblings and I progressed through school. Nevertheless my family's ways of knowing and making meaning, although not recognized in schools, were beneficial to my siblings and me. My father was a gifted storyteller, and my mother always sang. My parents spoke only Spanish to us and recounted stories of their home countries because it was important to them that their children have a sense of cultural and linguistic identity.

I believe it is our responsibility as educators to engage families in their children's learning in authentic ways, and that includes using their cultural and linguistic heritage as the foundation of the work we do with them. As a classroom teacher who served immigrant families, I sought ways to integrate their language, culture, and ways of making meaning into our classroom on a daily basis and did so by engaging them and their children in *pláticas literarias* [literature discussions]. As a researcher, *pláticas literarias*—authentic small-group discussions about books focused on topics of personal interest—remain my engagement of choice when working with Latino families and children.

Pláticas Literarias for Latina Mothers

Pine View Elementary is a public school in a rural area of a midsized southern city serving 520 children from prekindergarten through grade five; 84 percent of the children are African American, 12 percent are white, and 4 percent are "other." I have spent time over the years at Pine View teaching courses and working in classrooms, and have established relationships with the administrator and some of the teachers and families. Five Latina mothers joined me in this inquiry; all five were of Mexican origin and had been in the United States between three and nine years. Three of the mothers (Marissa, Elvia, and Marta) each had one child, one mother (Luisa) had two children, and one mother (Lily) had three children (the oldest was at the middle school across the street) with another on the way. The children ranged in age from five to eight years old, and all were biliterate, reading, writing, and speaking in Spanish and English. The mothers were all learning English and had differing levels of proficiency, so they preferred to participate in our group by using Spanish. We met for about one and a half hours, two to three times a month, in the school's reading resource room, which held a variety of books and reading assessments for teachers to check out for classroom use, from October through May.

I always conduct *pláticas literarias* in Spanish, allowing families to draw upon their linguistic strengths to talk about topics of personal interest from books that are either bilingual or completely written in Spanish. The books are ones in which the families can see themselves represented accurately. These *pláticas* provide the opportunity for families, in this case the mothers, to recognize that their life experiences and language are relevant to their children's learning and that these experiences can contribute positively to their children's success in school.

We engaged in weekly *pláticas* based mainly on Latino children's literature; my goal in using this specific body of literature was to facilitate connections, because I hoped that the mothers could personally connect and identify with it. Moreover, because "women have historically been considered the bearers of culture" (Villenas 2001, 8), I sought to use the literature as a tool to uncover their ways of knowing and learning and later to use them to make the link between home and school.

We read and discussed ten different books; I share excerpts from the *pláticas* of the four books that generated the most discussion: *Pepita Talks Twice/Pepita habla dos veces* (Lachtman 1995); *The Best Part of Me: Children Talk About Their Bodies in Pictures and Words* (Ewald 2002); *I Know the River Loves Me/Yo sé que el río me ama* (González 2013a), and *My Colors, My World/Mis colores, mi mundo* (González 2013b).

Establishing a Community of Practice

At the onset of our meetings, we participated in engagements to establish our community of practice (Wenger 1998). The domain of shared interest to which we were all committed was our small group; establishing a sense of community allowed us to build relationships in which we learned from each other and interacted in respectful ways. Our practice evolved as we shared stories and experiences.

In any community, time is needed to build trust among group members, and we allowed for that time. For all of the mothers, this was a new experience, and we tend to enter anything new with trepidation, particularly when dealing with sites, like schools, that have traditionally been hostile and unwelcoming toward children and families from linguistically and culturally diverse backgrounds. Additionally, because we strove for authentic and meaningful participation in the *pláticas*, everyone participated in the discussions when they were ready and no one was rushed into participating.

The first *plática* was based on the only non-Spanish book we discussed, *The Best Part of Me: Children Talk About Their Bodies in Pictures and Words* (Ewald 2002). This book is a compilation of photographs and observations written by first through third graders identifying their favorite body part and explaining why. Before the *plática,* we chatted about the book's background, growing out of a schoolwide project to engage young linguistically and culturally diverse children in thinking and writing about their cultural identities. We read a few selected pages and talked about the photographs and what the children had written. The mothers noticed that many of the children had Latino surnames. Lastly, we took a few minutes to think about our favorite body part and the reason or reasons why it was our favorite. A great discussion of favorite body parts and their reasons for being so followed.

Lily shared that her hands were her favorite part because *"con ellas cuido a mi familia"* [with them I take care of my family]. Marta echoed Lily's sentiment and said, *"mis manos, porque con ellas cocino y trabajo para mi familia"* [my hands, because with them I cook and work for my family]. Elvia said that her face was her favorite part: *"mí cara, porque me recuerda mucho de mi mamá a quien no he visto hace cuatro años"* [my face, because it reminds me of my mom, whom I have not seen in four years]. Once Elvia shared this comment about her mother, the others engaged in a discussion of the distance and time between them and their families in Mexico. All five of the mothers had not seen their mothers or fathers for an average of five years.

> **Luisa:** *Es muy difícil estar sin sus seres queridos. Es difícil hacer la decisión de dejar todo lo que uno quiere para montar viaje para acá, pero es algo que hay que hacer. Pues para mí, yo no tenía vida allá en México—no había trabajo y había tristeza. Hubiese tenido mi familia junta pero no valiera la pena. Hay que salir a buscar vida. Ahora estoy mejor, pero todavía me duele estar sin ellos.* [It is difficult to be without your loved ones. It is difficult to have to make that decision to leave everything that one loves to start the voyage here, but it is something that must be done. Well, for me, I had nothing in Mexico—there was no work, just sadness. Although I would have had all of my family together, it just is not worth it. You just have to leave to find life. Now I am better off, but it still hurts to be without them.]

> **Marissa:** *Sabes, tienes toda la razón—aunque duele, es necesario. También aquí tengo una vida nueva que un día ellos van a conocer. Eso es lo que me mantiene feliz, saber que un día muy pronto ellos vendrán a ver me.* [You know, you are totally correct—although it hurts, it is necessary. Also I have a new life here, and one day they will see it. That is what keeps me happy, knowing that one day soon they will come and see me.]

As the discussion continued, the mothers agreed that although it pained them to be so far away and physically disconnected from their families, they were better off in the United States; they had to leave their homes to "find a life." This resiliency, the strength to overcome the many obstacles in their paths, is something that they passed on to their children and something they need to be successful in American schools and society.

Establishing a community of learners allowed us from the beginning to discuss critical topics without fear of being shunned or ridiculed by others in the group. We had the trust that was necessary to engage in honest and very personal *pláticas* as we talked about other books closely connected to their Latina identities.

Language and Culture Are Important to Maintain

Pepita Talks Twice/Pepita habla dos veces (Lachtman 1995) is the story of a little girl, Pepita, who serves as a language broker for her community: she interprets for her mother on the telephone, helps the shopkeeper talk with his customers, and assists her aunt when the delivery truck arrives. One day, tired of having to talk twice, Pepita decides that she will no longer speak Spanish. The story continues as she must decide whether to speak Spanish when it comes to saving her dog, Lobo. In the end Pepita learns to appreciate the fact that she is bilingual and able to help others.

This book provided a very lengthy discussion, because all of the mothers connected to the story around issues of their children as language brokers (McQuillan and Tse 1995). Marta shared about the time when she took her six-year-old daughter, Sylvia, to the local drugstore because she needed to communicate with the pharmacist, who was a monolingual English speaker. She shared how she felt *vergüenza* [shame] for having to depend on her young daughter to communicate on her behalf. All of the mothers shared similar stories of having to depend on their children and of the sense of *vergüenza* that they felt for being unable to effectively communicate with other adults in necessary situations.

> **Elvia:** *"Es que son tan chiquitos, no deben tener que hacer estos para nosotros. Ellos son niños, deben estar jugando en cambio están con nosotros en las clínicas y quien sabe que más para poder hablar para nosotros. De veras que sí son como la Pepita."* [They are so young, and they shouldn't have to do these things for us. They are children; they should be playing instead of being with us at doctor's offices and other such places talking for us. They really are like Pepita.]

> **Julia [me]:** *Yo lo hacía para mis padres cuando era chiquita. Me recuerdo que venían a la escuela para reportes de mi hermano mayor, y él me amenazaba y me decía que si yo le decía a Mami lo que dijo la maestra, me iba a pegar. ¿Y yo, que hacia? No le podía mentir a mi mamá-decía lo que tenía que decir y llegaba a la casa con miedo."* [I did this for my parents when I was little. I remember that they would come to school to talk about my older brother, and he would threaten me and tell me that if I told Mamá what the teacher said, he would beat me up. And what would I do? I couldn't lie to Mamá, so I would say what I needed to say and then arrive home with fear.]

The discussion continued with stories of feeling uncomfortable with dependency on their children, and then the discussion shifted when Marta spoke:

Sí, pero chicas, hay que reconocer que es súper importante que nuestras niños mantengan nuestra idioma-y no solamente para ayudarnos pero para poder comunicar con nosotras y sus abuelitos allá en el otro lado y para seguir el orgullo en nuestra idioma y cultura. El idioma es parte de quienes somos. Yo conozco a una señora Mexicana que nunca le habla en español a sus niños porque cree que les va hacer daño y ya se les ha olvidado el español. Yo pienso que tienen que saber quiénes son, y nuestro idioma es parte de quienes somos. ¿Me entienden? [Yes, but girls, you have to recognize that it is super important for our kids to maintain our language, and not only for helping us but to be able to communicate with their grandparents on the other side and to keep that pride in our language and culture. Language is a part of who we are. I know a Mexican woman who never speaks to her children in Spanish because she thinks it will harm them, and they have forgotten how to speak Spanish. I think that our kids need to know who they are, and our language is part of who we are. Understand me?]

There were a few moments of silence after Marta spoke, as if everyone was gathering their thoughts, and then there was agreement amongst the group. Elvia spoke next:

Sí Marta tienes toda la razón. ¿Si uno no les da la lengua y cultura a los niños en donde la encuentran? [You are completely correct, Marta. If we don't give our kids the language and culture, then where will they find it?]

To close our discussion, Lily added the following:

¿Si uno no les enseña de la cultura e idioma a los hijos, quien lo hace? Nadie sabe la lengua o cultura mejor que un padre. Es nuestro deber: hay que hacerlo y además, es derecho de los niños hablar en su idioma. [If we do not teach our children their language or culture, who will? No one knows the language better than a parent. It is our responsibility. We have to do it. Furthermore it is their right to speak in their language.]

The mothers noted the role that language plays in identity, sharing that *"el idioma es parte de quienes somos"* [language is a part of who we are].

For the mothers, maintaining and passing on their heritage language to their children provides the necessary connection to the loved ones who are still on the "other side." Using the heritage language in school provides children the opportunity to think and communicate their thoughts, feelings, and understandings in a language that they understand. Lily summed up the discussion perfectly when she argued that it is the responsibility of parents to teach children about their language and culture and that it is also their right to have access to that language (Scott, Straker, and Katz 2008).

"Esa so yo": There Are Books Where I See Myself

The discussion on *I Know the River Loves Me/Yo sé que el río me ama* (González 2013a) was another important moment of connection for the mothers. In the excerpt at the beginning of this chapter, Marissa shared the importance of seeing oneself in books and explained that although the books she read in school were written in Spanish and about Mexico, she could not relate to them. A good part of our *plática* centered on the mothers sharing recollections of school days in Mexico and discussing the types of books they were given to read in school versus the types of books that their children brought home from school.

> **Elvia:** *Miren, pues yo miro los libros que me trae Dalila y veras que nunca veo una chiquita que se parece a Dalila. Fui a la biblioteca de la escuela antier y le pedí a Dalila que le hablara la bibliotecaria para buscar libros en español para que yo podía leer con ella en casa. Y sabes? La mujer nos enseñó unos libros bien usados y sucios. ¿Desde que estamos en éste grupito, yo sé que hay libros bonitos y con gente como nosotros, pero porque no hay en la escuela?* [Look, well, I look at the books that Dalila brings home and I never see a little girl that looks like Dalila. I went to the school library the day before yesterday and asked Dalila to talk to the librarian about finding me some books in Spanish so that I could read with her at home. And you know what? She showed us some very used and dirty books. Since we have been in our group, I know that there are pretty books with people like us, but why aren't they in school?]

> **Luisa:** *Pues tienes razón. Los pocos libros en español son viejos, y además son de gente de España o de D.F., y no de los pueblos como nosotros. Me acuerdo que la otra vez que leímos ese libro del señor esqueleto que a Sonia le encanto;*

le gusto contar con el libro y encontrar el gatito. Ese librito era de nosotras; había nuestra comida y hogares. [Well, you are correct. The few books that are in Spanish are old, and additionally the people are either from Spain or Mexico City, and not the pueblos like we are. I remember the last time that we read about the skeleton and Sonia loved it; she loved counting with the book and looking for the cat. That book was about us; our foods and homes were in there.]

Marissa: *Hay sí, ha David le gusto el de contar con el mismo señor esqueleto. Nunca había pensado que sería tan importante verse en un libro. ¿Yo pienso que ellos aprenden más cuando es algo familiar, no?* [Oh yes, David liked counting with Mr. Skeleton. I never thought that it would be so important to see yourself in a book. I think that they learn more when it is something familiar.]

The mothers raised an interesting question about why books like the ones we read in our group were unavailable in their school library. Instead they saw used and dirty books in Spanish and books about Spain or Mexico that did not represent pueblos or life as they knew it. Luisa and Marissa both referred to the books about "the skeleton," sharing that the books were about them—*"había nuestra comida y hogares"* [our foods and homes were in there]. The skeleton books are two readily available books by Latina author and illustrator Yuyi Morales, called *Just a Minute: A Trickster Tale and Counting Book* (2003) and *Just in Case: A Trickster Tale and Spanish Alphabet Book* (2008). The mothers' belief that children learn more when the books they read are about people and cultures like their own demonstrates that they were aware of what was happening with their children's education. Furthermore, their awareness of books being available elsewhere but not in schools calls into question efforts by schools to connect with the cultures of families. Both of these observations directly contradict the deficit rhetoric, which suggests that Latina mothers do not care about their children's education.

"Cuando era Chiquita"/When I Was Little

My Colors, My World/Mis colores, mi mundo (González 2013b) tells the story of a little girl, Maya, and her love of the brilliant colors that make up her world. Maya lives in the desert and shares the colors of the hot pink sunset and the flowers that go from vibrant purple to the color of sand when the desert dust storms kick up. The mothers talked about their lives in Mexico and recalled with fondness the colors of the sunset. Luisa and Marissa shared, *"Fíjense que tiene razón; los colores sí son tan brillantes al atardecer."*

[Look, the author is correct; the colors at sunset are as brilliant as she writes.]

As we continued our discussion, the mothers continued to make personal connections and shared stories of their childhood:

Lily: *Yo soy del rancho, y me recuerdo que yo tenía un columpio allá en el rancho. Eran una llanta que mi papá tenía que él, y mis tíos arreglaron así para nosotros. Me lo pasaba allí tan rico. Ser criada en el rancho es bonito; uno crece con confianza en la naturaleza.* [I am from a ranch, and I remember that I had a swing at the ranch. It was a tire that my father had, and he and my uncles fixed it for us. It was so enjoyable. Being raised on the ranch is lovely; it instills a confidence of being in nature.]

Marissa: *Yo no tenía eso, pero si tenía un carrito, y mi hermano me jalaba por todo el campo. Yo bien sentadita con mis muñecas y el empujándome. Vivir en el campo me sentía tan seguro. Como conocíamos todas las familias no había peligro.* [I didn't have that, but I did have a little car, and my brother would pull me all around the country. I sat with my dolls while he pushed me. I felt so safe living in the country. Since we knew all of the families, there was no danger.]

Marta: *Sabes, yo tenía uno también pero estaba al lado del rio. Allí nos dábamos unos empujones y saltábamos en el rio. Y como dices, Marissa, allá se conocía a todo el mundo. Salíamos los domingos, y parecía que todo el pueblo andaba allí en el rio. Hay, que rico, que memorias.* [You know, I had a tire swing too by the river. Oh, we pushed each other and jumped right into the river. And just like you said, Marissa, we knew everyone. We would go out on Sundays, and it seemed the whole village was out by the river. What great memories.]

Luisa: ¡Si, todos los domingos salíamos a la plaza y había música, *comida, y baile! Todos compartían y disfrutaban; era todo en familia, y todo el pueblo salía. Eso sí es cosa Mexicana creo yo, de pasar el domingo en la plaza.* [Yes, every Sunday we went out to the plaza. There was music, food, and dance! Everyone shared and enjoyed it; it was all families, and the whole village came out. That is a Mexican thing, I believe, spending Sundays in the plaza.]

Elvia: *No se olvide el rio. ¡Eso sí, cocinar afuera y bañarse en el rio—muy Mexicano! Siento que es cosa cultural bueno, el andar en familia, con nues-*

tra música, nuestra comida, y nuestra gente. Y aquí hay que hacerlo también para que los niños sepan lo que es vivir su cultura. Este librito como nos hizo pensar en tiempos pasados. [Don't forget the river. Oh yes, cooking outdoors and swimming in the river—very Mexican! I feel like it is cultural, well, spending time with family, our music, our food, and our people. And we have to do it here too so that our children will know how to live our culture. This little book made us think about past times.]

The picture where Maya is on her swing in this book sparked these memories and the sharing of stories about playing when the mothers were young. They connected to their identities as having grown up in different parts of Mexico, the ranch, river, pueblo, or country, and having place-specific ways of viewing the world, such as the belief that being raised on a ranch builds confidence in nature. They talked about playing on tire swings at the ranch, swings near the river, and being pulled in wagons by older brothers in the country. Although spending time with family can be considered universal, for these mothers, the mixture of food, music, place, and family was a "Mexican thing." These joyful times are ones that they wanted to share and create with their children to instill the *"cosa Mexicana"* [Mexican thing] of spending time with family sharing food and fun.

The memories the mothers shared demonstrate the value that they, regardless of their place of upbringing, held on to so that their children would learn "how to live their culture." The mothers instinctively understood the value of these stories, but the *pláticas* allowed a space where they could see them as more than family memories—as connections to their own cultural identities and therefore to their children's identities. They also were able to consciously make the connection between identity and success in school and to critique the ways in which the school had not provided the spaces their children needed to build on their cultural identities and thereby facilitate their learning.

Negotiating School Mandates

The Latino population was steadily increasing at Pine View, and the administrator was concerned that the Latino families were feeling neglected. He thought it was important for them to see themselves as part of the school community, and he was eager to find ways to build links between home and school. Although the school offered English classes and made efforts to have all school information available in Spanish, he thought this was not enough. He wanted something more personal to be put into place and invited me to work with the families.

The *pláticas* added to home/school partnerships already in place and provided a space for parents to explore their own cultural identities and recognize the need for their children to have these same spaces in their classrooms and the school library. Our major focus was not on standards and testing, nor did the *pláticas* take away from instructional time with children. Instead, they created a context that affirmed parents and their cultures as significant to the children and their success in school, and identified ways that schools might connect more significantly to the funds of knowledge within families to create more effective learning contexts.

Final Reflections

We know that books play a major role in the way children create meaning and form understandings about their culture and language and their place in society. Libraries, both school and classroom, need to have books that represent a variety of children from diverse linguistic, geographic, socioeconomic, and cultural backgrounds. Including books written in the languages represented in the school and making them accessible to children and families is essential for those families and children (see Figure 5.1 for recommended books around Mexican culture).

The *pláticas* with Latina mothers led me to think about ways that schools might open up spaces for families to connect with these books. For example, schools might host global literacy nights where the books are placed on display for families to peruse and provide commentary about their accuracy and authenticity. Families could be invited to discussions about the books with other families and teachers.

The school could host a family literacy night centered on family photos or pictures made by the children about their families, and teachers could bring photos of their own family events. Families and teachers could read selections from *Family Pictures* by Carmen Lomas Garza (2005) for ideas on writing about a family tradition. Once written, the separate pages could be organized into a book or series of books to be housed in the library or some other area of importance in the school. This family literacy night could grow into a yearlong project focused on family pictures and stories. Families could be invited to classrooms to talk about their culture, and children in classrooms could prepare for the visit by conducting research and preparing thoughtful questions for the families to respond to.

TITLE	AUTHOR AND ILLUSTRATOR	YEAR OF PUBLICATION	PUBLISHER
Just a Minute: A Trickster Tale and Counting Book	Yuyi Morales Tim O'Meara (Photographer)	2003	Chronicle Books
Just in Case: A Trickster Tale and Spanish Alphabet Book	Yuyi Morales	2008	Roaring Brook
Niño Wrestles the World	Yuyi Morales	2013	Roaring Brook
Viva Frida	Yuyi Morales	2014	Roaring Brook
My Abuelita	Tony Johnston Yuyi Morales (Illus.)	2009	HMH Books for Young Readers
What Can You Do with a Paleta/¿Qué Puedes Hacer con una Paleta?	Carmen Tafolla Magaly Morales (Illus.)	2014	Dragonfly Books
My Colors, My World	Maya Christina González	2013	Lee and Low
Dear Primo	Duncan Tonatiuh	2010	Harry N. Abrams
The Cazuela That the Farm Maiden Stirred	Samantha R. Vamos Rafael Lopez (Illus.)	2013	Charlesbridge
Tito Puente, Mambo King/Tito Puente, Rey del Mambo	Monica Brown Rafael Lopez (Illus.)	2013	Rayo
What Can You Do with a Rebozo?	Carmen Tafolla Amy Cordova (Illus.)	2008	Tricycle

Figure 5.1 Recommended Picturebooks to Explore Mexican and Mexican American Culture

Through this inquiry, the mothers came to identify the benefits that their experiences and culture could provide for their own children. Essentially, they came to realize that they already had cultural knowledge and social practices to draw upon to help their children succeed in a new culture. More importantly, they realized that their knowledge was rooted in their own culture as mothers and families, an understanding that parallels Norma González, Luis Moll, and Cathy Amanti's (2005) research on funds of knowledge. These mothers came to see their funds of knowledge as a bridge connecting their children to the "mainstream" culture of the school and community. This bridge, however, is not one that children cross to remain on one side; they cross back and forth, bringing tools from each side to succeed in each culture and build a truly bilingual and bicultural identity.

Recommended Books That Invite Global Perspectives

Morales, Yuyi. 2003. *Just a Minute: A Trickster Tale and Counting Book*. San Francisco, CA: Chronicle Books.

Señor Calavera arrives at Grandma Beetle's door unexpectedly and asks that she leave with him right away. Grandma Beetle tells him, "Just a minute." Señor Calavera ends up helping Grandma Beetle with chores until Grandma Beetle's grandchildren are gathered for the fiesta. When she is ready to go, Señor Calavera has disappeared.

Morales, Yuyi. 2008. *Just in Case: A Trickster Tale and Spanish Alphabet Book*. New York: Roaring Brook.

Señor Calavera is worried because he cannot figure out what to give Grandma Beetle for her birthday. A new friend, Zelmiro the Ghost, comes to his aid and gives him suggestions. Rather than give Grandma Beetle just one gift, Señor Calavera decides to find her a gift for each letter of the alphabet!

Morales, Yuyi. 2013. *Niño Wrestles the World*. New York: Roaring Brook.

Niño a luchador, a wrestler, is meeting some very fierce competitors: *la Llorona, la momia de Guanajuato,* and *el Chamuco* to name a few. He wrestles them all and wins fearlessly until he meets his last opponents, *las hermanitas,* his baby sisters.

Morales, Yuyi. 2014. *Viva Frida*. New York: Roaring Brook.

Morales created breathtaking figurines and art for this celebration of Frida Kahlo, set in Mexico. She painstakingly staged and photographed each figurine to create an exquisite book. Morales ends the book with an explanation of her connection to Kahlo.

References

Durand, Tina. 2011. "Latina Mothers' Cultural Beliefs About Their Children, Parental Roles, and Education: Implications for Effective and Empowering Home-School Partnerships." *The Urban Review* 43:255–278.

Freire, Paulo, and Donaldo Macedo. 1987. *Literacy: Reading the Word and the World*. New York: Praeger.

González, Norma. 2005. *I Am My Language: Discourses of Women and Children in the Borderlands*. Tucson, AZ: University of Arizona Press.

González, Norma, Luis Moll, and Cathy Amanti. 2005. *Funds of Knowledge: Theorizing Practices in Households, Communities, and Classrooms*. Mahwah, NJ: Erlbaum.

Huber-Smith, Madison, and Anne Williford. 2014. "Building Family Strengths Through Successful Parental Involvement Strategies: A Case Inquiry with Latino Immigrant Families and Elementary School Staff." *Journal of Family Strengths* 14(1): 1–16.

López-Robertson, Julia. 2012. "'Oigan, tengo un cuento': Crossing *la Frontera* of Life and Books." *Language Arts* 90 (1): 30–43.

McQuillan, Jeff, and Lucy Tse. 1995. "Child Language Brokering in Linguistic Minority Communities." *Language and Education* 9 (3): 195–215.

Scott, Jerrie, Dolores Straker, and Laurie Katz. 2008. *Affirming Students' Right to Their Own Language: Bridging Language Policies and Pedagogical Practices*. Urbana, IL: NCTE.

Short, Kathy, and Dana Fox. 2003. "The Complexity of Cultural Authenticity in Children's Literature: Why the Debates Really Matter." In *Stories Matter: The Complexity of Cultural Authenticity in Children's Literature*, ed. Dana Fox and Kathy Short, 3–24. Urbana, IL: NCTE.

Tenery, Martha Floyd. 2005. "La Visita." In *Funds of Knowledge: Theorizing Practices in Households, Communities, and Classrooms,* ed. Norma González, Luis C. Moll, Cathy Amanti, 119–130. Mahwah, NJ: Erlbaum.

Tschida, Christina, Caitlin Ryan, and Anne Ticknore. 2014. "Building on Windows and Mirrors: Encouraging the Disruption of 'Single Stories' Through Children's Literature." *Journal of Children's Literature* 40 (1): 28–39.

Villenas, Sofia. 2001. "Latina Mothers and Small-Town Racisms: Creating Narratives of Dignity and Moral Education in North Carolina." *Anthropology and Education Quarterly* 32 (1): 3–28.

Wenger, Etienne. 1998. *Communities of Practice: Learning, Meaning, and Identity*. Cambridge, MA: Cambridge University Press.

Children's Books Cited

Ewald, Wendy. 2002. *The Best Part of Me: Children Talk About Their Bodies in Pictures and Words.* Boston: Little, Brown.

González, Maya Christina. 2013a. *I Know the River Loves Me/Yo sé que el río me ama.* New York: Children's Book Press.

_____. 2013b. *My Colors, My World/Mis colores, mi mundo.* New York: Lee and Low Books.

Lachtman, Ofelia D. 1995. *Pepita Talks Twice/Pepita habla dos veces.* Illus. Alex Pardo Delange. Houston, TX: Arte Público.

Lomas Garza, Carmen. 2005. *Family Pictures/Cuadros de familia.* New York: Children's Book Press.

Morales, Yuyi. 2003. *Just a Minute: A Trickster Tale and Counting Book.* San Francisco, CA: Chronicle Books.

_____. 2008. *Just in Case: A Trickster Tale and Spanish Alphabet Book.* New York: Roaring Brook.

Weill, Cynthia. 2007. *ABeCedarios: Mexican Folk Art ABCs in English and Spanish.* Illus. Moisés and Armando Jiménez and K. B. Basseches. El Paso, TX: Cinco Puntos.

Chapter 6

Responses of Native American Children to International Indigenous Literature

Angeline P. Hoffman

Stories matter in the lives of Native American children, especially when they originate from Native perspectives that acknowledge Native nations. I have listened to, read, and learned from the oral and written stories of Indigenous peoples, and these stories have made a difference in my life. Native American literature offers a different perspective from European American stories, particularly in emphasizing dynamic self-esteem and a sacred relationship with nature. These stories are significant to Native American people because they portray our "way of life" and therefore must be heard and experienced by Native youth.

This chapter focuses on the connections of Native students on the White Mountain Apache reservation in Arizona to the unknown daily lives of Indigenous children living across the sea. Native children deserve a curriculum relevant to their lives and culture, and international Indigenous literature provides an experience that connects and extends their understandings of their identities as Apache and as members of a broader global community of Indigenous peoples. My hope was that Apache children would come to respect, acknowledge, and learn about other Indigenous peoples and gain a global perspective.

Cajete (2004), a Native American scholar, argues that Native literature can help Native children realize that "they are a part of greater human story of being and becoming and that their lives are part of the story of creation and life" (38). Traditionally, Indigenous literature takes the form of oral storytelling, but written literature provides a means of reaching a broader group of Native children with values embedded as deep knowledge in each story. The traditional cultural knowledge within each story connects students to other peoples and the natural world, and develops a relationship of respect and appreciation for cultures, conveying how one must behave to live well in the universe.

Although these stories matter, they are rarely taught in schools, particularly in urban schools. They are intended to strengthen mind, body, and spirit in the tribe and to create pathways to a better life; for those reasons, they need to be heard and experienced by Native youth. Stories have kept Native Americans alive for thousands of years amidst the trauma of foreign intrusion. These stories are remembered through oral literature from the elders and through novels and picturebooks with illustrations shared by teachers within classrooms.

This chapter shares my experience as an Apache educator working with a fifth-grade Apache/Navajo teacher to plan literature circles around books depicting Indigenous peoples from the Pacific region. Our goal was to enhance the reading experiences of Apache students and to encourage their cultural identities as Indigenous people and as Apache.

Classroom Context

The fifth-grade classroom is in a school at the center of the reservation, far away from modern urban settings, on the White Mountain Apache Reservation. With a population of around four hundred students in kindergarten through grade six, the community school is directed by Apache board members.

Because of my interest in children's literature, I was excited to introduce global literature into the curriculum and to follow up on my previous research as a teacher using Native literature with students (Hoffman 2011). The teacher who agreed to work on this inquiry is a fifth-grade teacher with many years of experience who is an insider as an Apache/Navajo person. We wanted to explore how to integrate our teaching practices with a culturally specific curriculum. After gaining the support of the board, Ms. Lupe and I introduced her class to international Indigenous children's literature about the Aboriginal peoples of Australia, the Maori people of New Zealand, and the Native Hawaiians of Hawai'i. We integrated social studies and language arts through literature circles and inquiry around these Indigenous groups. This inquiry was significant to Native students because, for the first time, they were reading about Indigenous people from other global cultures and being encouraged to appreciate and respect cultures as global citizens. We hoped that in the process of exploring other Indigenous groups, they would gain deeper insights into their own cultural identities with a sense of power and pride in what makes their identities as Apaches unique within the broader Indigenous community.

Framing Our Inquiry into Indigenous Literature

Ms. Lupe and I wanted to examine children's perspectives as they discussed the books in literature circles. I was particularly interested in how international Indigenous children's literature creates a "lived-through experience" so that students could immerse themselves in the cultures portrayed in the books (Rosenblatt 1938). Rosenblatt's theories support my belief that students have the potential to make sense of and come to new understandings of the world through experiences with literature. Rosenblatt (1938) argues that the "reader draws on past experience of life and language to elicit meaning from the printed words, and it is possible to see how through these words he/she organizes past experience to attain new understanding" (25). Students can reflect on what they read through evoking meaning from the text by critical engagement and allowing the relationship between the literature and their own life to connect.

I looked for these connections between literature and life in the responses of fifth graders who were born and raised on the Fort Apache Reservation. We framed our inquiry around these questions: What Native American textual features are identifiable in ten international Indigenous children's books? What type of talk about these textual features do children engage in through literature circles of international Indigenous children's literature? What are children's perspectives on reading and discussing international Indigenous children's literature?

Twenty-four students were in this fifth-grade classroom—twelve males and twelve females of different Native American nations (White Mountain Apache, Yavapai-Apache of Camp Verde, and Navajo), but primarily Apache. Over a two-month period, students participated in ten discussions around the literature of Indigenous peoples in Australia, New Zealand, and Hawai'i. We gathered field notes, audio recordings of the discussions, interviews, and student artifacts.

One of our goals was to explore how to integrate new teaching practices into the school and use time to provide space for these practices. We developed lesson plans and gathered resources, including maps, books, and online videos and books. The students engaged in discussion in small groups and wrote individual responses in journals as well as participated in interviews about their experiences. We read the books aloud to students, followed by talk in literature circles and writing and illustrating responses in journals.

Book Selection

The highlighted picturebooks authentically reflected several Indigenous cultures in the Pacific. These cultures were selected primarily because of the availability of picture-books, many of which were written by cultural insiders. Children need stories in their lives that authentically convey their own and other's cultures. Fox and Short (2003) affirm that stories influence the ways children think about themselves and their place in the world as well as the way in which they think about cultural perspectives and peoples.

Figure 6.1 indicates the authors, titles, tribes, and genres for the books we read with the children. Most of the genres were traditional literature and contemporary fiction. The ten books contain a mixture of stories by Indigenous and non-Indigenous authors and illustrators. The books were published within those countries or the state of Hawaii, and many are not available in the United States so are labeled as international literature. These books do not represent literature published in the United States for a mainstream audience but books published for children from those regions and cultures as the main audience.

AUTHOR	ILLUSTRATOR	TITLE	TRIBE	GENRE/FORMAT
Arone Raymond Meeks	Arone Raymond Meeks	*Enora and the Black Crane*	Australian Aborigine	Aboriginal realistic fiction: YouTube
Jeanie Adams	Jeanie Adams	*Going for Oysters*	Australian Aborigine	Australian Aborigine realistic fiction, folktale/legend
Percy Trezise and Dick Roughsey	Percy Trezise and Dick Roughsey	*Gidja*	Australian Aborigine	Myth
Tim Tipene	Henry Campbell	*Taming the Taniwha*	Maori	Realistic fiction: Digital book talk—YouTube
Peter Gossage	Peter Gossage	*In the Beginning*	Maori	Folktale, legend, myth, traditional story
Joy Cowley	Rodney McRae	*The Terrible Taniwha of Timberditch*	Maori	Realistic fiction, myth
Michael Nordenstrom	Michael Nordenstrom	*Pele and the Rivers of Fire*	Hawaiian	Myth, folktale, legend, traditional story
Chris Szekely	Malcolm Ross	*Rahui*	Maori	Realistic fiction, myth: YouTube

AUTHOR	ILLUSTRATOR	TITLE	TRIBE	GENRE/FORMAT
Kats Kajiyama	Kats Kajiyama	*Maui and His Magical Deeds*	Hawaiian	Myth
Dick Roughsey	Dick Roughsey	*The Rainbow Serpent*	Australian Aborigine	Myth: YouTube

Figure 6.1 Text Set of International Indigenous Literature

The genres we worked with were myths, folktales, legends, traditional stories, realistic fiction, and realistic nonfiction. We also used several digital books, including three available on YouTube and one from the International Children's Digital Library. Students enjoyed hearing the books that were read on YouTube videos, which included background sound effects and camera movements on the illustrations.

Literature Circles

Literature circles are small, flexible discussion groups of four to eight students that support readers in thinking critically about texts. We read the books aloud and then invited students to talk about what they had heard and to extend and deepen their understandings by sharing their thoughts and ideas. Literature circles are based in Rosenblatt's (1938) theory of transaction, in which an interpretation of a text develops through the transaction of a reader with the text and is not inherent in the words of the author. Each reader brings previous experiences to a text to create connections. In literature circles, readers share their questions and connections about the text or the author's style or motivation and then challenge their interpretations.

Vygotsky (1978) says that students' understandings are broadened and deepened when they collaborate on learning tasks. In literature circles, students share ideas with each other, as well as with the teacher, to clarify their thinking and to become more reflective and critical as readers. Literature circles provide an opportunity to gain a better understanding of how students engage in thinking and reflecting on books and interact with peers.

After completing our discussions of these books, I interviewed students in groups of two or three about their backgrounds, their experiences in literature circles, and their perspectives on the books. The interview provided a space for students to voice their perspectives about reading and discussing Indigenous literature.

Culturally Based Education

Our work was based in the conceptual framework of CBE (Culturally Based Education). Demmert (2005), a Native scholar, identifies critical elements of culturally based education as

- pedagogy in which teaching strategies are congruent with the traditional culture as well as contemporary ways of knowing and learning; and
- curriculum that is based on traditional culture, which recognizes the importance of Native spirituality and places the education of young children in a contemporary context.

From these theories, we implemented literature circles through an Indigenous stance by connecting the literature through cultural association with curriculum relevant to Native children. Students could thus reflect and validate who they are, along with the people they read about. This process involves the school, parents, and community in providing community knowledge, expertise, and cultural practices that shape the work of schools as relevant to the lived experience of children from Indigenous backgrounds.

In examining the children's responses to these books, I adapted categories developed in my earlier study of Apache culture and children's responses to authentic Native literature set in Indigenous cultures of the Southwest, their own region of the world (Hoffman 2011). These categories provided a strong Indigenous cultural perspective from which to examine children's responses. Their responses fell into two umbrella categories, Cultural Themes and Cultural Practice/Images, each of which included multiple subcategories. (See Figure 6.2.)

Cultural Themes

Cultural themes are responses that reflected ideas and topics significant to cultural ways of living for Indigenous peoples, particularly the significance of story, sense of place, relationships, and beliefs about creation.

Storytelling

The first cultural theme is storytelling, because many of the books included references to elders or family members telling traditional stories that provide knowledge and values significant to the Indigenous group from which that story originated. The stories were used to teach values based on the moral of the story around ways of life, learning from family and community members, and interactions with nature.

CULTURAL THEMES	CULTURAL PRACTICES AND IMAGES
Storytelling a. Ethics and Teaching b. Self-Images/ Knowledge of One's Own People	**Important Roles** a. Elders b. Woman c. Man d. Children (girl, boy)
Sense of Place a. Location: Places b. Time c. Journey	**Culture** a. Religion and Belief b. Lifestyle c. Hunting/fishing d. Sacred Being e. Dance and Music
Relationships a. Family/Kinship b. Association	**Images** a. Symbols/Illustrations
Creation a. Human b. World c. Animals	

Figure 6.2 Umbrella Categories of Children's Responses to Indigenous Literature

Both Aisaha and Clec talked about the need to listen and respect nature and people. In responding to *Enora and the Black Crane* (Meeks 2010), Clec said that he learned "to respect the animals and don't kill the animals." In this Aboriginal story, Enora kills a bird in the rain forest to show off its beauty to his parents. His mother cries because he wandered into the rain forest when warned not to do so, and the consequence of his actions turn him into a black crane. Aisaha responded to *Gidja* (Trezise and Roughsey 1988), saying that she learned "to not laugh about people because you might hurt their feelings." Gidja's physical features are different from those of everyone else in his tribe, so he is teased. Aisaha's statement indicates her awareness that laughing at someone who is different causes pain for that person.

Storytelling also provides a way for students to explore their self-image and to gain knowledge through comparing their cultural stories with those of other Indigenous peoples. From *The Terrible Taniwha of Timberditch* (Cowley 1982), Lynthianna made the connection, "It's like the Old Owl Witch of the Apache. The witch goes to the children's home at night and collects all the naughty children." In the book, the father tells his daughter not to go to the Timberditch because she will be alone; it would be dangerous, and she could fall into the water and drown. He warns her about the taniwha (an unknown creature) to stop her from going there.

Jhawndell responded to *Rahui* (Szekely 2011), saying, "A boy who died swim in the ocean. They close it for one year." The Maoris believe that when a person dies in a particular area, that area should be closed for a year in respect for that person. Jhawndell went on to connect the Maori respect for people who have died with the Apache belief in respecting the dead by not mentioning them again so they can continue on their journey without interruption.

The traditional stories provide important lessons about each Indigenous group's ways of living, learning, and acknowledging themselves as individuals. These stories have embedded values that Indigenous people incorporate into their way of thinking about themselves.

Sense of Place

The second cultural theme is sense of place, particularly the reverence of Indigenous peoples for the land where they live, focusing on why that place is so significant to a particular group. Biesha responded to *Maui and His Magical Deeds* (Kajiyama 2001) by commenting, "We need to leave the land the way it is." Maui was chosen to be trained with the gods and returned to Earth with powers greater than a normal human being. Biesha recognized that even though you have strength to move islands, sometimes it is better to leave them as they are.

Tailynn responded to *In the Beginning* (Gossage 2001), saying, "The kids wanted to get out to the real world, but in order for that to happen, they have to split Mother Earth and Father Sky up." Mother Earth and Father Sky are interconnected, with their children between them, but when one of their children lies on his back and stretches his legs upward with all his might, the parents are split, forming Mother Earth and Father Sky. The children are the wind, sea, war, forest, and storm and are made from their parents. Students' awareness of place is based on deep connections to a place within their own Apache culture.

Relationships

The third cultural theme focuses on the Indigenous respect for relationships through family, kinship, and connections between two beings or entities. Vriel responded to *Pele and the Rivers of Fire* (Nordenstrom 2002), saying, "Pele and her sister fight. Pele flows the lava and her sister is the water, so they form an island when they fight." Pele (Goddess of Fire) and her sister (Water) do not get along at all, and the book focuses on their fighting. Vriel also said, "I like the story and the illustrations. It was so colorful, with the lava and the ocean and to see how the fighting made the island." In this creation story of the Goddess of Fire, Pele is led by her brother, the shark, to an island to be alone, but her sister finds her and they fight. Pele does not survive but comes back in spirit to the people.

The relationships in this book are explained in the form of terrestrial and natural aspects as connected to the characteristics of humans. Family is not only immediate family, but also extends to clan (which is matrilineal—from the women), community, and tribe. Pele and her sister are immediate family, and their fight creates the islands of Hawai'i, a place for a network of extended family and clan as a significant foundation of responsibility and respect.

The theme of relationships also includes the association of individuals who come to know each other through an event. Gin responded to *The Rainbow Serpent* (Roughsey 1975), saying, "In the beginning of the story the Rainbow Serpent was looking for his people. When the serpent found the people, he taught the men how to dance." This story tells how the land was created by the slithering Rainbow Serpent making hills and mountains while searching for Aboriginal people. When he finally finds the people, he shows them how to dance. They trust him, but he deceives them by swallowing two young boys. When the people cut him open, the two boys turn into birds and fly out of him. He wakes and pursues his attackers, who turn into animals as they run. This event reveals how a relationship with the Aboriginal people led to the creation of animals and birds.

Creation

Explanations of the origin of people, creators, and the universe are at the center of thinking for Indigenous people. Indigenous stories of creation portray who we are and where we came from as well as help us know our function and responsibility in the world.

In the Aboriginal story of *Gidja* about the creation of the moon, Gidja is ridiculed but still sings a love song to a girl whom he marries. During a hunting trip Gidja's daughter dies in an unfortunate accident and the people blame Gidja, hunting him to kill him.

They push him higher and higher into the sky until he stays and becomes the moon. Gin focused on this creation aspect, saying, "I like it because Gidja turned into the moon." Milleo responded to *The Rainbow Serpent*, saying, "The story is about creation, when there were no people, no animals."

In both responses, students understood that they were learning sacred knowledge through these stories. Indigenous stories of creation are important to our way of life because they portray who we are and where we came from, and how things came in to being. This is significant in students' ability to understand and respect other Indigenous creation stories.

Cultural Practices and Images

The roles of elders, women, men, and children are significant within Indigenous practices, and students often commented on particular roles within books. Elders are important because they represent wisdom and insight. Several students talked about their learning from *Going for Oysters* (Adams 1993). Aneshia said, "It is about listening to your grandparents," and Ailynn said, "The grandpa told the children not to go there." Lec added, "The grandpa told the kids to get oysters for him. He was too old to go." All three students referred to grandparents, and their focus reflected their closeness to elders within Indigenous cultures. Even though children listen carefully to their elders, sometimes the events of daily life result in children forgetting their advice. In this book, the children get off the boat and run toward the area where they were told not to go because they are chasing an animal. One child remembers the warnings of the grandfather and reminds the others, so they stop and return to the boat.

The role of a woman is important because she gives life and conveys values and practices of daily life, so it is not surprising that students noticed this role in the books. The mother of *In the Beginning* is portrayed as Mother Earth. Randon commented, "Sky Father and Mother Earth were in love, and Mother Earth provides food." Ancesca continued, "The Mother Earth and Father Sky had a lot of children and had no room, so one of the kids pushed their father into the sky." This creation story tells how Mother Earth and Father Sky were separated from each other to bring light into the world. Their children became gods of War, Wind, Storm, Fish, Reptiles, and cultivated Food. Randon and Ancesca mention Mother Earth's affection for Father Sky and her role as co-creator and nurturer.

Men are considered to be protectors of the tribes, leaders of the people, teachers, storytellers, providers, dancers, medicine men, performers of ceremonies, and singers, and most are parents. Aneshia responded to *The Terrible Taniwha of Timberditch* by commenting on the father: "At the beginning of the story, Josephine's father told her not to go to the lake because of the Taniwha." Randon talked about the father in *Rahu*, saying, "The boy wandered off and the father found him dead, so they had a ceremony." In both responses, students comment on the male figure as protector, leader, and performer of ceremonies.

Children are socialized to learn through observation and pay attention to what goes on around them. In *Taming the Taniwha* (Tipene 2001), Tama is bullied by James (the taniwha) at school and turns to Aunty Flo, Uncle John, and his father for advice. Shawn noted, "Be a friend to everyone and no bullying. Children should not to be a bully." Gin, commenting on *Going for Oysters*, said, "The kids were going to an island for oysters." This book focuses on an extended Aboriginal family's weekend camping trip to an island where Grandad warns them to avoid the place of Yaatamay, the Carpet Snake. Traveling in two boats, the group lands on the beach, sets up camp, casts nets to catch fish, and collects oysters. The children get too close to the spot they have been warned about. In both responses, students talk about the influence of the socialization of family on children and the need to pay attention and understand what they are learning and what goes on around them. Children's lives are adventurous but lived within the protection of family.

Within Indigenous cultures, girls and boys are viewed as having different roles. Girls are viewed as free adolescent females, daughters, granddaughters, or goddaughters and one day as co-creators. In *The Terrible Taniwha of Timberditch*, Josephine wants to play at Timberditch, but her dad warns her about the taniwha. She is told that it might be a terrible beast, slimy monster, Chinese dragon, or a Greek Gorgon and decides it's better to just catch a taniwha. Yisha commented, "Josephine wants to know what a taniwha is, and her father tells her not to go to the Timberditch where the taniwha lives." Aitlynn responded to *Gidja*, saying, "I like the story because of all the colors and the events. Yalma agreed to marry Gidja and they had a daughter named Lilga." Both responses indicate that the girls in the stories played an important role as daughters, and both comments came from female students. In each story the girls were free adolescent females, living with parents who cared for them. The girls have a huge responsibility ahead, in the future, when they grow up and become co-creators and women.

Boys are viewed as free adolescents, sons, and grandsons, as well as having the responsibility of becoming future leaders of their tribes. After reading *Taming the Taniwha*, Ynthianna commented, "I learned not to be a bully, because if you don't get friends with that person again, it will keep going on." In *Enora and the Black Crane*, Enora turns into a black crane because he killed a bird. Iesha said, "Enora said he was getting attacked by birds. The people said, 'We need evidence,' so the next morning he brought back a dead bird and his mom started crying. Then Enora turned into a bird." Both responses to the male characters refer to a moral of the story and the story's ending. Ynthianna said that she learned to be friends with the bully. The boys in the books, Tama and Enora, were in a situation where they needed support, but they made different choices. The students liked these two books, because they could relate them to their own lives and paths of learning through everyday living.

Cultural Practices

Students talked about particular cultural practices in the books, including those related to religious beliefs, lifestyles, and hunting and fishing. Indigenous religious beliefs focus on the unknown—the Great Mystery—and the connections of these beliefs to purpose and need. In responding to *Rahui*, a story of happiness and death, Milleo said, "A boy drowned and the people came. They respect his death." Chris added, "The boys tried to look for this cousin but they thought he went home, and then Dad found him dead and they had the rahui." Students focused on how the Maori respect the deceased by not going to the area where that person died for one year. The Apache students mentioned that the belief of the Apache people is similar, since the family honors the passing away of a family member with a dinner a year later. The remembrance of the person a year later refers to the time when the year has ended and grieving is released. The Maoris conduct a ritual, a ceremony to show their respect for people who have passed over to the spirit world.

Cultural practices come together to create a lifestyle that reflects the attitudes and values of a person or group of people. Urrell noted that in *Going for Oysters*, "The family is going swimming and going to the camp." Hawndell continued, "It was fun going for oysters and families eating together during a trip. They're going fishing and going for oysters." These students' responses indicate their interest in reading about the lifestyles of contemporary Indigenous families as they camp, fish, collect oysters, and eat. This lifestyle of an Aboriginal family reflects how they work together and value each other through their daily living and the values of survival that come from the teachings of how to fish and collect oysters.

Another set of cultural practices related to hunting and fishing is the way the universe provides wild game and the respect and honor given to animals and fish that provide food. In *Enora and the Black Crane*, Urrell commented, "Enora killed the bird; then he turned into a bird," and Nthinna responded, "I learned not to kill the birds because Enora turned into a bird." In Indigenous cultures, prayers and rituals are performed before a hunt. In both responses, students imply that Enora had not performed these rituals and shown respect for birds.

Many cultural practices exist around Indigenous beliefs about the sacred being, an entity whose purpose is contained in teaching by elders, often as a metaphor in oral stories about things to be aware of. Phil talked about *The Terrible Taniwha of Timberditch*, saying, "Josephine wanted to know what the taniwha looked like and that she always wanted to catch the monster." Hawndell commented on *Pele and the Rivers of Fire*, noting, "It is about how the lava girl lives in the volcano and that Pele 'Goddess of Fire' and her sister 'Goddess of Water' fought and form the island."

The sacred being in the first story is the taniwha, and in the second story they are Pele and her sister. The taniwha is a thing to beware of, but Pele and her sister are goddesses and are to be respected as creators. Students were very interested in these stories from a different place and about sacred beings that are different from those found in Apache culture. They compared them with the Apache sacred being and found similarities to the Apache story about the old owl witch.

Music and dance are significant cultural practices. Dance reflects movements, signifying life and honoring life by evoking the universe made by the Creator. Gin responded to *The Rainbow Serpent*, saying, "In the beginning the serpent was looking for his people, and when he found his people, he taught them how to dance." Ani continued, "The snake went to the one that has a red mountain. But they didn't speak his language, so he went to a different tribe and they danced different, but that was his tribe." In the book, Rainbow Serpent journeys to find his people and sees that they are not dancing in the right way, so he teaches them how to dance. Both students recognized the importance of dance as a way to signify life and honor natural forces and the spirits as well as to emulate animals in honor of their existence.

Music is the sound of an invisible force, the sounds of movements and voices that sing the songs. Music of our inner silence can also be heard from within and during our visions and dreams. Milleo responded to *The Rainbow Serpent*, saying, "I like the story because of the songs of the Aboriginal people singing in the background." Ewayne responded to the same story, noting, "The story talked about a snake, how animals were made, and I liked the music." These students focused on the role of music in the book and hearing

Aboriginal people in the background as we watched a YouTube of the animated story. As the story was told, music was heard and the camera moved across the illustrations throughout the narration, putting a focus on Indigenous experiences through dreams, natural forces, and vision.

Images and Symbols

Images play an important role within Indigenous cultures through symbols, characters, figures, marks, icons, and pictograms that express a concept of existence and how things or events occur. Symbols and illustrations reveal that animation is the primary reality, which delves deep into the realities of Indigenous thought. Students often made comments about the illustrations in these books. As we discussed *Pele and the Rivers of Fire*, Milleo commented, "I like the story because the pictures are beautiful and it's entertaining." Citlynn made the same type of comment as we discussed *Rahui*, saying, "I like the illustrations. They are colorful and creative." In responding to *Maui and His Magical Deeds*, Milleo noted, "The illustration of the sun is bright and the shadow of Maui talking to the sun, very powerful." His comment reflects the ways in which students were drawn to the illustrations to construct their interpretations of stories. Students saw beautiful colors that created good feelings.

Student Perceptions of Indigenous Children's Books

Interacting with international Indigenous children's literature was a new experience for these Apache students, and many made comments about enjoying the books. As we talked about *Pele and the Rivers of Fire*, Ray said, "It was a good book. I like it." Ray commented about *The Rainbow Serpent*, "I like the story because it tells about the Aboriginal culture," and Eqayne responded to *Taming the Taniwha*, saying, "I think the story was great. It tells about not to be mean." Finally, Iesha's enjoyment of *In the Beginning* was evident in her comment, "I like the book. It is so soundful to my ears."

Students found learning about a new culture to be enlightening as a way to learn lessons about life. They loved to listen to the stories, finding that they were poetic and filled them with strong feelings. They constantly made connections to their own Apache culture, particularly at the heart of the stories, but found interesting differences that reflected the geographic and historical settings of these Indigenous groups, especially the contrast between the desert and ocean.

Reflections on the Books

This experience at a Fort Apache Indian Reservation school indicated the importance of providing international Indigenous children's literature to Native American children. The books supported the students' literacy development because their interest and enjoyment of the books encouraged them to engage in further independent reading. They also gained deeper insights into their cultural identities as Apache and broadened their views globally, seeing themselves as part of a global community of Indigenous cultures and youth.

This inquiry is placed within the theoretical framework of global literature and reader response theory, but through a Native American lens for examining children's talk and why they chose to focus on particular aspects of the books. This focal point took into account the cultural practices and values within international Indigenous children's literature as well as the interpretations that these Apache children brought to their reading.

My analysis of the ten books indicated that they reflected significant textual features that were deeply embedded within Indigenous cultures. Children were able to explore a diversity of Indigenous cultures and to engage with the cultural values and practices within these books. Because the books were written and published for children from those cultures, not a mainstream US audience, the ways in which the stories were told as well as their content reflected Indigenous ways of thinking about the world.

Across the books, the largest number of student comments related to the significance of storytelling as teaching, with most of the responses coming from *Rahui*. This story is filled with children playing and swimming, having fun together—and then a cousin drowns. A rahui, or restriction, is placed on the area where the boy drowned, and no one visits that place for a year. The students could relate to the story because of the realistic experiences and the cultural traditions in their Apache way of life. Cultural storytelling provides information about where people come from, why they were created, how familial and extended relationships are essential, and how we must attribute our existence to our environment.

The two books that encouraged the most comments about sense of place were *Taming the Taniwha* and *Gidja*. Students could relate to these stories because of their combination of realistic fiction and traditional stories, an important interconnection within Indigenous thinking. In one book, a boy is bullied, and the other is about a man who faces obstacles in his life. Both portray actual experiences in their world, but they also pull from traditional stories to deal with these experiences. The characters have a strong sense of belonging to a specific place that provides a sense of home, respect for nature, and communication with balance and harmony.

The book that encouraged the most comments about relationships was *Pele and the Rivers of Fire*. The book about Pele, her sister, and their shark brother was frequently mentioned as a favorite book. Students could see themselves in the characters' roles, because they had siblings who fought. This cultural story was relevant to their lives and was from another place, supporting them in experiencing that place and learning about another culture.

Students reported in the interviews that they enjoyed the dialogue about the different tribes in the books. They liked being able to connect their personal experiences to the literature and learn about themselves, particularly in thinking about family relationships. They also believed that they learned about the different Indigenous tribes and their cultures. They saw aspects of each Indigenous tribe that they realized were unique, but they also saw the similarities and gained a respect for the diversity within the broader Indigenous community.

Students indicated that the characters in the books reminded them of a relative or friends with similar experiences. The stories provided them with guidance for appropriate behavior and reminded them of what they had learned through past experiences. They believed that stories of international Indigenous peoples should be respected and the knowledge applied to their lives.

Final Reflections

Banks (1975) argues that students need to develop more sophisticated understanding of the diverse ethnic groups that make up not only the United States, but the world, and gain a greater acceptance of cultural differences. Furthermore, students need a conceptual understanding of culture and can gain a global understanding through viewing the diversity and complexity within each cultural group. This complex understanding is developed by examining expressions of culture in literature, music, drama, dance, art, communication, and food, as well as in everyday living and learning to live the "way of life" in balance and harmony.

Cajete (2004) notes that the "Indigenous community, here and far, becomes a story that is a collection of the individual stories, ever unfolding through the lives of the people who share the stories of that community. When a story finds that special circumstance in which its message is fully received, it induces a direct and powerful understanding; this becomes a real teaching" (124). The deep knowledge of this inquiry involves teaching embedded in literature circles and through books representing Indigenous people from around the world. Overall, the deep knowledge came from the students' responses and their personal investigations, sense of wonderment, and discoveries. The stories offered insights into Indigenous cultures different from their own and yet with significant connections to their own Apache way of life. Knowing your unique identity and therefore respecting each other for the uniqueness of each person, as well as seeing the connections across Indigenous nations, is a new understanding. Importantly, this perspective supported students in becoming more open-minded about people from global cultures.

Recommended Books That Invite Global Perspectives

Nordenstrom, Michael. 2002. *Pele and the Rivers of Fire*. Honolulu: Bess Press. Pele, the restless Goddess of Volcanic Fire, journeys across the sea and brings fire to the Hawaiian Islands, even though her sister, the Goddess of Water, continually puts her fire out. Pele continually destroys and rebuilds the land to bring new life to Hawai'i.

Szekely, Chris. 2011. *Rahui*. Illus. Malcolm Ross. Auckland, NZ: Huia. This story is composed of memories from the summertime of a Maori extended family in New Zealand, including holidays, the rocky shore, family, friends, fun, and sadness. The memories include the accidental drowning of a cousin.

Tipene, Tim. 2001. *Taming the Taniwha*. Illus. Henry Campbell. Auckland, NZ: Huia. Tama, a young Maori boy, is being bullied by a boy at school. He goes to his family, who offer a range of solutions for how to tame the taniwha. Set in New Zealand.

Trezise, Percy, and Dick Roughsey. 1988. *Gidja*. Sydney, Australia: Gareth Stevens. In Dreamtime when the world was created, Gidja the Moon and Yalma the Evening Star had a daughter named Lilga, who is killed in an unfortunate accident. Aboriginal tribal members thought they were immortal, and this event causes their lives to change forever.

References

Banks, James. 1975. *Teaching Strategies for Ethnic Studies*. New York: Allyn and Bacon.

Cajete, Gregory. 2004. *Look to the Mountain: An Ecology of Indigenous Education*. Skyland, NC: Kivaki Press.

Demmert, William. 2005. "The Influences of Culture on Learning and Assessment Among Native American Students." *Learning Disabilities Research and Practice* 20:1–16.

Fox, Dana, and Kathy Short. 2003. *Stories Matter: The Complexity of Cultural Authenticity in Children's Literature*. Urbana, IL: National Council of Teachers of English.

Hoffman, Angeline. 2011. *Stories That Matter: Native American Fifth Graders' Responses to Culturally Authentic Text*. Dissertation. Tucson: University of Arizona.

Rosenblatt, Louise. 1938. *Literature as Exploration*. Chicago: Modern Language Association.

_____. 1978. *The Reader, The Text, The Poem*. Carbondale, IL: Southern Illinois University Press.

Vygotsky, Lev. 1978. *Mind in Society*. Cambridge, MA: Harvard University Press.

Children's Books Cited

Adams, Jeanie. 1993. *Going for Oysters*. Chicago: Whitman.

Cowley, Joy. 1982. *The Terrible Taniwha of Timberditch*. Illus. Rodney McRae. Auckland, NZ: Penguin.

Gossage, Peter. 2001. *In the Beginning*. Auckland, NZ: Scholastic.

Kajiyama, Kats. 2001. *Maui and His Magical Deeds*. Honolulu: Barnaby Books.

Meeks, Arone Raymond. 2010. *Enora and the Black Crane*. Broom, WA: Magabala.

Nordenstrom, Michael. 2002. *Pele and the Rivers of Fire*. Honolulu: Bess.

Roughsey, Dick. 1975. *The Rainbow Serpent*. Sydney, Australia: Harper Collins. Aboriginal Dreamtime: *The Rainbow Serpent*. YouTube.

Szekely, Chris. 2011. *Rahui*. Illus. Malcolm Ross. Auckland, NZ: Huia.

Tipene, Tim. 2001. *Taming the Taniwha*. Illus. Henry Campbell. Auckland, NZ: Huia. Digital book talk—YouTube; www.childrenslibrary.org; Read the Book.

Trezise, Percy, and Dick Roughsey. 1988. *Gidja*. Sydney, Australia: Gareth Stevens.

Chapter 7

From Knowing to Feeling to Action: A Collaborative Inquiry on Culture and Identity

Wen-Yun Lin

Bishop (1990) reminds us that books act as windows through which children can look out at the world and learn about cultures other than their own as well as mirrors in which they can reflect on themselves. When children are unable to find themselves in books, however, or when the images they see are "distorted, negative, or laughable, they learn a powerful lesson about how they are devalued in the society of which they are a part" (ix). Her words are critically important to modern-day Taiwan, a culturally diverse society where children from minority groups rarely see themselves in children's books.

Taiwan is an immigrant society that is multicultural and multilinguistic. Sixteen tribes of Indigenous peoples are the original residents. Since Taiwan is close to China, immigrants from different Chinese provinces have come to Taiwan throughout history and are known collectively as Han Chinese, the largest ethnic group of Chinese in Taiwan. Among Chinese immigrant groups, the Ming have been the biggest group and the Hakka the second biggest since the seventeenth century. After World War II, in 1949, Taiwan's political status changed, and Chinese became the dominant culture and Mandarin Chinese the official language. However, different dialects, especially Ming and Hakka, are still spoken, and Indigenous languages are spoken mainly by tribal elders. According to the Hakka Affairs Council (2011), Taiwan's population is 67.5 percent Ming, 13.6 percent Hakka, 7.1 percent Chinese from other provinces of China, and 1.8 percent Taiwanese Indigenous peoples.

Since the 1980s, the origins of immigrants to Taiwan have expanded with a new type of arranged marriage (Hsia 2003). A large group of women from China and several South Asian countries have married Taiwanese men and become the new immigrants to Taiwan. These multiracial families bring cultures from different countries, including Vietnam, Indonesia, Thailand, and the Philippines. According to the National Immigration Agency of Taiwan, in 2012, 10.9 percent of elementary school students and 3.9 percent of junior high school students came from multiracial families. To respond to the growing number of multiracial families, the National Immigration Agency and the Ministry of Education (2012) have worked together to promote multicultural education, and the Ministry of Education has emphasized literacy projects for adult immigrants and their children. Although multicultural education is a hot issue, this focus is not reflected in textbooks. Social studies textbooks have information on new immigrants to Taiwan, but that cultural diversity is not reflected in textbooks for language and literature, where the majority of stories are about dominant culture groups. A few include Indigenous groups, but they focus on festivals rather than on families.

As a teacher educator, I agree that children need to find themselves in books. In Taiwan, this means that children need to find themselves in the textbooks, because they serve as major learning resources for the official curriculum. Since assimilation has long been the doctrine of official curriculum, the absence of culturally diverse stories in most of the language and literature textbooks is understandable. Children from multiracial families often hide the identity of their maternal culture, a consequence of societal views. I believe that it is the right of all children to be proud of their personal cultural identities, which leads to the inquiry in this chapter.

In this chapter, I share the stories of how preservice teachers worked with children from multiracial and Indigenous families to create their own stories. Based in the work on funds of knowledge (González, Moll, and Amanti 2005) and identity texts (Cummins 2006; Cummins and Early 2011), this inquiry began with reflecting on the lack of global literature from these children's cultures, which further led to a literacy project during which children wrote their own stories. Throughout the process, preservice teachers from dominant cultural backgrounds came to learn about children's cultures and appreciate their knowledge. This process was one of reading to know, to feel, and then to act for the preservice teachers, and one of nurturing personal cultural identities for the children.

Global Literature for Children in Taiwan

Martin (2008) argues that the worldviews of teachers, which include their assumptions, values, and beliefs, are a key factor in influencing teaching and learning. Intercultural education, therefore, needs to be a philosophy embedded across the curriculum, not a subject. I also believe that literature "once heard, can change other hearts" (Cai and Bishop 1994, 68) and view global literature as an important teaching resource to increase awareness of cultural diversity.

Taiwan is a highly literate society that values literacy education from early childhood, and many books are published each year. However, little trace of the diversity of cultural perspectives in Taiwan can be found in children's books. Most are about Han Chinese culture, and a few are about Ming, Hakka, and Indigenous cultures, all of which are considered local cultures. Indigenous writers are few although increasing in number, but no children's books written by new immigrants were available as of 2016. Most books about Indigenous cultures are informational texts or about holidays and traditions, with only a few on Indigenous peoples in modern life. A small number of books about new immigrants focus on holidays or festivals or on discrimination within mainstream society, indicating that publishers have not yet responded to the changing cultures in Taiwan.

Several years ago, local government officials invited local writers to write multicultural children's books, which were sent to the schools as resources, but many were written by a small number of Taiwanese writers who were not from the culture of the immigrants. For example, thirty different multicultural titles published by New Taipei City from 2008 to 2010 were written by the same author. The government shows a good heart to promote multicultural education and value the role of children's books, but overlooks issues of cultural authenticity, voice, and power (Short and Fox 2003).

In terms of global children's literature, translated books come primarily from the United States. Local Taiwanese writers also write multicultural books, but mainly about Ming and Hakka, and Indigenous people. Ming and Hakka cultures have their own traditional nursery songs, modern poetry, traditional literature, and nonfiction. Because Ming is the major minority culture, there are books about Ming culture in modern life. For other cultural groups, most books are about old traditions, and only a few are about life in modern society. The few Indigenous books are stories about festivals or cultural events, but even those that show modern life depict the people as wearing traditional costumes. Some authors who are outsiders of the culture mix different Indigenous cultural symbols to create their own perspectives. Thus, cultural authenticity is an issue in Taiwan.

Although there are stories about recent immigrants, none are written by insiders. Many are about the challenges of life and discrimination that immigrants face. The authors' goal seems to be to raise awareness of the challenges that immigrants face and to remind us to respect immigrants. However, they ignore many stories of successful immigrant women in Taiwan that are reported in newspapers and other media. In daily life, immigrant women who achieve a lot are easily seen and are not in an inferior position. Children of immigrants in multiracial families and children from the dominant group both need to read stories about successful immigrants.

Because all "children have a right to books that reflect their own images and books that open less familiar worlds to them" (Bishop 2012, 9), more global children's literature from insider perspectives is needed in Taiwan. These stories should highlight both similarities and differences in ways of thinking, as well as traditional and modern lifestyles among different cultural groups.

For these reasons, I engaged in an inquiry that involved preservice teachers in working with cultural minority students in an elementary school. My hope was to create authentic stories from insiders' perspectives and to nurture preservice teachers' intercultural awareness and understanding. Because of the lack of books about the children's cultures, we engaged children in presenting their stories by writing, drawing, or oral presentation as a way to share their identities and voices.

Theoretical Framework for Curriculum

In Taiwan, some of the research on children from minority and multiracial families considers these students culturally deficient and needing extra help through remedial teaching. Since most of these children are from working-class families, the school system tends to encourage them to assimilate into the dominant culture without the awareness that they might have rich cultural knowledge from their parents.

Funds of knowledge is a concept that grew out of research by González, Moll, and their colleagues (2005), where teachers as researchers collected household knowledge from students' families and communities and wove their findings into their classrooms. The goal was to bridge students' daily life knowledge with the school curriculum as teachers learned about students' cultures through interactions with people in the community. The philosophy and practice of funds of knowledge challenges the traditional deficit model and myth of minority students.

Funds of knowledge views students' household knowledge and everyday life knowledge as a resource instead of a problem (González, Moll, and Amanti 2005). In our inquiry, the stories the children created presented their personal and family funds of knowledge, which was valuable to them as well as to the teachers and the school.

Cummins (2006), a bilingual educator in Canada, encourages bilingual children to use their cultural and language background to create texts called "identity texts" that represent their knowledge and culture. Identity texts go beyond traditional print-based literacy to celebrate multiliteracy and encourage multimodal forms of presentation, such as writing, visual arts representation, and so on. According to Cummins and Early (2011), identity texts encourage students to represent themselves and their identities. Through sharing and communicating with audiences, students appreciate each other's cultures and identities and nurture respect among themselves.

Inspired by the research on funds of knowledge and identity texts, I used children's literature as a tool to mediate and to nurture mutual understandings among cultural minority students and preservice teachers. The core philosophy of our inquiry was that of teachers

- viewing students as having rich cultural knowledge and as the base of the curriculum. A teacher's role is to be a learner of students' cultures.
- helping students construct knowledge based on their current experiences and cultural backgrounds in making connections to the world around them and developing their identities.
- providing connections for students between their mother tongues and the school language and raising the awareness of the functions of both languages.
- encouraging students to create their own stories in different formats and providing opportunities for student authors to interact with their audiences.
- acting as inquirers in learning together with students—in our case, about our mutual cultures through personal stories and sharing.

Based on these principles, I worked with preservice teachers to enact a curriculum that is intercultural by engaging students in exploring their personal cultural identities and developing their voices. And through the process, teachers and students would mutually learn from each other.

The Identity Stories of Children

For preservice teachers, this inquiry went from reading to know toward reading to feel and take action. The curriculum began with their questions about the cultures and countries of minority and immigrant students in Taiwan. Preservice teachers collected and read books from university and city libraries. Their reflections showed that their knowledge about minority cultures expanded, but with little empathy for these cultures, primarily because most books were informational texts. I suggested they read realistic fiction, since I wondered if realistic fiction would be a way to encourage them to share their concerns and feelings. Their book talks and reflections about realistic fiction indicated that they were aware of current issues in Taiwan. Then, many of them joined a project to work with minority children in an elementary school. Their inquiry thus moved through reading nonfiction for knowing, to reading fiction for feeling, and then to working with minority children for action.

We applied pedagogical practice through funds of knowledge and identity texts in our work with minority students at Dan-Feng Elementary School of Taipei County, a neighboring area of the capital, Taipei City. Twelve preservice teachers worked for a semester in four classrooms, two for children with Indigenous heritage and two for children from multiracial families. The students and preservice teachers met for three hours once a week for ten weeks in an after-school reading-and-writing program.

The first week, we conducted a small book fair with a focus on global literature related to students' cultural backgrounds, and then we invited students to respond to the books. Most of the books were written by local authors. Initially, students responded positively to the books, but through discussion they came to question the authenticity of the content, saying these "stories of the book" were not their stories. Children criticized the stories as not representing their culture and current life. Along with the children, we were concerned about issues of voice and authentic cultural perspectives (Short and Fox 2003).

Here, I share stories from four preservice teachers who engaged children in reading picturebooks as a mediator to invite them to share their own stories as identity texts. Two stories are from classrooms, and two are from one-to-one interactions with children in the after-school program. Through these interactions, preservice teachers learned from children about their cultures. Their reflections show the power of instruction based in funds of knowledge and identity texts. These four stories show how preservice teachers came to appreciate children's knowledge and encouraged them to voice their identities.

The first story is from Ms. Lu's class, which had students from multiracial families whose mothers originally came from China and South Asia countries. Her students showed their cultural knowledge by criticizing a book on China by a foreign author. She encouraged students to represent their stories in multiple ways and was challenged in her own bias. The second story is from Ms. Tu's class, in which students came from Indigenous families that live in the Taipei City area. Ms. Tu was impressed by the knowledge students owned through their work.

The third and the fourth stories are from one-to-one interactions between a student and a preservice teacher. The third one is about how Ms. Lee worked with a student who grew up in Vietnam and immigrated to Taiwan with her mother, who married a Taiwanese man. A bilingual Vietnamese-Chinese book was chosen for Ms. Lee to teach the student Chinese and for the student to teach her Vietnamese, leading to a mutual exchange of knowledge. The fourth story is about how Ms. Shy worked with a student who grew up in Boston and moved to Taiwan with his Taiwanese mother and American father for one year. The student drew to share his experience, and the teacher learned the difference between the family life of a boy in the United States and that depicted in American movies.

Sharing Personal Stories to Increase Intercultural Understanding

This class was made up of children from multiracial families in which the wives became immigrants to Taiwan by marrying Taiwanese men. The fifteen students from grades five and six included ten whose mothers were from South Asian countries such as Vietnam and Thailand and five whose mothers were from different provinces of China.

Ms. Lu, the preservice teacher, introduced a picturebook called *To Grandmother's House: A Visit to Old Town Beijing* (Keister 2007) to invite students to share their experiences. She read the story aloud and encouraged students to respond through discussion. She chose this book because it depicts going to the mother's hometown, which she thought might inspire children to write similar experiences of their own. Surprisingly, students criticized the story for not being interesting in that it did not include details about what the characters did at the grandmother's house. Besides, from students' perspectives, the pictures looked old and some of the language did not sound like conventional Chinese. Perhaps because the book had been written by an American and then translated into

Chinese, Chinese-origin children were critical about its cultural authenticity.

Students' responses indicated that children whose mothers came from China had a good sense of Chinese culture and some had been to China to visit grandparents. Since none of the students' mothers came from Beijing, the capital city of China, and since there is great diversity among different provinces of China, they decided to find other books about China to read after they finished reading the book set in Beijing. While reading this book, students were very engaged in talking about their own experiences in China, and that inspired Ms. Lu to look for books connected to her students' experiences and interests.

However, we could not find children's books about other provinces in China, so Ms. Lu decided to share her personal story. She talked about growing up in a small town near Taipei City as part of a family that had lived for many generations in Taiwan. Even though her story differed from their stories of the immigration of their mothers, her stories of childhood invited students to share their stories.

Students worked in small groups to share their experiences and continued to raise more questions about the book. By questioning the book, they felt a need to share their own stories. Some students talked about visiting their relatives, and others talked about visiting grandparents in China. Children wrote about their trips to China, visits to relatives in South Asian countries, visits to relatives in Taiwan, and family trips in Taiwan. The stories from children represented their real, current life experiences.

From their sharing, we realized that not all of the children from multiracial families had visited their mothers' hometowns. Surprisingly, a high percentage of children in this class came from single-parent families. We appreciated the trust evidenced by children sharing their personal stories, and we especially respected their positive attitudes about the difficulty of their lives.

Children in this class represented a diversity of multiracial family cultural backgrounds. Given the rich diversity of their mothers' backgrounds, Ms. Lu invited students to share and talk about the similarities and differences between the local culture and their cultures. Through sharing and discussion, both students and teachers learned. More importantly, they learned from each other's firsthand experiences. This process improved the teachers' cultural understanding of the students, both their out-of-school experiences and their academic learning. Understanding that not all students liked to write, Ms. Lu provided different ways for children to present their stories. They could write, do an oral interview, or make a comparison chart. Ms. Lu was touched by the personal stories that students shared and learned that when students use different ways of presenting their stories, they can represent themselves better, a reminder from Cummins (2006) about different formats of identity texts.

Teaching children with diverse cultural backgrounds challenges teachers' attitudes toward students. Ms. Lu had a strong identity as Taiwanese and was challenged to teach children from China, who share the same Chinese cultural heritage but with different political identities. She was touched by how much children opened their hearts to her, and that reminded her to treat children equally, without stereotypes. Cross-cultural understanding was emphasized not only for students but also for the teacher. Through reflection and dialogue, Ms. Lu changed her biases and raised her awareness of students' cultural identities, which helped her be a better teacher of students with diverse cultural backgrounds.

In this class, the teacher and students used their personal stories to make connections between one another and to learn from each other's stories. This experience showed us how powerful personal stories are in raising intercultural understanding.

Dialogue to Represent Cultural Knowledge and Identities

Ms. Tu, a preservice teacher, worked with sixteen third- and fourth-grade students from six Indigenous backgrounds. Their hometowns were in different areas of Taiwan, including the east coast, the south, and mountain areas in the middle of Taiwan.

We researched children's books about Taiwanese Indigenous peoples and cultures and found stereotypes. Most of the picturebooks were myths or folktales, and some were about festivals, with only a few representing contemporary life in Indigenous families. The illustrations showed Indigenous people wearing traditional costumes no matter what they were doing. Authors seemed unaware that Indigenous families live a modern life even in their tribal hometowns.

Ms. Tu believed all Indigenous children needed to see themselves represented in contemporary ways of life and that mainstream children also needed stories about the modern lifestyles of Indigenous families. We used two stories for children to respond to and then encouraged them to share their experiences and stories.

The first book we read, *Amis Grandma* (the title is translated from Chinese; Lee 2009), is about a young girl and her grandmother living a contemporary lifestyle on the east coast of Taiwan and depicts the wisdom of the Amis Indigenous culture in terms of plants and vegetables. The second book, *Kaleidoscope of the Indigenous* (the title is translated from Chinese; Chen 2012), introduces the uniqueness of different Indigenous cultures and tribes in Taiwan, including their lifestyles, family and social systems, festivals, music, and fine arts. Indigenous children could all find descriptions of their own cultures.

Ms. Tu used these two books to invite children to tell their own stories. When she read the stories aloud, she often stopped for the children to respond, and they did so with enthusiasm. Throughout the engagements, children showed that they were capable storytellers and loved to share their stories orally or in drawings. They did not like to write, they said, because writing reminded them of schoolwork. Although some children did not speak their tribal languages, they showed their knowledge about their own Indigenous culture even though they lived in the city.

Ms. Tu found that children with different Indigenous cultural backgrounds have different perspectives on certain traditions. In conversation, children with the same Indigenous background supported each other by adding details to the story they were reading, and that led to deeper discussion. The conversations showed us that they were knowledgeable about their own cultures. For example, when they were talking about a tribe's hunting culture and cultural events, Ms. Tu learned more details from the children than from the book. There were also discussions among children with different tribal backgrounds, and students' pride seemed to increase as they shared their different perspectives about certain traditions.

Besides whole-class and small-group discussion, Ms. Tu conducted one-to-one conferences with students so they could share their stories. She found that their stories were very special to her, a teacher who is not Indigenous, as she learned about their experiences as normal daily life events. Ms. Tu had never been to the various tribal communities and realized she had misconceptions about them. She was surprised when several children told her that their grandparents' houses in the tribal communities were much prettier and bigger than their houses in the city. Most had participated in cultural festivals and enjoyed traditional and local foods, which were different from those in the city. In class, children often worked together in groups and sang, behaviors that were different from those Ms. Tu had experienced in teaching mainstream students. These experiences helped her understand the importance of everyday knowledge (Vygotsky 1978) as a starting point of inquiry.

Through their discussion and stories, students proudly showed their identities. That sense of identity came from where they lived and how they interacted with their families and connected to their tribal cultures. From the students' stories, we came to understand that children in modern-day Taiwan share similar experiences in knowing their own uniqueness no matter where they come from. Both the similarities and the unique qualities of students are important for teachers to be aware of and appreciate.

Global Literature as a Mediator for Culture and Language

"I am forgetting my Vietnamese," Jen said sadly. A new immigrant girl who had grown up in Vietnam and come to Taiwan a year earlier, Jen was twelve when Ms. Lee, a preservice teacher, worked with her. At that time, Jen went to a public school in Taipei, the capital city of Taiwan, and was considered deficient in language and literacy. Unlike Jen's teachers, Ms. Lee treated Jen's mother tongue as a resource and mediator to help her read and write Chinese, using Vietnamese/Chinese bilingual picturebooks to create dialogues between herself and Jen. In their first conference, Ms. Lee told Jen that she wanted to learn Vietnamese language and culture from her, and in return she could teach Jen to read and write Chinese.

Vietnamese Cinderella (the title is translated from Chinese; Ming-Ko 2010) was the first book that Jen picked to read together. She was not satisfied with some of the translation and explained to Ms. Lee how it should be translated. Jen also explained about the costumes and foods in the book. Ms. Lee often asked questions about Vietnamese culture while they read together, questions that were posed out of curiosity, not with an instructional purpose. As they worked together, Jen gradually showed her confidence in her knowledge of her culture and language. Many times, Jen acted as if she were the teacher. For example, she would ask Ms. Lee to read the Vietnamese sentences in the book aloud and ask her comprehension questions.

Toward the end of the semester, Jen was invited to the university to present Vietnamese stories to college students and answer their questions about Vietnamese language and culture. Jen's language and cultural knowledge were valued, and her voice was heard. She showed her confidence in the presentation. It was a valuable intercultural encounter for Ms. Lee, the college students, and Jen. After the presentation, Jen decided to write her own version of *Vietnamese Cinderella* because she was not satisfied with the translation. Her act of writing showed her cultural identity as Vietnamese and her confidence about her cultural knowledge.

Ms. Lee was touched by the power of a funds of knowledge perspective and suggested that if a teacher is humble enough, he or she can access students' cultural knowledge. Ms. Lee and Jen's story reminds us to value children's multilingual and multicultural backgrounds as resources instead of regarding them as problems (Ruiz 1984).

Student's Drawings as a Portfolio of Identity Texts

Dong was an eight-year-old boy who grew up in Boston and moved to Taiwan for one year. His father is American, and his mother is Taiwanese. He was placed in the second grade, one year below his age, because his language proficiency was below grade level, and assigned to attend a pull-out language class.

Ms. Shy was the preservice teacher who worked with Dong. Since Dong understood by listening but did not speak much Chinese, Ms. Shy spoke Chinese to him most of the time with the support of English as needed. Dong could talk in English or mix Chinese and English as long as he was comfortable. The first time when they met in October, they talked about their families and where they came from. When Dong talked about his parents, grandparents, and extended family, he drew maps to show Boston, the city in which he used to live, and Connecticut, where most of his family lives. He also drew a family tree to introduce the members of his extended family he loved and played with. Dong missed his large extended family and always drew when talking about family events. He drew the drive from home to Connecticut, where his grandparents lived, indicating his knowledge about transportation and cities in the United States.

Dong often drew houses, trees, and plants to show Ms. Shy what his home and grandparents' house looked like. He always drew to help her understand him better, and he explained details when she asked questions. As Dong talked and drew about his relatives in the United States, his drawings become a portfolio of his family stories.

Dong loved to talk about basketball, his favorite sport, and the food he loved in America. Since it rarely snows in Taiwan, Dong drew a map to show where it snows in America. Dong also told Ms. Shy who he used to play with in the snow. They often talked about different kinds of ice cream products in the States and in Taiwan. Although Ms. Shy spoke Chinese and Dong spoke English most of the time, Dong gradually began to speak some Chinese in their conversations.

Ms. Shy brought *Good Night, Boston* (Gamble 2006), a book for young children, to share with Dong, asking questions out of curiosity that Dong was happy to answer. Their conversations were authentic, with the purpose of satisfying personal curiosity rather than instructional objectives. Through conversation, Ms. Shy got to know Dong and his family life and hometown. The family life that Dong shared changed her conceptions about American life as perceived from TV programs and movies.

Based on the philosophy of cross-cultural exchange, Ms. Shy and Dong shared their cultures as a mediator for learning language. They challenged the traditional relationship between teachers and students in which the teacher teaches and students learn. In this case, the teacher and student came from different cultural backgrounds and created a partnership to learn from each other. This sharing also supported the student in gradually improving his Chinese language skills.

Through this interaction with Dong, Ms. Shy questioned the school's decision to place him a grade level below his age. The school had judged his competence only by his fluency in a second language without valuing his knowledge of his first language. This experience also revealed the importance of providing different mediators or sign systems, such as pictures, drawings, graphic organizers, and charts, for students to represent their knowledge.

Final Reflections

Preservice teachers learned a great deal from students during the process of inquiry. In helping children create their stories as identity texts, they learned to be facilitators who listen to children and appreciate their stories. More importantly, they learned about children's cultures, engaged in creating authentic intercultural identity texts, and grew in practicing their social responsibilities.

Preservice teachers' reflections indicated enhanced understandings about students and their cultures:

- Differences between cultures mean that teachers need be aware of the diversity inside diversity. Children are aware of differences between cultures in different geographic areas within the same country. It is important to identify the culture in general and the specific cultures within that culture. By sharing and comparing, students gain a better understanding of their own cultures.

- Children's perceptions of their own cultures are influenced by how society views them. Much of teacher knowledge about minority cultures comes from society and schools, which means it is full of stereotypes. Unfortunately, some Indigenous children do internalize these stereotypes.

- Children show pride in their identities when they share their cultural knowledge. Many know their culture much better than teachers do, but did not consider their knowledge important before this experience. It was through conversations facilitated by teachers that students were willing to share their stories and gradually felt that their knowledge was valuable. Teachers can nurture intercultural understanding not only for the students but for themselves.

- Symbols and colors are two major elements by which children make connections to their cultures. As long as they are willing to explore by making connections, they show their rich knowledge about their cultural heritages.

Preservice teachers' reflections indicated understandings about teaching:

- Dialogue is a powerful way to invite students' funds of knowledge into classrooms. The conversations and questions posed by students among themselves helped them reflect deeply on their experiences and stories. Questions posed out of curiosity inspired children to put more details into their stories.
- Conversations and discussions among children with similar cultural backgrounds resulted in collaborative talk that inspired them to create deeper understanding and knowledge about their cultures.
- Making comparisons among languages and cultures inspired students to share their knowledge and to learn more about their languages and cultures. Some children, however, did lose their mother tongues because their mothers or fathers could not speak these languages fluently.
- Children's interviews of parents were a good way to collect family stories. These stories showed differences between minority and mainstream cultures, and between their culture's past and present.
- Drawing can be an important mediator for children to share their stories. By drawing, they share knowledge and experiences not available in their writing.
- Publication and presentations inspired children to write and draw as a way to share their stories. In turn, sharing their stories continued the conversation.
- Teachers need to learn children's languages to show an appreciation of children's cultures. After teachers learned some of children's languages, even only a few words of greeting, children felt closer to their teachers and were inspired to share more of their knowledge and culture.

Trust is an issue when we work with children from minority backgrounds because of their anxiety about being accepted by someone from the mainstream culture. They needed time to find balance and identity in growing up as both bilingual and bicultural.

This collaborative inquiry began with a concern for authentic global children's literature that included insiders' perspectives (Bishop 1990) and grew into a process of localizing global knowledge. We engaged in a pedagogical approach of funds of knowledge using global literature to create identity texts of minority children in Taiwan. If books were not available, we found ways for children to create their own texts.

Throughout this process, all participants learned. As a teacher educator, I learned to put theory into practice to address my concerns about intercultural education in Taiwan. Preservice teachers learned to work with children from culturally diverse backgrounds and to celebrate intercultural differences. Students of minority backgrounds developed pride in their personal cultural identities and created identity texts. The books created by children became resources for curriculum in the schools. This inquiry thus leads to new inquiries as we work together within schools and share students' stories with other teachers and students to demonstrate a way of nurturing intercultural understanding.

Recommended Books That Invite Global Perspectives

Chen, Chih-Yuan. 2003. *On My Way to Buy Eggs*. LaJolla, CA: Kane Miller. On her way to the grocery store to buy eggs for her father, a young girl explores the neighborhood, enjoying her interactions with animals and nature. This simple story shares a child's perspective of her world with the illustrations depicting a community with independent grocery stores in Taiwan.

Sun, Xin-Yu. 2008.一日遊 [*One Day Trip*]. Taipei, Taiwan: Hsin-Yi Foundation. This wordless book has two story lines on each page. The lower part of the page is a family trip to a zoo where all the animals have disappeared, and the upper part of the page is about the animals' one-day trip. The animals take Sunday off and use the MRT (Mass Rapid Transit) to visit famous sights in Taipei City, joining humans at the end of the day to enjoy the sunset over the Tamsui River.

Zeng, Qing-Yang. 1988. 媽媽,買綠豆 [*Mama, Buy Mung Beans*]. Illus. Guo-Hua Wan. Taipei, Taiwan: Hsin-Yi Foundation.

This wordless book consists of short interactions between a boy and his mom. The boy likes to go with his mother to the market, where they buy mung beans to make sweet mung-bean soup and mung-bean ice pops, popular desserts in Taiwan. The boy often keeps a few seeds to make mung-bean sprouts. The illustrations show daily life in Taiwan as well as local foods.

Zhu, Xiu-Fang. 2001. 走,去迪化街買年貨 [*Go to Di-Hua Street Shopping for Chinese New Year*]. Illus. Li-Ya Chen. Taipei, Taiwan: Children's Publications.

The Chinese New Year is important to Chinese people, with food playing a significant role in the celebration. People shop for these special foods on Di-Hua Street, an old community that mixes the traditional with the modern. The book follows a boy and his grandfather on Di-Hua Street, visiting temples, clothing stores, groceries, and Chinese medicine shops as they enjoy the crowds of people bustling with noise and excitement.

References

Bishop, Rudine Sims. 1990. "Mirrors, Windows, and Sliding Glass Doors." *Perspectives* 6 (3): ix–xi.

_____. 2012. "Reflections on the Development of African American Children's Literature." *Journal of Children's Literature* 38 (2): 5–13.

Cai, Mingshui, and Rudine Sims Bishop. 1994. "Multicultural Literature for Children." In *The Need for Story*, ed. Anne Haas Dyson and Celia Genishi, 57–71. Urbana, IL: National Council of Teachers of English.

Cummins, Jim. 2006. "Identity Texts: The Imaginative Construction of Self Through Multiliteracies Pedagogy." In *Imagining Multilingual School: Language in Education and Globalization*, ed. Ofelia Garcia, Tove Stutnabb-Kangas, and Maria Torres Guzman, 51–68. Clevedon, UK: Multilingual Matters.

Cummins, Jim, and Margaret Early. 2011. *Identity Texts: The Collaborative Creation of Power in Multilingual Schools*. London: Trentham Books.

González, Norma, Luis Moll, and Cathy Amanti. 2005. *Funds of Knowledge: Theorizing Practices in Households, Communities, and Classrooms*. Mahwah, NJ: Erlbaum.

Martin, Fran. 2008. "Mutual Learning: The Impact of a Study Visit Course on UK Teachers' Knowledge and Understanding of Global Partnerships." *Critical Literacy: Theories and Practices* 2(1): 60–75.

Ruíz, Richard. 1984. "Orientations in a Language Planning." *NABE* Journal, 8(2): 15–34.

Short, Kathy G., and Dana Fox. 2003. "The Complexity of Cultural Authenticity in Children's Literature." In *Stories Matter: The Complexity of Cultural Authenticity in Children's Literature*, ed. Kathy G. Short and Dana Fox, 3–24. Urbana, IL: National Council of Teachers of English.

Vygotsky, Lev. 1978. *Mind in Society: The Development of Higher Psychological Processes*. Cambridge, MA: Harvard University Press.

Chinese References

Hakka Affairs Council. 2011. 2010–2011 National Survey of Hakka Population.
(行政院客家委員會99-100年全國客家人口基礎資料調查2011.)

Hsia, Hsiao-Chuan. 2003. The Localization of Praxis-Oriented Research: The Case of "Foreign Brides Literacy Programs." (A Case Study of a Literacy Program for Foreign Brides.") *Taiwan: A Radical Quarterly in Social Studies* 49:1–47.
(實踐是研究的在地實踐: 以"外籍新娘識字班"為例.台灣社會研究季刊 49:1–47.)

National Immigration Agency. 2012. First Project Report of Torch Project for Immigrant
(全國新住民火炬計畫推動小組第1次會議業務報告).
http://www.immigration.gov.tw/np.asp?ctNode=32967&mp=1.

The 20th Forum of Taiwan Sociology of Education. 2014.
(第20屆台灣教育社會學論壇. 2014.)
http://www.ed.ntnu.edu.tw/IS/index.php?id=1209&parent_id=1217.

Children's Books Cited

Gamble, Adam. 2006. *Good Night Boston*. Illus. Joe Veno. Boston: Our World of Books.

Keister, Douglas. 2007. *To Grandmother's House: A Visit to Old Town Beijing* (bilingual edition). Layton, UT: Gibbs Smith.

Chinese Children's Books Cited

Chen, Jia-Chi. 2012. *Kaleidoscope of the Indigenous: Introduction of Taiwan Indigenous*. Illus. Feng-Young Ho. Taipei, Taiwan: Council of Indigenous Peoples. (原住民萬花筒:台灣原住民簡介兒童繪本.文:陳佳淇;圖:侯方揚.出版項：臺北市:行政院原民會.)

Lee, Mong-Fen. 2009. *Amis Grandma*. Taitong, Taiwan: National Dong Hwa University.
    (阿美野菜奶奶 李孟芬 文圖 台東市: 東華大學出版.)

Ming-Ko. 2010. *Vietnamese Cinderella: Folktale of Ancient Vietnam*. Trans. into
    Chinese by Jun Feng Liu. Taipei, Taiwan: Go Go Books Co., Ltd.
    (Tam Kam. 越南民間故事:古越南灰姑娘傳奇.明國著,劉君方譯.狗狗圖書.)

PART 3

Cross-Cultural Studies

Chapter 8

Sliding Glass Doors That Open South Korea for American Children

Yoo Kyung Sung and Genny O'Herron

mong educators who embrace and promote multicultural and global literature as a tool to develop readers' social responsibility, the metaphor of windows and mirrors is an expression and concept that is referenced frequently (Bishop 1990). This metaphor conveys the belief that children deserve a balanced curriculum in which they see themselves and their worldview reflected in the books, posters, conversations, and activities that surround them in the classroom. Those are the mirrors.

Too many mirrors create a distorted reflection, however, like a hall of mirrors at an amusement park. It is unlikely that children will develop a disposition for global citizenship or an active examination of social justice and responsibility surrounded by images of only themselves. We have to provide windows, opportunities to look out onto the landscape of natural human variation with a penetrating gaze of curiosity and acceptance. In a balanced ratio, windows and mirrors affirm and expand everyone's life.

Yet it isn't that simple. Even with lots of windows and mirrors, children still resist and reject books and activities that emphasize global citizenship. The opportunity to consider, explore, and integrate facts and feelings about people and places far away from us, different from us, and unfamiliar to us is lost, a frustrating experience for teachers who care about global education. What can be changed?

For starters, it is not enough to have windows and mirrors. They are important, but if children don't have an accessible "entry point" to these multicultural and global perspectives and awareness, they are irrelevant. It is like a high-rise building of craftsmanship construction, with level after level of large windows and an interior full of ornate mirrors, *but no entryway*! No one can enjoy or appreciate the views from these windows or self-reflections from these mirrors if they cannot get into the building. The same tension exists with text sets, read-alouds, and cultural studies that are replete with global perspectives and awareness. If students cannot "get into" those materials and resources, they don't enjoy or appreciate anything being offered, including new perspectives, information, or insights. For the hypothetical high-rise and our real-world lesson plans, we need an appropriate, accessible entrance. It is helpful if the entrance is clearly marked, but at minimum, it needs to be functional. We need to know where the door is, and so do our students if we want them to pass through it.

This chapter is a reflective account about how we, a third-grade classroom teacher at a charter school (Genny) and a South Korean collaborator (Yoo Kyung) from a local university in Albuquerque, New Mexico, built a "sliding glass door" so that students could access a five-week inquiry about South Korea. For the sake of simplicity, we use the terms *South Korea* and *Korea* interchangeably throughout this chapter. We share details, detours, and discoveries from this cross-cultural study. We also discuss how we reframed our curriculum to better support students' growth in intercultural understanding, and, perhaps most importantly, we examine how students transitioned from passivity into making passionate connections through the use of a proactive critical literacy lens.

Our cultural study involved typical third graders: adorable, clever, boisterous, opinionated, funny eight- and nine-year-olds. Our setting, Mountain Mahogany Community School, is not a typical school. This small charter school focuses on the development of the whole child and joyous learning. The faculty is encouraged to take creative risks to enhance their teaching, and the school uses a heart-vulnerable relational model for communication systems, discipline, and pedagogy. The small campus in New Mexico's largest city has about two hundred students who attend grades K–8. More than twenty zip codes are represented in the student body, with more than 50 percent of the children qualifying for free or reduced lunches and more than 30 percent receiving special education services.

Selecting South Korea for our first collaborative cross-cultural study was intentional. As a cultural insider, Yoo Kyung, who grew up in South Korea and teaches children's literature courses at a local university in Albuquerque, could easily serve as an intimate sounding board for curricular decisions and provide feedback about cultural authenticity. To capitalize on this background knowledge, we brainstormed throughout the fall, both of us reading, thinking, sharing ideas, and getting excited. Yoo Kyung purchased Korean children's books during a trip back home to see family and friends, and Genny shopped at a local international market for Korean treats and trinkets. Together we developed lesson plans and gathered resources and candidates for guest speakers. The "windows" and "mirrors" were in place when the unit was scheduled to begin. But, even with all of this support and collaboration and these resources, Genny still froze at the "doorway" of this cross-cultural study. Understanding our guiding framework helps to contextualize this paralysis.

Our Guiding Framework and Unit

We developed our inquiry unit with the ambitious intention that students were not simply going to learn about South Korean culture but were also going to observe and reflect on their own cross-cultural growth throughout this learning journey. Of course, as with all inquiry learning, discoveries led to rediscoveries and multiple new discoveries, and a range of strategies and materials were used to facilitate a circular and organic unfolding and deepening. At the blueprint level, though, we had a focus question and a basic plan and a series of experiences. Our guiding question was how to encourage the curiosity and compassion of students who are more familiar and comfortable with looking at the mirrors and get them to gaze out expansive windows into the world beyond. To this end, the unit was shaped around the following sequence of engagements:

- Read and discuss children's books about New Mexico to explore the common literary portrayal (and possible stereotypes) of our home state
- Engage with the inquiry focus of South Korea
  - Provide a familiar way of learning about Korean culture through an author study of Linda Sue Park
  - Explore Korean culture through global children's literature
  - Investigate issues about authorship to encourage students to consider cultural insider/outsider perspectives and the issue of cultural authenticity and stereotyping in learning about South Korea
  - Think about Korean cultures in the roles of reader, reviewer, and pen pal writer
- Use a critical lens to identify and examine pervasive South Korean stereotypes
  - Connect to common stereotypes found in fiction about New Mexico
- Correspond with Korean-student pen pals in Seoul

Two intercultural education models illuminated our questioning and reflections: the Continuum of Intercultural Learning (CIL) by Fennes and Hapgood (1997) and the Developmental Model of Intercultural Sensitivity (DMIS) by Bennett (1993). DMIS provides explanations for the reactions people commonly have to cultural difference. Bennett defines the underlying premise, saying that as people's experiences with cultural differences become more complex and sophisticated, they increase their competence in intercultural relations. "By recognizing the underlying cognitive orientation toward cultural difference, predictions about behavior and attitudes can be made and education can be tailored to facilitated development into the next stage" (Bennett 2003, 158). The first three stages—denial, defense, and minimization—are ethnocentric. The second three DMIS stages are ethnorelative and involve acceptance, adaptation, and integration.

Similarly, Fennes and Hapgood (1997) note that there are seven major steps in Continuum of Intercultural Learning (CIL) to move toward intercultural competence: ethnocentrism (resistance), awareness, understanding, acceptance and respect, appreciation and valuing, change, and intercultural competence. We found it helpful to interpret students' increasing intercultural competence—particularly their transition from active resistance to engagement—using both models. It was also fascinating to trace Genny's growth and movement through the various stages as a way to understand why so many teachers conceive well-intended cross-cultural studies that are actually poorly implemented because they never move past an ethnocentric worldview.

Curriculum Reframing Requires Vulnerability

The inquiry unit we designed had impressive windows and mirrors and even plenty of "window dressing." It was a unit to be proud of, but Genny still found herself struggling unexpectedly with resistance when it was time to turn adult theoretical planning into a shared child-centered classroom reality. For her, there was self-doubt and insecurity about her capacity to facilitate a meaningful exploration of South Korea. She felt awkward, uncomfortable, and unsure, worrying about perpetuating stereotypes. She was also concerned about being able to identify examples of cultural authenticity and inauthenticity in the books students explored. She wondered if she would be an academic version of the "ugly American" of exploitative tourism. That thought turned into fear—she didn't want to be seen that way or see herself in that manner. She felt embarrassed and self-conscious. With deeper reflection, she was able to identify that her discomfort and reluctance stemmed from a fear of not being able to do it "right," even though—and especially since—she didn't know what "right" was! It was an emotionally painful and confusing time.

This awareness gave us considerable insight into the resistance that teachers experience and must penetrate in order to reframe curriculum with a global lens. Beneath resistance, typically, there is fear of one kind or another that must be faced honestly and ultimately transformed. This was our first adjustment: helping Genny reframe her fear. Intercultural education, after all, is not a vehicle for instant transformation. It is a gradual process that takes a particular combination of humility, openness, perseverance, and surrender to leave what is comfortable and familiar. For educators this includes leaving behind an authoritative attitude of knowing and teaching in order to venture into a realm of learning with, learning from, and unlearning. This stance challenges core identity politics of white privilege for white teachers, first-world assumptions and arrogance, and the iconic perceptions of teachers as knowledge holders. The sage-on-the-stage, all-knowing-teacher paradigm that has persisted, even though it is contradicted by current best practices, falls away entirely. In a word, reframing the curriculum requires vulnerability.

Using the doorway metaphor, this fear is like knowing where the entry point is for a book, activity, or unit but still needing to disarm the building security system in order to enter the material with students. The fear of judgment, failure, parental disapproval, administrative disapproval, poor student reception, or incompetence needs to be turned off. Eventually Genny was disarmed through frequent collaboration with Yoo Kyung and classmates at the university where she was taking graduate classes. Even with the entrance alarm inactive, though, she was still alone—her students were not with her. They were on the outside of the study that she and Yoo Kyung had designed, and they needed help moving into it and through the stages of intercultural competence—from denial, defense, and minimization toward acceptance (Fennes and Hapgood 1997). It was time to say, like any friendly door staff, "Welcome, kids! Come on in!" Empowered by her conscious shift on the Continuum of Intercultural Learning, Genny was able to make this invitation and entry through the doorway easier and more effective for students.

Children's Books as Entryway

The US Census Bureau 2010–2014 American Community Survey (2016) reveals that 2.6 percent of the Albuquerque population identifies as Asian American (1.4 percent of the state population).Accordingly, we anticipated that our students might have little knowledge or cultural sensitivity about different Asian American groups. This lack of information and empathy was not the main problem, though. True to the models on intercultural understanding (and similar to Genny's process), with little or no background knowledge about this area of the world, most third graders seemed neither curious nor comfortable learning about South Korea.

Initially, there were three distinct reactions to the content we brought: interest, indifference, and aversion. Aversion—both comic and serious—gripped the class at first. Comments of disdain and ridicule erupted about what the students found "dumb" and "stupid," and it would have been easier to just exit our endeavor altogether at that point. Alarmed but committed, we relied on various books that we hoped would have strong visual appeal. The results were mixed but, thanks to our guiding framework, promising.

On the first day that students looked at picturebooks and nonfiction texts about South Korea (see Figure 8.1), Jeff kept repeating, "This is freaky—this is so freaky" as he paged through pictures of a people and place that were completely foreign to him. Ryan insisted, "I don't want to learn about this place. I hate Korea!" after admitting that he knew nothing about South Korea. (Note that all names are pseudonyms.) Other children pointed and laughed at unfamiliar objects and activities in the books. Some appeared bored and were barely looking at the books. A few found sections of text about the Korean War and were deep into discussions about the military and video games.

FICTION	LANGUAGE AVAILABILITY
Choung, Eun-hee. 2008. *Minji's Salon*. Kim, Young Jin (illus.). La Jolla, CA: Kane/Miller.	Available in Korean and English
Go, Dae Young. 2007. 용돈 주세요 *[Allowance, Please!]*. Kim, Young Jin (illus.). Paju, Korea: Gilbutkid.	Available only in Korean
Go, Dae Young. 2008. 손톱 깨물기 *[My Sister Is Nail Biting]*. Kim, Young Jin (illus.). Paju, Korea: Gilbutkid.	Available only in Korean
Kwon, Yoon Duck. 2007. *My Cat Copies Me*. La Jolla, CA: Kane/Miller.	Available in Korean and English
Lee, Hyun Young. 2008. *Something for School*. La Jolla, CA: Kane/Miller.	Available in Korean and English
Lee, Suzy. 2007. *The Zoo*. La Jolla, CA: Kane/Miller.	Available in Korean and English

FICTION	LANGUAGE AVAILABILITY
Park, Linda Sue. 2005. *Bee-Bim Bop!* Lee, Ho Baek (illus). New York: Clarion Books.	Available in Korean and English
Park, Linda Sue. 2006. *Archer's Quest*. New York: Clarion Books.	English
Lee, T. J. 2007. 엄마마중/*Waiting for Mama*. New York: NorthSouth.	Korean and English bilingual book
NONFICTION (ENGLISH LANGUAGE)	
Cheung, Hyechong, and Prodeepta Das. 2008. *K Is for Korea*. London: Frances Lincoln.	
Haberle, Susan E. 2005. *South Korea: A Question and Answer Book*. Mankato, MN: Capstone.	
Han, Heung-Gi. 2006. *Let's Visit Korea*. Elizabeth, NJ: Hollym.	
Park, Kyubyong, and Henry Amen. 2001. *My First Book of Korean Words*. New York: Clarion Books.	
Stickler, John. 2003. *Land of Morning Calm: Korean Culture Then and Now*. Illus. Soma Han. Fremont, CA: Shen's Books.	

Figure 8.1 **Text Set on Korean Cultures**

Without the CIL and DMIS models, the initial lack of engagement and the intensity of words such as *hate*, along with the dismissiveness of words such as *freaky* might have derailed us. Instead, we had a context in which to understand their deeper meaning. Ryan's word choice of *hate*, for example, was probably a young child's protective strategy toward something unfamiliar, even though it had the tone of racism or nationalism. Pardy (2011) notes, "Hate then might be understood as vehement closure, a defensive and offensive response to a traumatic libidinal intrusion of the other . . . Hate is an emotional strategy for pulling oneself together" (56). Ryan's way of describing an uncomfortable feeling about unfamiliarity is the first response—resistance—in intercultural understanding development. Jeff's "freaky" comment had similar nuances.

Within the framework for the Developmental Model of Intercultural Sensitivity (Bennett 1993), each stage for developing intercultural sensitivity indicates a particular cognitive structure expressed in certain kinds of attitudes and behavior related to cultural difference. When Jeff insisted that the images he was viewing of Korean culture were "freaky," he was demonstrating verbally that he was in the ethnocentric stage, meaning his own culture was still being experienced as central to reality. Although it could look like uncensored xenophobia on the surface, such strong resistance expressed in the language of *freaky* and *hate* is actually natural resistance toward anomalies and difference. If left in this stage, tremendous damage is done in terms of alienating, "othering," and adopting superiority constructs of self, but we made sure to stretch students forward.

The first stage of resistance can be graphic and is probably the most challenging for classroom teachers. However, along with outspoken students disgruntled about aspects of unfamiliarity, there were also a few children who were excited about the new things they were seeing and reading. They were clearly in an ethnorelative stage. As they perused the books, the common exclamation was "Wow, this is cool!" Bennett (2003) defines *ethnorelative* as experiencing one's own culture in the context of other cultures. Both the "freaky/hater" kids and the "this-is-cool" kids were in stages that reflect the worldview of "Difference-seekers" (159). However, students who named Korean culture "cool" were in the stage of acceptance in which they were curious about and respectful toward cultural difference (Bennett 2003). Both reactions indicated that students had seen the doorway to our cross-cultural study, but that door remained closed because the stage of acceptance still involves judging cultural difference negatively. To shift that, stories were needed to push the door open.

Stories to Help the Heart and Mind Expand

Nigerian poet and novelist Ben Okri (1993) has said, "Stories can conquer fear, you know. They can make the heart bigger" (46). As third graders began their cross-cultural study about South Korea and Korean culture, we started a new lunchtime read-aloud of the Newbery Medal winner *A Single Shard* by Linda Sue Park (2001). Since third graders were familiar with the Newbery Award, they weren't resistant to listening to Genny read Park's book about twelfth-century Korea. Simultaneously, creating an author study of Linda Sue Park during the afternoon literacy block was another powerful avenue through which to expand our knowledge of Korean culture. We were able to discuss the author's identity and the cultural authenticity of a Korean American author who writes about Korean culture. Interestingly, Linda Sue Park was raised in a family and extended environment that did not intentionally emphasize her cultural heritage. Her determined effort to research and study Korean culture eventually helped her overcome her biologically-Korean-raised-in-America obstacles (Pereira 2008).

A Single Shard was not only the winner of the Newbery Award, but was also republished in South Korea in the Korean written language, Hangeul. In Genny's hands, reading it every day, ancient Korea immediately came alive in the classroom as the story of Tree-

Ear activated imaginations and warmed hearts. Every morning when the class resumed the cross-cultural study, thoughts and questions were refined; during every lunch period, interest and engagement increased. It was a powerfully reinforcing dynamic. And it started with one book—a book that functioned like an automatic door opener that is easily pressed and immediately responsive.

Multiple Entry Points

The fancy, main entrance of a building has its universally accessible door opener, but all large buildings have multiple entryways, not just one grand doorway. All large inquiry units do as well. In our South Korea unit, in addition to the Linda Sue Park read-aloud and author study as our door opener, spanning the entire time of the inquiry project, we had five sub-units or distinct entryways into deeper learning about the country and culture of South Korea. These sub-units are interrelated and part of a continuum of our learning journey, but they each had a specific focus and intended purpose. Most children progressed through them in a linear fashion; one door opened the next door, and so on. But some children found one favorite entrance and used it repeatedly. We begin with doorway number one.

The Land of Enchantment: Beginning with Our Culture

"In books, New Mexicans are often portrayed as poor," Adriana observed. "I think all the Hispanics makes our state special," Ivanna asserted. "In books, New Mexicans are often portrayed as eating Mexican food," Malik shared. These are some of the observations students made as they spent three mornings examining the images and storylines found in picturebooks about New Mexico before discussing anything about Korea. Children were guided to answer these two questions: How do we see ourselves as New Mexicans in books? What do we know about the area where we live?

There aren't a lot of children's books about New Mexico, but Genny read *Los Ojos del Tejedor: The Eyes of the Weaver* by Cristina Ortega (1998) and one of the books from the Carlos series by Jan Romero Stevens (1993). In the classroom, the rest of Jan Romero Stevens's books were on display along with *Miguel and the Santero* by Sandra Guzzo (1993), *The Farolitos of Christmas* by Rudolfo Anaya (1995), *ABC in Albuquerque* by Robin Segal (2009), and *E Is for Enchantment: A New Mexico Alphabet* by Helen Foster James (2004).

We included activities where partial statements were listed that children had to complete, such as "New Mexicans like to eat _____" or "New Mexicans enjoy _____." Genny emphasized that there were no right or wrong answers, that we were just trying to capture impressions, and it soon became apparent to third graders from the books and conversation that there is no one monolithic New Mexican experience. Some New Mexicans *are* poor, for example, but most students didn't feel like that label applied to them. Some New Mexicans have chile *ristras* hanging outside their home (a common image in picturebooks); none of the third graders did. Some New Mexicans are Latino; most of the class didn't self-identify as Latino and felt their ethnicity was special.

Next, students looked at nonfiction books about New Mexico and started recording facts. The question posed was, "What do we know about our state?" The following day, Genny read *Carlos and the Squash Plant* by Jan Romero Stevens (1993). Stevens is a New Mexican author, and the story is set in Espanola, New Mexico. Afterward, students were in pairs reading more Carlos books. They were given a piece of paper with four questions: How is landscape pictured? What foods are described? What do houses and buildings look like? What do you notice about the way people dress, speak, and act? As they read, they jotted notes. Genny modeled this first with a book she read earlier in the week, *Los Ojos del Tejedor: The Eyes of the Weaver* by Cristina Ortega (1998). Students looked through two other books, *The Farolitos of Christmas* (Anaya 1995) and *Miguel and the Santero* (Guzzo 1993).

Genny continually asked students to consider how New Mexicans are portrayed in books. Observations were enumerated on the board with lots of animated conversation. Persistent images (especially the ones that didn't relate to these third graders, such as the preponderance of rural images) were also noted. The class explored the word *stereotype*, and Genny alluded to the fact that they would be studying another place soon: a country called South Korea. She felt confident that they now had enough grounding in their own regional culture, the Land of Enchantment, to be able to begin exploring perspectives from the Land of the Morning Calm (South Korea's nickname).

Initial Steps Toward Intercultural Understanding

The third-grade class hopped continents after thinking about the fact and fiction of New Mexico as we know it and as shown in the limited collection of picturebooks that emphasize rural, traditional realities. Genny showed students the continent of Asia, South Korea, and neighboring countries on a large map. Because Bennett's stage of denial includes an inability to differentiate national cultures, this geography focus was critical.

Genny prompted students to consider, "What do we know or think we know about South Korea?" Some answers were confusing: "Women who have children don't have a lot of money." "Korean beef is different" (this child thought that the cows or actual meat was different as opposed to simply being prepared differently). Other responses included these:

- Korea is a country in Asia.
- Psy is a South Korean musician.
- *Miyok* (seaweed) and kimchi are Korean food. (This was provided by Sam, whose grandfather is Korean.)
- People can swim across the Yellow Sea. (This became a contentious debate, with one boy insisting that it was impossible because the Yellow Sea is a thousand miles wide.)
- There was a Korean War.

After children generated these ideas as a whole group, Genny asked them to list something they knew about Korea on an index card (Figure 8.2). Some insisted they didn't know anything. Genny told them they could copy an idea from the list they had generated. This time, their responses were more elaborate and richly personalized. For example, Sam wrote about her grandfather's escape from North Korea. Others wrote about their grandfathers' participation in the Korean War. Psy was recognized as a "fun" singer who sang "Gangnam Style," a recently released song they loved. Personal connections were made with the limited facts they had brainstormed earlier in a positive manner. This movement in CIL, from resistance to awareness and understanding, and the progression in DMIS, from ethnocentrism to enthnorelativity, continued as we used fiction published in the United States and informational texts to learn as much as we could about the culture and country of Korea.

After several days of open-ended investigation, Genny encouraged students to begin their research by looking specifically at the nonfiction books about Korea on a book display shelf. Many of these texts emphasized the "five Fs" of food, fashion, festivals, famous people, and folklore. To balance this limited depiction, Genny told third graders they would also be using the Internet to see more images of South Korea.

At this point, most students were straddling the middle stages of acceptance in both frameworks. Viewing contemporary pop culture immediately advanced them into the

CIL stages of respect and appreciation and the DMSI ethnnorelative stages of acceptance and adaptation. Adaptation is marked by a curiosity and eagerness to experience other cultures. Accordingly, attempts are made to learn how to act in ways that are more or less appropriate in those cultural contexts, which was evidenced by the students' interactions with guest speakers.

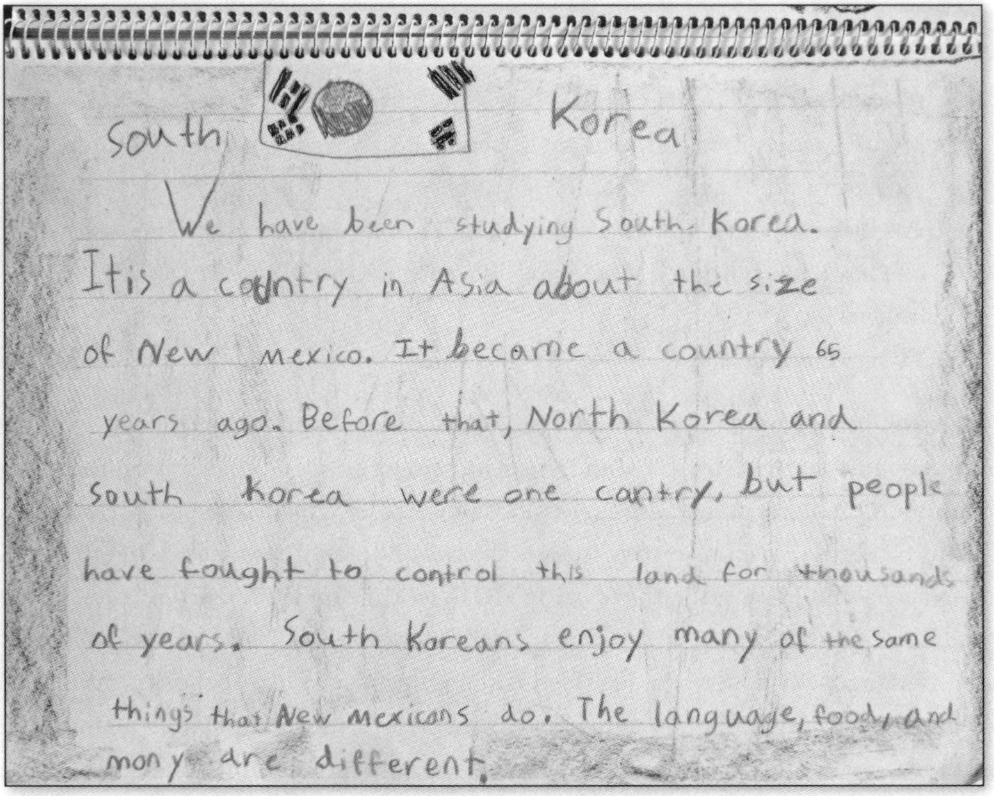
South Korea

We have been studying South Korea. It is a country in Asia about the size of New mexico. It became a country 65 years ago. Before that, North Korea and South korea were one cantry, but people have fought to control this land for thousands of years. South Koreans enjoy many of the same things that New mexicans do. The language, food, and mony are different.

Figure 8.2 Example of Children's Open Investigations of Korea

The "Whopum Gangnam Style" Entrance

Students watched a YouTube video about Olympic gold skater Yu-Na Kim. After the video Genny asked them what they noticed and what surprised them. The surprises all revolved around the modern images. Then the class broke into groups. Small groups looked through nonfiction books with the assignment to record impressions and questions while one group at a time watched a Korean travel video. Again, the aspects of modern life they viewed surprised them—they were attuning to similarities now, not just differences. Other clips of famous Korean celebrities were discussed, but none were embraced as much as Psy's song "Gangnam Style." After gesticulations and a spontaneous sing-along—complete with dancing—concluded, Yoo Kyung described the affluent Gangnam District of Seoul, class differences in her country, and what the song was about. Class issues were now on the children's radar, as well as rural and urban differences and traditional and contemporary distinctions.

The Door of Different Perspectives

Providing access to cultural insiders is one of the surest ways to excite and expand children's intercultural learning. In our case, because so much scaffolding was in place, third graders were primed to have an ethnorelative experience. When Yoo Kyung came in to meet the class as a guest, for example, the classroom was set up not only to welcome her, but also to proudly present the depth and breadth of students' learning. Looking like an interactive museum exhibit (Figures 8.3 and 8.4), the room had a listening center for audiobooks and Korean music. There were dioramas and essays displayed about Korean housing, clothing, and food. Hand-drawn maps and flags hung on the walls, and there were tables and baskets full of fiction and informational texts about Korea. There were also text sets written in English and Korean and a collection of books published in South Korea in Hangeul without translations into English (Figure 8.5).

Figures 8.3 Interactive Museum Artifacts from the Children's Inquiry

Figure 8.4 Interactive Museum Artifacts from the Children's Inquiry

Figure 8.5 Picturebooks in Two Languages to Examine the Portrayal of Korea

Before Yoo Kyung's visit, two Korean graduate students from the university had already been guests in the classroom, so students were extra-excited and prepared for her. They had learned a lot of interesting things from the previous presentations and were enthusiastic about demonstrating their knowledge. They were also clear about wanting to learn Hangeul, the written Korean language. To oblige, Yoo Kyung first shared several popular children's books written in Hangeul. She translated the books they had affectionately called the Naughty Boy and Sister series (2006–2013), a fitting title for a collection of books about a young boy who is constantly in trouble—which is all they could understand from the illustrations before Yoo Kyung read to them (Figure 8.6). Then she gave them a mini-lesson on how to read the Korean alphabet. Korean Hangeul is easy to learn because of its simple decoding, so they immediately wanted to learn to spell their names.

The questions the third graders' posed at this point were almost exclusively about contemporary Korea. Instead of simple compliments about certain things they liked, they had serious, thoughtful questions, asking, among other things, what their same-age Korean peers do for fun and inquiring about the popularity of Legos among Korean children. Yoo Kyung noticed that many of their questions were related to the picturebooks that were published in Korea for Korean audiences, which they had looked at together earlier. It was as if students recognized and wanted to categorize subtle cultural differences and similarities that they noticed in books. Stephanie commented, for example, "You have a woman on some of your money. We don't have any women on our money because we've never had a woman president."

The time with students was not Yoo Kyung's first experience talking about Korean culture in a question-and-answer format. In her previous presentations, however, it always seemed that her country of origin was too foreign for most of the children, which was a disappointing experience for her. In contrast to that experience of minimization, these students had insightful questions and such a proactive manner of seeking answers that she was compelled to share extensively. She even brought up intricate details about topics such as the spectacular blossoming of the cherry trees in spring, because students were so fascinated and engaged.

Initially, Yoo Kyung credited the pop sensation Psy's "Gangnam Style" song for this authentic interest in contemporary Korea, but as soon as children asked her to translate the Korean picturebooks, she came to appreciate the power of those cultural artifacts. It was clear that these students cared about the culture, people, and places they had encountered in books. They had developed relationships with Korean protagonists, scoured informational texts, and treasured other environmental print that traveled home with a different child each night in a Korean backpack. This bag contained English-Korean bilingual audiobooks, vocabulary magnets, Korean schoolbooks, and Korean snack food in colorful packaging that students could enjoy with their families. The backpack was one of their favorite windows into South Korea.

Figure 8.6 Yoo Kyung Sharing *A Naughty Boy*

Practicing Critical Literacy: Our Pen Pal Project

We believe our cross-cultural study was successful because we provided different ways for students to look out the many windows of nonfiction and fiction books published in the United States, books published in Korea and republished as translations in the United States, and books about Korean Americans and Korea written by Linda Sue Park. With all of these windows, Genny invited students to think like book reviewers and critics. As a class, they explored issues of cultural authenticity, positionality, and stereotyping by asking increasingly complex questions about specific descriptions or images in books about Korea that were published in the United States or only in Korea. They made connections to their early experience of exploring how New Mexican culture was represented in books and what elements of our local cultures were missing from them.

We knew we were on track several weeks into the unit when Gabe posed the question, "How come Korean children in American informational books always wear dance outfits or masks? Korean children in Korean books don't wear special dresses or masks." This was the comment of a child who was clearly reaching toward intercultural competence, and his peers were right there with him. We were pleased that we had essentially created sliding glass doors for these youngsters. They could see into and out of their cultural study with ease (i.e., questioning the different representations that appeared in books published in the United States and books published in Korea). They could easily access new ideas and information about the Land of the Morning Calm as genuine inquirers for intercultural learning. They had arrived authentically at self-driven critical literacy.

By the end of our unit, third graders had developed such a strong relationship with Korean culture and fictional characters (see Figures 8.7 and 8.8) that they were perfectly poised to begin personal relationships with elementary school pen pals in Seoul. Yoo Kyung's friend Hee Young, an elementary school teacher at GangDong Elementary School, facilitated that experience with her students. In carefully written letters, Genny's students attempted to sign their names and add short phrases in Hangeul. They asked both personal and cultural questions and shared vulnerable and tender aspects of their own lives. They added pictures, origami, photographs, and little trinkets to lengthy letters and sent them parcel post to Seoul six times. Eight- and nine-year-olds communicated across cultural boundaries with intercultural competence—Genny and the South Korean teacher Hee Young were comparing notes and realities in the same ethnorelative manner. These changes occurred because both teacher and students experienced and embraced the early, confusing stages of resistance.

Negotiating School Mandates

This cross-cultural study took place in the educational landscape of irony and entitlement. As a charter school, Mountain Mahogany Community School affords great autonomy, leadership, and empowerment to its faculty. It also invests sizably in professional development that helps teachers wrestle with issues of race, diversity, and systems of oppression. It strives to provide rich, meaningful intercultural education at the same time that its faculty and student body do not reflect the ethnic or racial demographics of the city or state. The school is a predominantly white space, while the Greater Albuquerque metropolitan area is 40.3 percent White, 48.1 percent Hispanic or Latino, 5.1 percent Native American, and 2.1 percent Asian (Albuquerque Economic Development 2015).

Figure 8.7 **Reading and Connecting to Korean Characters**

The school is bound by the same state and national mandates as every other public school, and is also accountable to its charter, which has explicit goals in the areas of joy and security, literacy and critical thinking, school life as real life, individualized learning, universal empathy, environmental awareness, ongoing school growth, and media literacy. This makes it both easier and surprisingly harder to incorporate global and intercultural perspectives and curricular innovation. It is easier because there is unwavering support to teach with a critical framework and a creative spirit. It is harder because being well meaning does not make one culturally competent, and yet there is an expectation in an institution like this that one automatically is (which seems to perpetuate an invisible ethnocentrism). The faculty does not always admit that "they don't know what they don't know," and being stretched thin, like all teachers today, they don't actively embrace and support their own progression through intercultural learning and intercultural sensitivity.

Nonetheless, we were highly encouraged and satisfied by the intercultural learning that began in third grade, and we were extremely grateful to be in such a flexible, accommodating environment to tinker and explore. It struck us, too, that negotiating mandates is like negotiating intercultural learning: it requires perseverance and commitment.

Figure 8.8 Girls Reading Korean Picturebooks

Final Reflections

Windows. Mirrors. Doors. Before the Individuals with Disabilities Act (IDEA) legislation in the 1970s there were all kinds of buildings that were not universally accessible. Renovations were extensive, and innovative architecture was necessary. Reframing a cross-cultural curriculum for intercultural accessibility can be quite involved and requires just as much thoughtfulness. In many ways, teachers are both the demolition crew and the curriculum architects.

Models like CIL and DMIS are helpful tools in the reframing process. So are collaboration, contact with cultural insiders, and a positive, humble attitude. A stance of openness to learning right alongside the students is probably most important, and when that is cultivated, a disposition for global citizenship is fostered for everyone. Over time, students become engaged, and the teacher can be more of an observer, like a proud doorman or doorwoman inviting self-directed guests through sliding glass doors. Doors that open effortlessly. Doors that one can see through, looking in and looking out. Doors that are marked with a great big "Welcome" sign.

Recommended Books That Invite Global Perspectives

Go, Dae Young. 2007. 용돈 주세요 [*Allowance, Please!*]. Illus. Young Jin Kim. Paju, Korea: Gilbutkid.

Byung Kwan has a long list of toys, snacks, and stationery that he wants to buy. He helps his mom with house chores, and although things do not go exactly as he plans, he eventually earns some allowance. (Naughty Boy and Sister series)

Go, Dae Young. 2008. 손톱 깨물기 [*My Sister Is Nail Biting*]. Illus. Young Jin Kim. Paju, Korea: Gilbutkid.

Jiwon bites her nails. She is stressed because of schoolwork and her increasing weight. Byung Kwon thinks his big sister occupies too much of their parents' attention because of this nail-biting issue. To get more attention and his own reward, he starts biting his nails too. (Naughty Boy and Sister series)

Park, Linda Sue. 2006. *Archer's Quest*. New York: Clarion Books.

An ancient Korean king, Chu-mong, arrives at Kevin's room in Dorchester, New York. Kevin is a twelve-year-old Korean American, and he is too stunned to believe what is happening to him. Korean heritage is highlighted from the moment Kevin encounters the Korean time traveler.

Park, Linda Sue. 2001. *A Single Shard*. New York: Clarion Books.

A young homeless boy in twelfth-century Korea, Tree-ear, becomes an apprentice to the potter Min because he mistakenly breaks one of Min's pots. Tree-ear grows in courage and agency while tasked with delivering Min's exquisite wares to the emperor.

References

Albuquerque Economic Development. 2015. Albuquerque Demographics. http://www.abq. org/Demographics.aspx.

Beach, Richard. 1997. "Students' Resistance to Engagement with Multicultural Literature." In *Reading across Cultures*, ed. Theresa Rogers and Anna O. Soter, 69–94. New York: Teachers College Press.

Bennett, Janet. 2003. "Turning Frogs into Interculturalists: A Student-Centered Developmental Approach to Teaching Intercultural Competence." In *Crossing Cultures: Insights from Master Teachers,* ed. Nakiye Avdan Boyacigiller, Richard Alan Goodman, and Margaret Phillips, 157–170. New York: Routledge.

Bennett, Milton. 1993. "Towards Ethnorelativism: A Developmental Model of Intercultural Sensitivity." In *Education for the Intercultural Experience*, ed. R. Michael Paige, 21–71. Yarmouth, ME: Intercultural Press.

Bishop, Rudine Sims. 1990. "Mirrors, Windows, and Sliding Glass Doors." *Perspectives: Choosing and Using Books for the Classroom* 6 (3): ix-xi.

_____ . 2012. "Reflections on the Development of African American Children's Literature." *Journal of Children's Literature* 38 (2): 5–13.

Fennes, Helmut, and Karen Hapgood. 1997. *Intercultural Learning in the Classroom*. London: Continuum International.

Jordan, Sarah, and Alan Purves. 1993. *Issues in the Responses of Students to Culturally Diverse Texts*. Albany, NY: National Research Center on Literature Teaching and Learning.

Ladson-Billings, Gloria. 1994. "Who Will Teach Our Children?" In *Teaching Diverse Populations: Formulating a Knowledge Base,* ed. Etta R Hollins, Joyce E. King, and Warren C. Hayman, 129–158. Albany: State University of New York Press.

Naidoo, Jamie. 2014. *Diversity Programming for Digital Youth: Promoting Cultural Competence in the Children's Library*. Santa Barbara, CA: Libraries Unlimited.

Okri, Ben. 1993. *Songs of Enchantment*. New York: Nan A. Talese.

Pardy, Maree. 2011. "Hate and Otherness: Exploring Emotion Through a Race Riot." *Emotion, Space and Society* 4:51–60.

Pereira, Aline. 2008. Interview with Linda Sue Park. http://www.papertigers.org/ interviews/archived_interviews/LSPark_2.html.

U.S. Census Bureau. 2016. American Community Census. http://factfinder.census.gov/ faces/tableservices/jsf/pages/productview.xhtml?src=bkmk.

Zeichner, Kenneth. 1993. *Educating Teachers for Cultural Diversity.* East Lansing, MI: National Center for Research on Teacher Learning.

Children's Books Cited

Anaya, Rudolfo. 1995. *The Farolitos of Christmas: A New Mexico Christmas Story.* Illus. Richard C. Sandoval. Santa Fe, NM: New Mexico Magazine.

Guzzo, Sandra. 1993. *Miguel and the Santero.* Illus. Richard C. Sandoval. Santa Fe, NM: New Mexico Magazine.

James, Helen Foster. 2004. *E Is for Enchantment: A New Mexico Alphabet.* Illus. Neecy Twinem. Chelsea, MI: Sleeping Bear.

Ortega, Cristina. 1998. *Los Ojos del Tejedor: The Eyes of the Weaver.* Santa Fe, NM: Clear Light.

Park, Linda Sue. 2000. *The Kite Fighters.* Illus. Eung Won Park. New York: Clarion Books.

———. 2001. *A Single Shard.* New York: Clarion Books.

———. 2005. *Project Mulberry.* New York: Clarion Books.

———. 2006. *Archer's Quest.* New York: Clarion Books.

Segal, Robin. 2009. *ABC in Albuquerque.* Illus. Jean-Pierre Fournier. New York: Murray Hill Books.

Stevens, Jan Romero. 1993. *Carlos and the Squash Plant.* Illus. Jeanne Arnold. New York: Scholastic.

Chapter 9

Investigating Nigeria in a Cross-Cultural Inquiry

Deanna Day

This chapter looks inside a middle school class of twelve- and thirteen-year-old students who were struggling with reading and needed literacy support. Their classroom teacher believed that despite their reading levels and test scores, they deserved opportunities to read global literature to help them wonder and think about the world. Freeman and Lehman (2001) say that global literature helps students travel the world, come together and bridge differences, and rejoice in common joys and triumphs.

Within a curriculum framework of interculturalism, these seventh graders participated in a cross-cultural study by reading children's literature and newspaper articles that took place on the continent of Africa, specifically the country of Nigeria. Kurtz (2007) notes that the African continent seems to be invisible in American schools, yet through the power of words and children's books Africa can become visible. One of the goals of this inquiry was to help students think beyond their own views and realize that their perspectives are one of many ways to think about and view the world. Huck (1989) believes that through children's literature, students develop a sense of humanness and gain insights into the behavior of others and themselves. This inquiry's aim was to create an awareness and sensitivity to people in African nations and to reach the seventh graders' hearts as well as their heads (Bishop 1994).

Inquiry Journey

Over a three-month span, Penny, a middle school reading specialist, invited me into her classroom to help her teach a cross-cultural inquiry two or three days a week for part of a class period (all names are pseudonyms). In Penny's first-period class there were eleven students—four girls and seven boys—who qualified for assistance because their state comprehension scores and quarterly literacy assessments were low. Students took this reading intervention course in place of an elective. In addition, each student was enrolled in a seventh-grade English course.

Penny's classroom was organized around the Daily 5 model where students listen to reading, read to self or a partner, work on writing, and complete word work (Boushey and Moser 2014). Furthermore, students completed the CAFE Menu, which consists of instruction in comprehension, accuracy, fluency, and expanding vocabulary (Boushey and Moser 2009). Penny believed in mixing instructional and independent work time so that students changed or moved every ten to fifteen minutes to maximize their attention spans and to challenge them. For example, the middle school students usually participated in a fifteen-minute mini-lesson around the CAFE Menu, wrote for ten minutes, and then read nonfiction and answered comprehension questions on the computer using a program called MobyMax for fifteen minutes.

Personal Cultural Identities

We began the inquiry by having students think about their own cultures, backgrounds, and traditions through creating cultural autobiographies, so they could understand why culture matters in the lives of others around them. We hoped that by examining their own histories, they would understand how those experiences and interactions determine their views of the world. During the first week, I introduced myself to students by sharing my own cultural autobiography: ten objects that reflected my background and culture (Swiss chocolate, maps of Switzerland and Great Britain, a plastic saguaro cactus, a stuffed turtle, a Yahtzee game, a can of black-eyed peas, a wooden cross, a favorite book, and a photograph of my family).

Seventh graders were invited to gather artifacts and information from home to help them discuss their family's ethnicities, heritages, cultures, customs, religions, and languages. Each student was asked to think about his or her favorite family foods, hobbies, literature, and traditions. A letter was sent home to families describing the project (see

Figure 9.1). One week later students brought in their cultural autobiographies to share in small groups. They then completed a museum walk where they viewed photographs and maps, asked questions about cultural objects, touched religious artifacts, and examined items representing hobbies (see Figure 9.2).

Dear Families,

*As a way to get to know everyone in our class and to understand each other's diverse backgrounds, we are asking every seventh grader to think about his/her life and find five objects to describe their culture and heritage. Families, could you please help your child by discussing your family's ethnicity, heritage, culture, customs, religion, and languages. Please talk about favorite foods, hobbies, favorite art or literature, and/or other traditions your family participates in. These questions might help: Where did your family come from? What is important about your culture—traditions, religion, etc.? On special holidays what does your family eat? Is there a special saying or advice that is shared often in your family? Every child needs to bring at least **five objects** to share their culture and heritage with classmates (gift bag provided to bring objects). Please have your child practice sharing each object at home so that they will be comfortable discussing them at school. Possible objects could include a flag, a map, a photograph, a food item, an image, an object, and so on. Please, no toys or expensive objects. We look forward to learning about every student's culture and heritage!*

Figure 9.1 Family Letter About the Cultural Autobiography

The students came from diverse backgrounds: three boys were from Russia, one girl was from Cambodia, and the other children said their families were from Germany or Great Britain. Both the seventh graders and Penny exclaimed that they learned about each other after listening and viewing the cultural autobiographies. Nathan remarked, "I never knew that Mia was from Cambodia. It was fun seeing money from that country." Penny said, "I enjoyed learning about their hobbies outside of school. Martin likes to draw city landscapes, and Owen plays in a soccer club."

Cross-Cultural Studies

To build understanding and appreciation for others, I read aloud several picturebooks whose stories took place on the continent of Africa such as *Goal!* (Javaherbin 2010), *Amadi's Snowman* (Saint-Lot 2008), and *14 Cows for America* (Deedy 2009). After each read-aloud, students were invited to share their thoughts and feelings. Some were silly or were reluctant to communicate their opinions. Andy exclaimed, "Reading picturebooks is boring and dumb." These students hadn't participated in many discussions and were hearing stories far removed from their own lives. Furthermore, many middle school teachers do not use picturebooks for instruction, unaware of their potential.

Figure 9.2 (Above and Opposite) Examples of Cultural Autobiographies

To promote more discussion and participation, Penny wrote down what each student said on chart paper, signaling to all of them to participate. In addition, I explained that their opinions and thoughts were valuable and important for all of us to hear, because we could gain new perspectives. Picturebooks are "everybody books" because everyone can learn and grow from them, even adults and seventh graders. One title, *Brothers in Hope* (Williams 2013), about the Lost Boys of the Sudan, inspired a lot of thinking and discussion from students. They listened intently and talked about how the stronger boys cared

for the weaker boys and never gave up. Gabe mentioned, "It was very sad and emotional, because tons of boys lost their families." Desiree said, "I think there was a lot of bravery because they had to risk their lives. And they had no food and water." Nathan shared, "Even though they lost their families, they had faith they'd get out."

Next, a global novel that takes place in Nigeria, *The No. 1 Car Spotter: Best in the Village—Maybe in the World!* by Atinuke (2011), was chosen for students to read. Since their reading and comprehension levels ranged from third to sixth grade, an easy-to-read book that was part of a series was selected. This novel is about a boy who keeps track of every car that drives through his town. His family sells produce in a market and feeds tourists who pass through their village. My hope was that students would learn about Nigerian traditions and cultures. In an author's note, Atinuke states that she names Africa rather than a specific African country as the setting, even though she is Nigerian, because there are so few books set in Africa. She wants all African children to see themselves in a book and so chose not to name the specific country in which the story takes place. Throughout this inquiry, however, we referred to Nigeria when talking about this book because I did not want students to make the common American mistake of treating Africa as a country rather than as a continent made up of many nations.

Over the course of three weeks, students read *The No. 1 Car Spotter* with a partner for fifteen minutes two times a week. As the students read, they wrote down their thoughts, feelings, predictions, and questions on sticky notes in preparation for literature circles. In addition, at the end of a page or two, partners summarized or retold what they'd read. Some student pairings were highly engaged with this novel, even though two boys grumbled about the illustrations because they contained stick figures. I wondered if students were looking at how differently the No. 1 Car Spotter's family was compared with their own families, not noticing the complexity, diversity, and cultures within all families.

To help students expand their perceptions of culture we brainstormed and talked about the cultural aspects in the book. As they talked, I wrote down their thoughts on language, food, values/morals, relationships, and economics (see Figure 9.3). We returned to this poster several times, adding to it after reading time. Slowly students began to recognize similarities they shared with the main character. Just like No. 1, they had family and friends who supported and encouraged them. Students identified global issues such as poverty when they noted that No. 1's family had no refrigerator or electricity, putting sodas in a nearby river to keep them cool. Marcus mentioned that even though No. 1 knew all the names of the cars that passed through his village, his family did not own a vehicle for transportation. In regard to economics, students noticed that fathers worked in the city to support the mothers, children, and grandparents. One boy said that the family worked together to feed the tourists who drove through their village.

Gradually, seventh graders developed an appreciation for the cultural differences they were reading about along with the similarities. This increased knowledge about others and an awareness of differences is essential to dispelling stereotypes about people from cultures other than their own (Freeman and Lehman 2001).

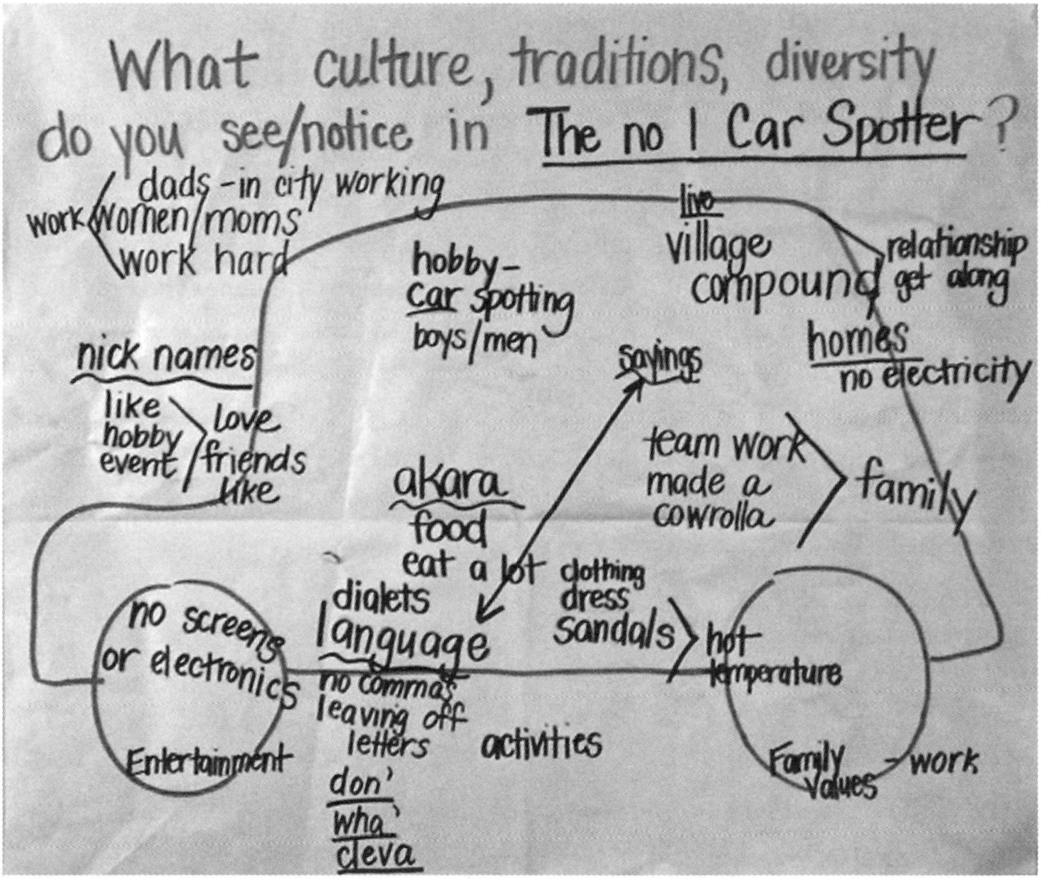

Figure 9.3 **Brainstorming Cultural Aspects in** *The No. 1 Car Spotter*

As students read *The No. 1 Car Spotter,* Penny continued teaching comprehension mini-lessons from the CAFE Menu and the Common Core State Standards. One day, students wrote a quick summary about what they had read in the book that day. On another day I taught a mini-lesson about author's purpose that involved visiting Atinuke's website (http://atinuke-author.weebly.com/). To ease reading the information, Atinuke's story was printed out, and students coded or tracked their thinking in the margins (Harvey and Goudvis 2007). They made a star when they read about how and why she became a writer, drew a question mark when they had a question, and wrote the letter *C* for "connections." After reading, students asked what boarding school was and what Atinuke meant by "African diaspora." They discovered that Atinuke's "roots go deep into the rich soil" in Africa. She writes and tells stories about Nigeria so that others can learn about her homeland. In addition, they learned that she wrote *The No. 1 Car Spotter* for her two sons, who listened to draft after draft as she wrote the book.

When seventh graders finished reading the novel, two small-group literature circles were organized. Since many of these students had been in intensive reading programs for several years, it wasn't a surprise that they hadn't participated in literature circles. I reminded them that they had been talking about the book all along with their partners and when we brainstormed about the cultural aspects in the book. I taught several mini-lessons on how to talk about a book and how to grow discussion (Villaume et al. 1994).

Students returned to the sticky notes where they had been writing comments and questions as they read the book to think about which of them their classmates might find interesting to talk about. We discussed what "seed ideas" or effective notes might look like with the goal of growing discussion. Students were given a list of seed starters that could help build and sustain discussion, which helped them write additional sticky notes in preparation for the literature circles (see Figure 9.4).

I wonder why . . .	*How could . . .*
How did you change . . .	*I was confused by . . .*
I didn't understand . . .	*What should . . .*
How would this be different . . .	*Explain . . .*
What would you do . . .	*What did you think of . . .*
Compare and contrast . . .	*The author's style . . .*

Figure 9.4 **Seed Starters (adapted from Villaume et al. 1994)**

Over the course of two days, students talked about the novel in their small groups. Seventh graders asked many questions to help them understand the book further: "What is *akara*?" "Where did the welder come from?" and "I wonder if they ever get to drink any of the soda they sell." One question that was discussed in detail in both groups was No. 1's hobby:

Henry: How does it come natural for him to know all the car names?

Gabe: His entire life, like learning the ABCs, he's known cars.

Pete: I have the same question on page 91.

Martin: He has seen a Lamborghini, Porsche, Bentley.

Gabe: Rolls Royce.

Martin: Probably lots of Jeeps, Land Rovers.

Gabe: The number one car is Land Rover for safaris. That's what I've seen on TV.

Martin: Is Golf even a car?

Gabe: Yes, a five-mile-hour golf cart.

Both Martin and Gabe helped answer Henry and Pete's question, building comprehension and understanding, and sharing some of the vehicles No. 1 spotted throughout the book. Later the only girl in this group, Desiree, asked why Atinuke chose car spotting for No. 1's hobby and focused on cars. Gabe answered, "Remember we read on her website that she has boys." Henry then exclaimed, "I don't think this book is all about cars. It's about living in Africa!"

The student-led discussions gave seventh graders opportunities to ask questions about an unfamiliar culture and language. Students asked, "Does *Na-wa-oh* mean 'sorry'?" and "I think *wahala* means 'no playing around.'" In another portion of a discussion Desiree asked, "Why did she write the book this way?" Atinuke left the last letter off of some of the words, and students noticed this as they read the novel. Martin confirmed, "The grammar is different." Henry said, "How would they know how to speak if they don't [go] to school?"

In another group, Lisa commented on the illustrations, asking, "Where is all of their hair?" Owen exclaimed, "It's too hot for hair!" When Lisa noted, "They don't have shoes,"

Nathan answered, "They're used to walking without." The seventh-grade boys could re-late to hot weather and going barefoot, thus helping Lisa understand the book.

No. 1's family lived quite differently from these students, who had access to grocery stores. The students were aware of No. 1's economic situation:

Gabe: Everyone has bony legs and arms in the drawings.

Martin: The legs are poorly drawn.

Henry: It's because they don't have much food or money.

Gabe: They may have only one meal a day.

Martin: Otherwise they'd live somewhere else if they could.

Desiree: I think they're making and selling food to survive.

Later, this group discussed how Coca-Cola's family moved quickly to complete their specific chores to make meals for the tourists who stopped in the village. The seventh graders agreed that the family members worked well together and that feeding the trav-elers was a smart way to make money.

In another discussion students discussed the nicknames of the different family mem-bers:

Nathan: On page 9 they had weird nicknames.

Andy: They are cool names—Nike.

Owen: Who'd want a name like Mama B or Auntie Fine Fine?

Me: Do any of you have a nickname?

Mia: My name is Mia, but I go by Mimi for my family only.

Andy: Why would a mom give him the name Coca-Cola?

Nathan: Remember, he gets it from his job, getting Coca-Cola from the river.

They went on to discuss their own personal nicknames, and then it dawned on them that families give nicknames to each other, even families on another continent.

By immersing students in discussion, we encouraged them to carefully examine this novel. They talked about how it was written. They drew on their own backgrounds to make meaning. They gained insights into how people feel and live in a different part of the world. They thought provocatively about nicknames, hobbies, chores, and families. And they came to appreciate the cultural and individual differences of the characters in the book. At the beginning of this inquiry, students looked at *The No. 1 Car Spotter* superficially, but their discussions led them to be more engaged and see a world larger than their own.

A collection of global novels and picturebooks was available for students to read and explore when they finished reading *The No. 1 Car Spotter* or the nonfiction stories on MobyMax (see Figure 9.5). Freeman, Lehman, and Scharer (2007) suggest pairing global books to help readers make connections and contrasts. A text set of books was provided to extend students' understandings of culture in Nigeria and surrounding countries. Students chose books that interested them and read them silently at the close of the class period for five to ten minutes. Originally Penny wanted students to summarize or retell what they read in their journals and discuss them in small groups, but we ran out of time.

TITLE	AUTHOR/ILLUSTRATOR AND YEAR OF PUBLICATION	COUNTRY
The No. 1 Car Spotter Goes to School	Atinuke. 2014.	Nigeria
The No. 1 Car Spotter and the Car Thieves	Atinuke. 2012.	Nigeria
The No. 1 Car Spotter and the Firebird	Atinuke. 2012.	Nigeria
Lost Boy, Lost Girl: Escaping Civil War in Sudan	Dau, John Bul, and Martha Arual Akech. 2010.	Sudan
A Gift from Childhood: Memories of an African Boyhood	Diakité, Baba Wagué. 2010.	Mali
Our Stories, Our Songs: African Children Talk About AIDS	Ellis, Deborah. 2005.	Malawi, Zambia
What You Wish For: Your Favorite Authors Write to Honor Darfur	Book Wish Foundation. 2011.	Darfur
The Red Bicycle: The Extraordinary Story of One Ordinary Bicycle	Isabella, Jude. Illus. Simone Shin. 2015.	Burkina Faso
Sahwira: An African Friendship	Marsden, Carolyn, and Phillip Matzigkeit. 2009.	Zimbabwe
Beatrice's Goat	McBrier, Page. Illus. Lori Lohstoeter. 2001.	Uganda

Figure 9.5　Text Set of Books on Africa Available for Free Reading

TITLE	AUTHOR/ILLUSTRATOR AND YEAR OF PUBLICATION	COUNTRY
Peaceful Protest: The Life of Nelson Mandela	McDonough, Yona Zeldis. Illus. Malcah Zeldis. 2002	South Africa
Mimi's Village: And How Basic Health Care Transformed It	Milway, Katie Smith. Illus. Eugenie Fernandes. 2012.	Kenya
One Hen: How One Small Loan Made a Big Difference	Milway, Katie Smith. Illus. Eugenie Fernandes. 2008.	Ghana
Cry of the Giraffe	Oron, Judie. 2010.	Ethiopia
A Is for Africa	Onyefulu, Ifeoma. 1997.	Nigeria
Emeka's Gift: An African Counting Story	Onyefulu, Ifeoma. 1999.	Nigeria
A Long Walk to Water	Park, Linda Sue. 2011	Sudan
Every Human Has Rights: A Photographic Declaration for Kids	Robinson, Mary. 2009	
The Mangrove Tree: Planting Trees to Feed Families	Roth, Susan L., and Cindy Trumbore. 2011.	Eritrea
Chanda's Secrets	Stratton, Allan. 2004.	Sub-Saharan Africa
Ryan and Jimmy: And the Well in Africa That Brought Them Together	Shoveller, Herb. 2006.	Uganda
Out of Shadows	Wallace, Jason. 2010.	Zimbabwe
Wangari's Trees of Peace: A True Story from Africa	Winter, Jeanette. 2008.	Kenya

Figure 9.5 **Text Set of Books on Africa Available for Free Reading (continued)**

Inquiries into Global Issues

To help seventh graders build intercultural understandings about global issues that were occurring in Nigeria, we read newspaper articles from Newsela (https://newsela.com/). This website publishes daily news stories in five different reading levels, grades three to twelve. Penny shared her thinking as she read aloud an article about the United States helping Nigeria search for kidnapped girls. The seventh graders followed along and highlighted the main idea and supporting details as well as wrote questions in the margins. Then students read the remainder of the article with a partner, sharing their thinking aloud. Afterward we had a class discussion about this world event and learned that this was the first time the seventh graders had heard about this kidnapping. The event had not been mentioned or discussed in any of their classes. The students shared many questions: "I thought slavery was over." "Were the girls on a field trip? Is this how they were kidnapped?" "Why would they kidnap the girls?" "What does *fundamentalist* mean?" "Is Boko Haram against gender equality?" They thought critically about the article, noticing the control Boko Haram possessed and the girls' lack of power.

The next day students sketched their thoughts, feelings, and questions about the newspaper article in a sketch to stretch (Short, Harste, and Burke 1996). Some complained because they felt they weren't very good at drawing or couldn't remember what the article was about. A handful of students skimmed the article to refresh their memories and were given more time to think and sketch. Eventually every student swapped sketches with a partner, and they discussed what they noticed. Students then wrote their interpretations of their own sketches.

Nathan said, "I feel enraged in the way that makes me want revenge on the people [who] took other people." Owen wrote, "They are going to do anything to get what they want or what they need. They will kidnap and kill." Every seventh grader was angry that the girls were kidnapped and that they were still in captivity ten months later. Sketching and writing encouraged them to personally and emotionally connect to the kidnapped girls. In addition, many expressed compassion and empathy for the families. Mikaelsen (2007) says empathy is a necessary step in moving toward world peace.

The next step within the intercultural framework would have been to take social action, but because of time constraints we had to conclude the inquiry. This project took longer than we expected, and Penny had mandated curriculum that needed to be taught to help seventh graders prepare for state testing in late May.

Negotiating School Mandates

Because the Common Core State Standards testing was coming up soon, Penny couldn't give up more instructional time for this cross-cultural inquiry. She needed to concentrate on preparing students for the Smarter Balance assessments. Throughout our study on Nigeria we integrated the Common Core State Standards into our lessons and activities. For example, we taught mini-lessons on summarizing at the end of reading, thinking about the author's purpose, determining the theme or main idea of a newspaper article, and analyzing elements of a novel and how they interact. In addition, students practiced and participated in these literacy standards in the student-led literature circles as they discussed the craft, structure, and author's purpose of *The No. 1 Car Spotter*.

The goal of this reading intervention class was to teach skills and strategies to improve literacy test scores. The pressure from the middle school to help these struggling readers meant there was less time available to complete the inquiry and engage meaningfully in developing intercultural understandings.

Final Reflections

At the beginning of this inquiry, I found it difficult to engage these middle school students in global literature. They resisted listening to and discussing the picturebooks, and a couple of them grumbled as they read the novel *The No. 1 Car Spotter*. This resistance may have occurred because the students were unfamiliar with the continent of Africa and viewed the Nigerian culture as "exotic or strange" (Short 2009). Students were introduced to a new author, Atinuke, whose book invited them to think about poverty, culture, and perseverance in new ways. Furthermore, the news articles helped students learn about what was occurring in Nigeria. They noticed that the conflict between Nigeria and Boko Haram was about cultural and religious differences, along with human rights. These experiences took them beyond resistance into engagement.

Banks (2004) notes that literacy in the twenty-first century should include a focus on global issues and problems as well as action that can help resolve them. One of the goals of intercultural education is to help students develop a sense of responsibility and a commitment to making a difference in the world. Originally I hoped this inquiry would lead to some kind of action to create a better, more just world. When the students read about the 230 girls who were kidnapped, they were shocked, and their emotions were heightened. Their interest provided an opportunity for them to think about what they could do about the girls' abduction. The "Bring Back Our Girls" campaign called for citizens around the world, including children and adolescents, to wear red to remember the girls on the one-year anniversary and to write letters to members of Congress. In addition, the text set of books the students read during the five to ten minutes before the class period ended contained issues of war, discrimination, freedom, basic needs, and the environment. One of these books could have inspired the students to focus on an issue, research the problem, and come up with a way to take action. These examples may be simple forms of developing agency, but they build on the lived experiences of students that move them toward multiple perspectives and social action (Short 2012). Unfortunately, we ran out of time to think about how they could make a difference in the world.

Overall, students explored their own identities in relation to global citizenship by creating and viewing cultural autobiographies. They learned about Nigeria and Africa and developed an awareness of and respect for different cultural perspectives as they read a novel and picturebooks. They also discussed and reflected on a significant global issue, the kidnapping of the Nigerian girls, leading to questions about issues of injustice and oppression. Students sympathized with the girls and their families, wondering how something like that could happen in today's world. This inquiry demonstrates that these adolescents' perspectives and views of the world were intensified and altered through this cross-cultural study.

Recommended Books That Invite Global Perspectives

Atinuke. 2011. *The No. 1 Car Spotter: Best in the Village—Maybe in the World!* London: Walker.
No. 1's hobby is identifying and memorizing vehicles that pass through his village in Nigeria. When the family cart breaks down before market day, No. 1's hobby becomes helpful to his family.

Javaherbin, Mina. 2010. *Goal!* Illus. A. G. Ford. Somerville, MA: Candlewick.
A group of friends in South Africa play soccer in the streets with a federation-size ball until bullies stop the game. With some quick thinking, the ball is hidden, and later the game resumes.

Williams, Mary. 2013. *Brothers in Hope: The Story of the Lost Boys of Sudan.* Illus. R. Gregory Christie. New York: Lee and Low.
Many Sudanese boys lost their homes and families during a civil war. They endured numerous hardships, traveling many miles to find a place of safety. They eventually came to live in a refugee camp, dreaming of freedom.

References

Associated Press. May 8, 2014. "U.S. to Help Nigeria Bring Back Kidnapped Girls." https://newsela.com/articles/nigeria-kidnapping/id/3926/.

Banks, James. 2004. "Teaching for Social Justice, Diversity, and Citizenship in a Global World." *Educational Forum* 68:289–298.

Bishop, Rudine Sims. 1994. *Kaleidoscope: A Multicultural Booklist for Grades K–8*. Urbana, IL: National Council of Teachers of English.

Boushey, Gail, and Joan Moser. 2009. *The CAFE Book: Engaging All Students in Daily Literacy Assessment and Instruction*. Portland, ME: Stenhouse.

_____. 2014. *The Daily 5, Second Edition: Fostering Literacy Independence in the Elementary Grades*. Portland, ME: Stenhouse.

Freeman, Evelyn, and Barbara Lehman. 2001. *Global Perspectives in Children's Literature*. Needham Heights, MA: Allyn and Bacon.

Freeman, Evelyn, Barbara Lehman, and Patricia Scharer. 2007. "The Challenges and Opportunities of International Literature." In *Breaking Boundaries with Global Literature: Celebrating Diversity in K–12 Classrooms*, ed. Nancy L. Hadaway and Marian J. McKenna, 33–51. Newark, DE: International Reading Association.

Harvey, Stephanie, and Anne Goudvis. 2007. *Strategies That Work: Teaching Comprehension for Understanding and Engagement*. Portland, ME: Stenhouse.

Huck, Charlotte. 1989. "Shared Book Experience: Teaching Reading Using Favorite Books." In *Whole Language: Beliefs and Practices, K–8*, ed. Gary L. Manning and Maryann Murphy Manning. Washington, DC: National Education Association.

Kurtz, Jane. 2007. "An Anchor for the Wandering Heart." In *Breaking Boundaries with Global Literature: Celebrating Diversity in K–12 Classrooms*, ed. Nancy L. Hadaway and Marian J. McKenna, 38–39. Newark, DE: International Reading Association.

Mikaelsen, Ben. 2007. "Children of the World—Becoming Authors of Their Lives." In *Breaking Boundaries with Global Literature: Celebrating Diversity in K–12 Classrooms*, ed. Nancy L. Hadaway and Marian J. McKenna, 117–118. Newark, DE: International Reading Association.

Short, Kathy G. 2009. "Critically Reading the Word and the World: Building Intercultural Understanding Through Literature." *Bookbird* 2:1–10.

_____. 2012. "Children's Agency for Taking Action." *Bookbird* 50 (4): 41–50.

Short, Kathy G., and Jerome Harste, with Carolyn Burke. 1996. *Creating Classrooms for Authors and Inquirers*. Portsmouth, NH: Heinemann.

Villaume, Susan Kidd, Thomas Worden, Sandi Williams, Linda Hopkins, and Connie
    Rosenblatt. 1994. "Five Teachers in Search of a Discussion." *The Reading Teacher* 47 (6):
    480–487.

Children's Books Cited

Atinuke. 2011. *The No. 1 Car Spotter: Best in the Village—Maybe in the World!* London:
    Walker.

Deedy, Carmen Agra. 2009. *14 Cows for America.* Illus. Thomas Gonzalez. Atlanta, GA:
    Peachtree.

Javaherbin, Mina. 2010. *Goal!* Illus. A. G. Ford. Somerville, MA: Candlewick.

Saint-Lot, Katia Novet. 2008. *Amadi's Snowman.* Illus. Dimitrea Tokunbo. Gardiner, ME:
    Tilbury House.

Williams, Mary. 2013. *Brothers in Hope: The Story of the Lost Boys of Sudan.* Illus. R. Gregory
    Christie. New York: Lee and Low.

Chapter 10

Encouraging Cultural Awareness Through an Exploration of Muslim Cultures

Seemi Aziz

The increasing diversity in the United States makes it necessary to develop sensitivity about cultural differences. Children are an ideal population to begin teaching about a range of peoples, because they are in a formative stage of life. Books about diverse cultures can invite children to explore their own cultures as well as provide access to the unfamiliar. The premise of this chapter is to share classroom experiences with books on immigration that led to a deeper exploration of picturebooks about Muslims.

The lack of high-quality global literature within classrooms became evident through my work with teachers in urban and rural areas in Oklahoma. These experiences provided an opportunity to see the kinds of literature that preservice teachers were using within class inquiries and that inservice teachers were using with their mostly white student populations. These experiences made it clear that there was a need for teachers and children to become more aware of global cultures through intercultural studies and to explore how to use this knowledge in their practice. This inquiry involved a cross-cultural study introducing a rural school community and an urban/rural school community to global books about multiple Muslim societies, a population that is often misunderstood and stereotyped.

The main focus of this inquiry was to create culturally and socially responsible readers through familiarizing them with an inquiry-based curriculum informed by children's investigations and to raise children's awareness of issues of immigration and Muslim cultures through multiple interactions with literature. I collaborated with four teachers on this inquiry involving two groups of first-grade students and a group of English language learner (ELL) children to observe and record their responses to the literature.

Rhonda Hover (2011), an ELL teacher in Perkins, Oklahoma, framed the rationale of the inquiry this way:

> Our student body has little to no contact with people from the Arab world or Islamic cultures. I grew up in the same area in which I now teach. My exposure to the Muslim people and their culture was limited to cartoons with flying carpets and rich sheiks, as well as occasionally seeing people outside of my community wearing traditional Arab clothing. Similar to my experiences, my students are exposed to subtle stereotypes of Arabs through the cartoons and television programs they watch, in the books they read, and the commercials they see. Those who pay attention to world events hear a barrage of news reports about trouble in the Middle East, including the involvement of our military. As the vastness of our world seems to shrink with new advances in technology, children need to have multiple exposures to cultures different from their own in order to build tolerance and respect as well as understanding of people unlike themselves. Children's books, with their combination of picture and text, are well suited to this endeavor. Thus with the issues presented by the educators to such a diverse population of children was indeed an undertaking worth the effort.

This cross-cultural inquiry was based on the concept of interculturalism as an orientation that pervades our thinking and curriculum. Our premise was to provide multiple examples of how interculturalism as a curriculum framework can play out in a classroom and create spaces for learning respect for other cultures to create understanding and empathy for Muslim ways of living and being.

Our Inquiry Context

Texts we initially identified for this inquiry ranged from picturebooks to novels to informational texts, but we decided to focus on picturebooks, given the limited amount of time allotted to us by the administration. We explored the books and read them as a group to decide which ones to use in the classrooms. We also decided on various classroom interactions as a group in our weekly meetings. I went into classrooms during these interactions to observe, and then our group met to debrief and plan. We worked together to reflect on the teaching experiences and plan future book experiences. Based on what we observed about children's responses during their small-group discussions, we decided whether a book needed further investigation and what texts to use next (Aziz 2011).

The text set used in this inquiry comprised the books in Figure 10.1.

BOOK	AUTHORS/ILLUSTRATORS	YEAR OF PUBLICATION
Mirror	Jeannie Baker	2010
One Green Apple	Eve Bunting. Illus. Ted Lewin	2006
Sami and the Time of the Troubles	Florence Heide and Judith Gilliland. Illus. Ted Lewin	1995
Big Red Lollipop	Rukhsana Khan. Illus. Sophie Blackall	2010
My Name Is Bilal	Asma Mobin-Uddin. Illus. Barbara Kiwak	2005
The Best Eid Ever	Asma Mobin-Uddin. Illus. Laura Jacobsen	2007
Nasreen's Secret School	Jeanette Winter	2009
The Librarian of Basra: A True Story from Iraq	Jeanette Winter	2005
My Name Is Sangoel	Karen Lynn Williams and Khadra Mohammed. Illus. Catherine Stock	2009

Figure 10.1 Text Set of Muslim Literature

We used literature discussion strategies and other activities once a week in one-hour sessions within the three classrooms to observe student interest. We also wanted to know if the students' perspectives and knowledge of Muslims in different regions of the world shifted as we progressed through the inquiry. Students participated in multiple activities that built understandings of new ideas and unfamiliar cultures, including Venn diagrams, literature circles, and graffiti boards. We also used Smartboards to look up the geographic regions represented in the books. Students were asked to explore their own cultures before they were exposed to the various texts.

Four teachers from two first-grade classrooms within Stillwater and a third-grade ELL classroom in the adjoining Perkins school district were involved in this inquiry. Jackie and Melanie were first-grade teachers at a school in Stillwater. Their classes varied between nineteen and twenty-two students as the student population changed over time. The inquiry was undertaken as a whole-class activity that was an extension of a unit on immigration. Jackie had taught first grade for seven years. Her students were fairly evenly divided among boys and girls. Both Melanie and Jackie worked with a culturally diverse student population, including children from Middle Eastern regions. Zeinab was a native Arabic speaker who had been an elementary teacher. Her role in this inquiry was to take field notes of classroom interactions and coordinate our work. She also sometimes worked with smaller groups using response strategies. In both Melanie and Jackie's classes, children worked as partners or in groups to participate in book talks and discussions after read-alouds. They created records of their conversations and thinking, which provided us with work samples as well as material for reflection and evaluation.

Rhonda was a Title 1 reading teacher in Perkins, Oklahoma, working with small groups of children who struggled with reading in first to third grades in a rural school that is not diverse. For this inquiry, she worked with seven third graders who struggled with reading fluency and comprehension. Rhonda's group met twice a week for thirty-minute sessions. Her students interacted with seven books that depicted Muslim cultures. After reading each book, they discussed the books in literature circles.

We met as a group to collaboratively make decisions about books and engagements and to reflect on student responses. Teachers also had the opportunity to write about this inquiry in classroom vignettes published by each teacher on *WOW Stories* (http://wowlit.org/on-line-publications/stories/storiesiv1/).

Classroom Connections

Our group was focused on inquiry-based learning, so we decided to use multiple interactive reading and response engagements with the texts. When we examined field notes of the interactions and children's artifacts, we identified three major themes in students' learning and intercultural understandings. Children made connections to the texts and gained awareness of differences; built knowledge, perspective, and understanding; and, most significantly, confronted stereotypes. Experiences from the three classrooms are shared in the next sections within these three areas of learning.

Making Connections and Gaining Awareness of Differences

In each of the classrooms, we began with students knowing themselves better and making connections between literature and their lives. With each text we invited students to relate with the story through interactive read-alouds and literature discussion strategies that helped them consider the books more deeply.

Melanie's class had read texts and participated in interactive activities to create a two-week social studies unit on immigration. This unit laid a foundation for students upon which to build awareness of the struggles and difficulties of immigrant peoples. Melanie introduced the inquiry unit by creating a KWL chart—which held what students knew (K), wanted to know (W), and learned (L)—so that the students could retain most of the information on immigration and build on that knowledge base. Given the curriculum framework that guided this inquiry, in Melanie's class we decided to use personal cultural identities as an entry point into this inquiry (Bradley and Mohammad 2011).

Melanie and Zeinab sent home a survey asking parents to share the meaning of their child's name, its origin, and why they had selected it for the child. The first book we decided to use was *My Name Is Sangoel* (Williams and Mohammed 2009) in which Americans struggle to accurately pronounce a boy's name, a key part of his cultural identity as a Sudanese refugee. Students initially thought he was from America, because he was playing soccer. We discussed new terms from the book: *sky-boat, the moving stairs in an airport,* and *the doors that open magically when a person walks by.* Students immediately knew that his lack of knowledge came from living in a refugee camp where these items were not present. Even though their response was that of sympathy for Sangoel and his situation, they thought that if they were in his place, they would change their own names to something easier to pronounce. With further interactions and discussion they came to realize the emotional attachments people have to their given names. After reading about how Sangoel represented his name as a sun and a soccer goal to help others pronounce it, students thought about their own names and created pictorial representations of them. I modeled mine with an eye, signifying "see," and added the word *me.*

In both Jackie and Melanie's classes, the early exposure to diverse cultures in the immigration study had nurtured their awareness and acceptance of different-sounding names. The significant indicator of empathy developed through these intercultural interactions was that students asked others from their classroom who were from different countries about the correct way to pronounce their names in, for example, Mexico or Iraq. They also commented that names do not change just because someone moves to a different country; several strongly expressed that one should be proud of his or her name.

Students filled in a story map about three main characters: Sangoel, his father, and his sister, Lili. When thinking about the story's setting, students remembered that it transitioned from Sudan to the United States, and compared the two. They described Sudan as a war zone that was dangerous and America as a safe place. They did, however, mention that Sangoel missed Sudan even though it was dangerous, because he felt at home there. Through these interactions students not only retained the key elements of the story but also connected to a story that was dissimilar from their lived experiences to embrace a new way of looking at the world.

In Jackie's class, students had practiced text connections through think-alouds as comprehension strategies. Jackie knew that to help students become critical thinkers and deepen their understanding of texts, they needed to be able to make strong text-to-world connections. A student discovered that the title can help a reader predict something that might happen or be represented in the story. One noticed while reading *Big Red Lollipop* (Khan 2010) that Ami did not know what a birthday party was. Jackie asked what his group thought:

José: Maybe she never went to a party.

Lupita: Everybody goes to parties.

Amna: In my country [Iraq], we have birthday parties.

Jackie: Why do you think Ami does not know what a birthday party is?

Amna: Maybe she just came to America and doesn't understand it in English yet.

Others: I think that's right!

When Melanie's class read *One Green Apple* (Bunting 2006), we looked at the book's cover, which shows a girl with a head covering, to make connections and predictions about the book. One student said, "Ms. Mohammad [Zeinab] has the same things, but hers is blue and white."

Building Knowledge, Perspective, and Understanding

Through interactions with the texts, children gained knowledge of language, dress, and other aspects of Muslim cultures and widened their perspectives about how other people lived. In Jackie's class, picturebooks were used to promote intercultural awareness and sensitivity. The class had discussions about the hijab, Islam, languages, and the beliefs of diverse cultures in the weeks before reading texts for the inquiry. Students were initially introduced to *Big Red Lollipop* (Khan 2010) through an interactive read-aloud. The following week, they formed small groups of three to four and again read and responded to the story. Before students broke up into randomly selected groups, they discussed what they remembered and shared personal connections. Initially, they individually wrote about what was important to them about the story. Then they used a large sheet of paper to draw and write about their connections to the story. Their main connections were about experiences with siblings whom they were forced to take with them to a party or the excitement of being invited to a party. They noticed the mother wore a hijab, but it was not a main topic of discussion or curiosity, because most students saw women wearing hijabs on a daily basis at Jackie and Melanie's school. Further, they had read other stories in which characters wore hijabs and had several guests wearing hijabs visit their classrooms. When asked what they wanted to write or draw about, one student responded this way:

Alexander: I am writing about when she was chasing her sister around the living room.

Jackie: Why was that important to you?

Alexander: Because that's what my sister does to me.

Jackie: Okay, so you had a connection there! What kind of connection was that?

Alexander: I had a text-to-self connection.

On the other hand, unfamiliarity with the hijab was one of the common elements in the reactions to the books Rhonda's group responded to. Much of her students' discussion focused on the hijab worn by the female characters in *The Best Eid Ever* (Mobin-Uddin 2007), *Big Red Lollipop* (Khan 2010), and *Nasreen's Secret School* (Winter 2009). For these rural students, a hijab was an item of clothing that was unfamiliar and fascinating.

Most did not understand the reasons why girls and women would wear a scarf to cover their hair. One student believed that the women were required by their husbands to wear the head covering because the husbands did not want their wives seen by others. This was an excellent example of children's inaccurate beliefs about Muslim culture, and it was good to observe that students were interested in finding out more about why Muslim women wear the hijab. They also wondered where the places of worship like the one mentioned in the story might be. It is interesting to point out that they lived within twenty minutes of one of these places of worship but had no idea it even existed before this inquiry.

When students in Rhonda's classroom read *Mirror* (Baker 2010), they looked for connections between the areas of rural Morocco and urban Australia that are contrasted in the book. They noticed similarities in such things as consumerism (people in both books buy stuff, although in different places and ways), and both have phones and animals (but as pets in Australia). Both have tables, but children commented that "people sit in chairs like us in Australia and on the floor in Morocco." They noticed that the hijab worn in Morocco was different from the ones represented in other literature we had read in that it covered the whole face with slits for the eyes. They also noticed that both communities had family units. They noted that shoes were not worn inside the house in Morocco. Rhonda's students made connections between their world and that of Muslims with *The Best Eid Ever* (Mobin-Uddin 2007) where they were able to connect the celebration of Christmas to Eid (an Islamic celebration held twice a year: once at the end of Ramadan and then again two months and ten days later to celebrate Abraham's willingness to sacrifice his son in Allah's name).

Confronting Stereotypes

The most significant breakthrough in this inquiry came through interactions with texts that challenged students to confront stereotypes about Muslims in a safe environment. Even though Jackie's students were told the settings in *Mirror* (Baker 2010) were Australia and Morocco, a few referred to the places as America and Iraq. We compared and contrasted the first few pages as a whole group. An Arabic-speaking boy recognized some of the Arabic characters and was able to sound out some of the individual characters he recognized in the book. Students then formed small groups. Caucasian students from one group surmised that people in "Iraq" live underground and people in "America" do not. A student from Iraq said there are no cars in Iraq, just donkeys, and that buildings in Iraq are made of dirt and of bricks, thus reinforcing widely held views. Another group noticed that people in Australia ride horses and people in Morocco ride donkeys.

A student from Iraq came up to Jackie later and said she thought two boys in her group were making fun of her country. They had been looking at a picture of a covered woman wearing a veil, and one boy said the person was a robber and looked like a "terrorist." When asked what that meant, he said he had seen the label "terrorist" on a picture in a book he had bought. When asked, he told Jackie that a terrorist is a person who is Arabic and fights against "our country." He also said that the person in the picture looked like a man and that he was stealing food. The student from Iraq told him that sometimes people from her country wear that type of dress and her impression was that the woman was merely waiting to pay for the things she had shopped for. Jackie said that wearing certain attire does not mean a person is a terrorist. She reminded students that they might have been influenced by television or home conversations, but that we shouldn't make assumptions about all people based on those depictions.

In Melanie's class, during a discussion of *Mirror* (Baker 2010), students compared the lack of cars and the color of the characters' skin on the Moroccan side of the book. They noticed that one side had "outside stores" and the other had "inside stores." When looking at the market in Morocco, they made connections with a farmers' market in Stillwater and also connected it to Melanie's trip to a Belizean market that she had previously mentioned to them. They noticed that in the book, only Australia had electronics, buildings, and roads. They discussed magic carpets, saying they were carpets that fly, but noted "they're not real." They saw magic carpets as fantasy items, because "there is no such thing as magic." When asked how they knew about magic carpets, they unanimously cited the Disney movie *Aladdin*. When comparing the cultures of the two sides of the *Mirror*, they referred to "us" and "them." They automatically viewed the light-skinned and contemporary, familiar world of Australia as America, and the desert-like illustrations of Morocco to be "them."

When the teachers and I met to discuss how to challenge children's stereotypes and assumptions, we decided to gather additional images of the two countries. We were particularly concerned that the book contrasted rural Morocco with urban Australia, an unfair comparison, and so gathered a slide show of diverse images from Morocco and Australia, including images of the Australian Outback as well as urban Morocco. Once students realized that the book portrayed only one view of these countries, they decided that the book was not accurate, and talked about what they would change to make it more authentic. They were encouraged to write and illustrate changes to the story.

Using the observations from their think sheets and the slide show, students discussed and represented overwhelming misconceptions in the text. Many discussed limited portrayals of skin color, the lack of big buildings in Morocco, and the omission of the Outback in Australia. Jackie noted they were better able to compare and contrast after they took a deeper look at urban and rural lives in both countries. The majority of students were surprised to see that Morocco had modern cities that looked like American cities. They also talked about the difference in traditional and modern settings. Even though it was difficult for them to make the distinction between the look of Australia and the look of America, the activity generated great discussion and definitely increased awareness and understanding of the cultures. Jackie reflected on this experience, saying, "The use of global literature is so important in our classrooms today. Classroom teachers must be innovative in finding ways to include all cultures in today's diverse classrooms" (Iob 2011).

When Melanie's class read *One Green Apple* (Bunting 2006), students did not know that the "thing" covering the girl's head on the cover was called a hijab. Melanie asked where students thought the girl was from and they named quite a few logical places, such as South America, Egypt, Sudan, Libya, Africa, and Iraq. We had previously discussed the fact that not all Islamic countries are on one continent. While reading the story, they stopped periodically for discussion as the main character, Farah, expresses her feelings about being in a new country. We compared her feelings with those of other characters they had already been introduced to during the immigration study. When Farah refers to her head covering as a *dupatta*, students compared her language with other examples of hijab. The students observed that this character is probably from a different country, since she has a different term for a head covering.

When creating a Venn diagram comparing Sangoel and Farah in the two books, students focused mostly on how the characters were treated, who their friends were, and where they were from. Also, students recalled the unfamiliar elements that Sangoel came across in America, and connected them to Farah's struggles. Sangoel was introduced to an escalator, an airplane, and automatic glass doors. Farah was introduced to a juicer in the apple orchard. In both books, the authors, through the immigrant voice, describe unfamiliar items through a sensory experience so that students as readers were able to make connections to the actual objects.

Both Jackie and Melanie's classes had some assumptions about Muslims. Through exposure to Baker's book these negative images surfaced and led to discussion. The intercultural understandings that both first-grade classes developed allowed them to begin to confront their misunderstandings about Muslims.

Rhonda's main goal through this inquiry was to challenge stereotypes and fears that often accompany ignorance by exposing students to children's literature that depicts Muslim cultures. She believed that "introducing students to intercultural children's literature is a beneficial step in the process of eliminating stereotyping and prejudice . . . and we experience not only change, but also an increase in empathy and knowledge when we read about another culture" (Hover 2011).

Rhonda hoped that with each connection students made throughout this inquiry they would be less inclined to make prejudicial or stereotypical judgments. As students looked at *Big Red Lollipop* (Khan 2010), one asked, "What is that headband thingy they wear?" and Heather commented, "She's wearing that thingymabob." They readily recognized the hijab as part of the culture and seemed to accept it. Students continued to make connections to their own lives as we read *My Name Is Bilal* (Mobin-Uddin 2005). They automatically predicted that Ayesha, Bilal's sister, would be subject to bullying because of what she was wearing. Despite their predictions, they gasped when we read Scott's words, "This is America . . . We don't wear dumb things on our heads." Ironically, one student responded as a bully herself, and another simply expressed her disbelief.

Elizabeth: Oh, I'd punch him so hard . . .

Victoria: This is a free country. She can wear that if she wants.

Rhonda chose more books and began read-alouds with open-ended questioning about the various regions represented in the books. Students came away with additional knowledge about each of the Muslim cultures in these books. After reading *My Name Is Bilal*, they engaged in freewriting as a literature discussion strategy. Every free-write dealt with the issue of bullying, indicating they were transacting with the literature through personal connections to build understanding. Although they did not discuss the clothing, several included Ayesha's hijab in detail in their pictures during graffiti-board responses (see Appendix D). While reading *Nasreen's Secret School* (Winter 2009), students were upset that girls were treated so unfairly in Afghanistan, but did not indicate recognition of the Taliban.

We read *The Librarian of Basra* (Winter 2005) around the anniversary of the Oklahoma City bombing, and students made many connections to that event. As they discussed the book while completing a consensus board, they came up with an interesting question (see Appendix D for a description of consensus boards). One student wondered, "If the books were not safe in the library, then why were they safe in her house?" Several guessed that she must have lived in the country, and that "as long as you were outside of the city, you were safe from the bombs." Their discussion was thoughtful and deep as they talked about and questioned what the military commanders think about when they decide to bomb an area and if they choose a place that is more heavily populated. Student's thoughts were deep even though they had not personally experienced war.

In *Sami and the Time of the Troubles* (Heide and Gilliland 1995), students again related the war to the bombing in Oklahoma City. As we discussed the literature through a sketch to stretch (Appendix D), only Britany drew a picture that related to the book. She included the blue sky and the sun, details mentioned in the book. Adam commented that he thought the sky should be black because the feelings evoked by the war in the story seemed more black and dreary than blue. They worked to come up with solutions that fit in with their perspectives and their understandings of these issues in their discussion:

Oliver: On this page, whenever it says, "Stop. Stop. Stop the fighting," they probably want them to stop fighting because the kids are always stuck inside and stuff, and they want freedom to be outside all the time, probably like kids here [in the United States].

Victoria: Well, probably the people there that fight, they probably get bored and don't want to stay in the whole time . . .

Elizabeth: Well, this is what I think they should do: I think they should stop the war for a day and let the kids play.

Victoria: Mmm . . . and then the other day [they can fight]. That's what I mean.

Elizabeth: 'Cause, you saw, like, all that was destroyed, so I don't think there's, like, any peaches growing.

Oliver: Um, I think they have this market close by that, beside them, that a bomb did not go off around [so the peaches could be growing there].

Rhonda: So, where did the market get the peaches?

Elizabeth: It's hidden. [The peaches were grown in a place safe from bombing.]

Oliver: And they probably went there to get a peach for the two kids to share, and it takes two days or something [to get to the hidden growing area].

Victoria: Why can't they just take one half for the kids to play on like this book [pointing to one side of the page] and the army can keep this side? [She was referring to the earlier part of the discussion, indicating they could divide the area and use part for play and part for fighting.]

It was evident that through these interactions students were building better understandings of the experiences of children in other areas of the world.

Discussion

Through observations and field notes, we witnessed movement toward understanding and realization that the issues children of the world face are connected to students' lived experiences. By using multiple literature discussion strategies independently and responsibly, students demonstrated to teachers that they are capable of exercising agency in making sense of the myriad of meanings within the texts. We grew in our belief that to create discerning readers of the word and the world, interactions with challenging global and international books is imperative, including books that a particular community might find controversial (Short 2009). Children and teachers came away from these experiences convinced that high-quality global literature engages students through

- increasing participation of international students,
- gaining empathy and awareness for children in global cultures, and
- trusting inquiry and critical literacy.

Jackie thought that it was interesting to see that international students made connections beyond the scenes described in the books. Their reasoning for some of the situations reached into their background knowledge of places outside the United States. Most had not returned to their home country since arriving in the United States but did have a grandparent come to visit for an extended time. Working with these books increased their willingness to contribute to class discussions because they had knowledge beyond that of classmates.

Jackie believed that teachers are challenged with the question of how to enhance the strategies children need to interact effectively with individuals from diverse racial and ethnic backgrounds. She came away recognizing that instilling intercultural sensitivity is important to helping children develop strong social competence, especially given an increasingly diverse society. At the conclusion of this inquiry she asked students what they liked or disliked about the stories they had read, and the most common response was that they had had fun. Students especially enjoyed seeing pictures of another country where a friend was from. Members of one group said they were happy to know they could still go to a birthday party if they moved to a new country.

Another significant outcome of these intercultural interactions was that teachers learned they could embrace a more democratic classroom. Jackie, Melanie, and Rhonda had not conducted student-led literature circles and were unsure about whether students could read and discuss with each other without direct supervision. Jackie was impressed with students' level of responsibility and attention. Melanie and Zeinab commented that students were able to comprehend the text and participate in student-led literature circles with their peers as well as engage with critical literacy.

After engaging in interactions with the literature, students became more empathetic and accepting of others, especially those immigrating to America. Their awareness of common misconceptions about Muslims grew as well, and they became more familiar with various world cultures and peoples. They better understood why people immigrate to other countries and what it feels like to do so. Teachers saw the significance of students making their own meaning as readers. Incorporating new knowledge into their own experiences with books and the world around them was especially beneficial for first graders because they could build on their background knowledge about immigration and were given more time for the inquiry than third graders were. Teachers also found less cultural bias and fewer stereotypes among students than they had anticipated. Students were curious and open-minded when introduced to new ideas.

Rhonda culminated this inquiry by asking students if they thought their feelings toward Muslim cultures had changed. All of the students felt that they were more familiar with these cultures and would not be as wary when they came into contact with Muslims in the future. A student from a military family who had lost an uncle in the occupation in Afghanistan and Iraq was the only one who hesitated when asked this question. Rhonda believed that this exploration familiarized students with Muslim cultures that are sometimes associated with fear in the United States. She thought that this familiarization was just a baby step, however, toward dispelling the fears and stereotypes that we develop without even realizing it (Hover 2011).

The public school systems in Oklahoma in particular and the US in general tend to shy away from teaching about Muslim cultures; in doing so, they fail to teach students the difference between extremists and those who desire to live peacefully. The result is an unfounded fear of all Muslims. Rhonda, like the other educators, thought that much more needed to be done in schools to address this problem and to create a future in which diversity and acceptance are the standard rather than the exception.

The most significant overall learning experience for all of us was the realization that one book is never enough. Students need to be exposed to more literature about a range of Muslim countries to help them develop deeper understandings of these regions of the world.

Negotiating School Mandates

Using literature was never a question for us as a literacy group. We knew that we could augment learning and meet standards through this inquiry. We informed the school principals about the literature discussion strategies that we would be using and the effect on student learning that we were envisioning. The response strategies connected to the school literacy standards, particularly around comprehension.

For Jackie and Melanie, the inquiry fit into their social studies curriculum and connected to the school unit on immigration. Rhonda's group benefited in a way that was not expected as the mostly white students came to understand and be empathetic toward multiple Muslim cultures. Despite the pressures of standardized testing this inquiry was welcomed and its effect was positive.

Final Reflections

As educators, we challenged ourselves to be drawn into a curriculum process that let us explore interactions with global literature focusing on a cultural group that is often stereotyped and misunderstood in mainstream society. Throughout this inquiry we used literature discussion and responses as a means of drawing student voices into the process of meaning making. In particular, we integrated personal cultural identity and cross-cultural studies into our inquiry. Our curriculum focus addressed fostering a sense of culture and personal cultural identities, developing an awareness of different cultural perspectives, and valuing the diversity of cultures while developing as knowledgeable, thoughtful, and caring inquirers.

Edelsky (2004) lists multiple ways in which educators can think about democratic classrooms. As we worked toward democratic classrooms through this inquiry, we noticed how effective the interactions were when students took responsibility for the content as well as the literature discussions. Student knowledge of and respect for the various regions and the challenges faced by immigrant characters in adjusting to Western communities also enhanced empathetic feelings within the groups. As a community we observed that literature presents human experience, and because of this "the reader seeks to participate in another's vision—to reap knowledge of the world, to fathom the resources of the human spirit, to gain insights that will make his own life more comprehensible" (Rosenblatt 1938, 7). The world is rapidly evolving as a place where children are linked globally in numerous and multimodal ways.

The interactions around global literature brought new insights and empathy for all of the children, even though there was ethnic diversity in two classrooms and a lack of diversity in the third. We came away from this experience with the realization that students are ready for thoughtful transactions with global literature and are prepared to explore new knowledge and wrestle with words through dialogue instead of merely walking on top of them (Freire 1970).

Recommended Books That Invite Global Perspectives

Baker, Jeannie. 2010. *Mirror*. Somerville, MA: Candlewick.
This wordless picturebook from Australia compares the lives of two children residing in Morocco and Australia to explore global connections. In an innovative two-books-in-one concept, it explores a simultaneous reading experience of two opposing worlds, but also reinforces stereotypes through the comparison of rural Morocco with urban Australia.

Bunting, Eve. 2006. *One Green Apple*. Illus. Ted Lewin. New York: Clarion.
Farah has migrated from an unknown Muslim region to the United States and is having difficulty fitting in at school. On a field trip to an apple orchard, she mixes her green apple with the red ones of her classmates to produce the same juice. The story conveys a problematic message of cultural assimilation.

> **Mobin-Uddin, Asma. 2005.** *My Name Is Bilal.* **Illus. Barbara Kiwak. Honesdale, PA: Boyds Mills.**
> Ayesha is bullied at school because she wears her hijab. Her brother, Bilal, does not want to be associated with anything Muslim, including his name, and he walks away when his sister is bullied. His view changes when a Muslim teacher enlightens him about the significance of his name and his religion.

> **Williams, Karen Lynn, and Khadra Mohammed. 2009.** *My Name Is Sangoel.* **Illus. Catherine Stock. Grand Rapids, MI: Eerdmans.**
> A young refugee child from the Sudan takes action by insisting that his new classmates in the United States pronounce his name correctly. He uses innovative multimodal ways to express his name, which is tied to his Dinka heritage and identity.

References

Aziz, Seemi. 2011. "Interactions with Literature About Immigration and Middle Eastern Cultures." *WOW Stories* 4: (1). http://wowlit.org/on-line-publications/stories/storiesiv1/7/.

Bradley, Melanie, and Zeinab Mohammad. 2011. "Cross-Cultural Understanding Through Children's Literature." *WOW Stories* 4: (1). http://wowlit.org/on-line-publications/stories/storiesiv1/8/.

Edelsky, Carol. 2004. "Democracy in the Balance." *Language Arts* 82: (1) 8–15.

Freire, Paulo. 1970. *Pedagogy of the Oppressed.* New York: Continuum.

Hover, Rhonda. 2011. "Third Grade Connections to Middle Eastern and Arab Cultures." *WOW Stories* 4: (1). http://wowlit.org/on-line-publications/stories/storiesiv1/10/.

Iob, Jackie. 2011. "First Grade Explorations of Global Literature About the Middle East." *WOW Stories* 4: (1). http://wowlit.org/on-line-publications/stories/storiesiv1/9/.

Rosenblatt, Louise. 1938. *Literature as Exploration.* New York: Modern Language Association.

Short, Kathy G. 2009. "Critically Reading the Word and the World: Building Intercultural Understanding Through Literature." *Bookbird* 2:1–10.

Children's Books Cited

Baker, Jeannie. 2010. *Mirror*. Somerville, MA: Candlewick.

Bunting, Eve. 2006. *One Green Apple*. Illus. Ted Lewin. New York: Clarion.

Heide, Florence, and Judith Heide Gilliland. 1995. *Sami and the Time of the Troubles*. Illus. Ted Lewin. New York: Houghton Mifflin.

Khan, Rukhsana. 2010. *Big Red Lollipop*. Illus. Sophie Blackall. New York: Viking.

Mobin-Uddin, Asma. 2005. *My Name Is Bilal*. Illus. Barbara Kiwak. Honesdale, PA: Boyds Mills.

_____. 2007. *The Best Eid Ever*. Illus. Laura Jacobsen. Honesdale, PA: Boyds Mills.

Williams, Karen Lynn, and Khadra Mohammed. 2009. *My Name Is Sangoel*. Illus. Catherine Stock. Grand Rapids, MI: Eerdmans.

Winter, Jeanette. 2005. *The Librarian of Basra: A True Story from Iraq*. San Diego: Harcourt.

_____. 2009. *Nasreen's Secret School*. New York: Beach Lane.

PART 4

Integration of Intercultural Perspectives

Chapter 11

Understanding the Past and Present Through Intercultural Perspectives on Forced Journeys

Whitney Young and Janelle Mathis

The topic of journeys is not a new one for teachers. We go on a journey every day we walk into the classroom. Our journey is emotional, physical, unpredictable or too predictable, and sometimes chaotic. But when we set the right conditions, our journey can be exciting, enlightening, and encouraging. It can be one that leads children to global citizenship, new perspectives, and the empathy needed to identify with those from backgrounds differing from their own. Unfortunately, our freedom to set those conditions has become more restricted. That means we have had to work a little harder and become more creative with the frameworks we provide to support children in becoming global citizens.

In a similar vein, students embark on journeys every day they enter our classrooms. Their journeys, too, are both predictable and unpredictable, much as their lives outside classrooms are when encountering new experiences and people. Becoming a citizen is not always an easy task. Taking on perspectives that differ from our own, an important part of becoming a global citizen, requires even more information and space in which to contemplate one's own perceptions and integrate understandings of others. To support student development of an intercultural perspective that is a design for actions, beliefs, and values, teachers search for ways to bring intercultural perspectives into everyday classroom experiences, not just as special units of study, an important component of our curriculum framework. This can be achieved by integrating a variety of authentic, well-selected multimodal texts inclusive of global literature across multiple cultures. In doing so, a space for children emerges so they can reflect on their personal identities, consider their place in the larger society, and engage in conversations that connect local and global issues.

More than just setting conditions for students to interact with intercultural perspectives, teachers must also assist students in asking critical questions, exploring inquiries, and making their own decisions about the reality of the world and their place in it. Janks (2012) and Shannon (1995) point to children's need for access to language to critique the texts that position them as citizens. This practice encourages children to acknowledge whose voice is present, whose is silenced, and what perspectives are left out, and consider why a certain perspective was shared over another (Lewison, Leland, and Harste 2015).

With all of the mandated curricula, teachers may find it difficult to add *anything* else to their daily schedule. However, many realize the imperative nature of the journey they facilitate for themselves and their students as they relate global, local, past, and present perspectives to students' lives. For these teachers, literature is often a vehicle for this journey. Whitney is one such teacher. She engaged in experiences with global literature in a university class taught by Janelle, and the two of us share a concern about supporting young readers and writers as they discover more about their global community.

The remainder of this chapter is told from Whitney's point of view. It reveals a classroom teacher facilitating the journey of her students and herself that begins with an exploration of personal cultural life experiences and continues along a path toward understanding others by integrating intercultural perspectives.

The Context of Our Journey as Educators

South Trails Elementary is in an urban school district in Texas. It is one of twenty elementary schools, having the third-highest percentage of low-income students in the district and a diverse makeup of students. I had forty fourth graders who were split into morning and afternoon language arts classes. Students of more than eight ethnicities made up my two classes. Having six Tongans, thirteen African Americans, four Caucasians, six Hispanics, and the rest inclusive of Thai, Indian, Pakistani, and Vietnamese heritage clearly added to the diverse range of perspectives with which my classroom began. With more than 80 percent of students on the free or reduced lunch program, a low socioeconomic status was a label many shared. Another label I would add to the children is *curious*. They wanted to know why things happened the way they did, why people were treated the way they were, and what events had brought us to where we are now.

At one point I shared with Janelle that the students were very interested in current events, especially refugees. Many followed the story of ISIS on the news and reported this news at school. Their interest seemed to be sparked by the violence occurring, so I began putting an image of refugees on the board each day and asking them to write a response to it. Through this effort to add another perspective, students became interested in the journey these refugees had embarked upon. Seeking to create venues that would invite continued critical thought, I turned to literature.

As a resource to support my planning, Janelle suggested a framework of Forced Journeys (Mathis 2012) to engage the students in the notion of journeys—both their own and those of others. In selecting books, I looked for literature in which the characters embark on a journey that is forced upon them by an outsider or outside event or is the only option for survival as well as books located in many different global areas. The resulting Forced Journeys unit, planned initially for twelve weeks, used children's literature and other modes of text to support students as they engaged in global perspectives, critically analyzed historical and political events, and connected to characters and contexts that otherwise could seem foreign. Three phases that built on one another were put into place to ensure that children started with the local by connecting to their own lives and experiences and branched out to global topics and issues as we progressed through the unit.

Going into the Forced Journeys unit, most students thought a journey was no more than an adventure or exploration. But, what my two classes came to realize over the next twelve weeks was that journeys can be as simple as a stroll through the neighborhood or as grand as a hot air balloon trip across the ocean. Journeys can be brief, extended, positive, or negative. They can be imaginative, chosen, forced, physical, or emotional. And most important, they learned that journeys are happening in every part of our lives, locally and globally, all the time.

Literacy Events That Build on What Children Bring

In any literacy unit, it is important to consider the literacy events that will drive the content. Literacy events in our classroom are structured in such a way that they provide insight into the children, their lives outside of school, and their understandings of what is being studied. To truly relate the teaching and learning to children's lives, we first have to take the time to get to know them beyond a surface level.

I have found classroom talks, quick-writes, open-ended responses, and read-alouds—strategies that are not new to literacy instruction—to be useful in gaining a deeper understanding of who children are as cultural, social, political, and emotional beings. If used in strategic ways, read-alouds offer time and space to listen and respond to new local and global perspectives, stories, and issues. This insight leaves teachers with the information needed to situate the teaching and learning "within the lived experiences and frames of reference of students" (Gay 2002, 106). As a result, children may begin finding relevancy, as they make connections, to the learning experiences we set before them.

Literature, paired with other modes of texts, can serve as a safe entry point into critical issues in our classrooms. Well-chosen picturebooks allow children and adults to experience people, times, and power structures as readers make connections and examine various issues and events through a critical lens. In the Forced Journeys unit, picturebooks brought authentic perspectives into past and present historical, cultural, social, political, and emotional journeys and gave children the opportunity to connect both locally and globally to texts. When choosing literature for this unit in particular, in addition to authenticity, Janelle and I chose picturebooks that met two or more of the following four criteria. In almost all cases, at least three of the criteria were met for text selection:

- Assists in building knowledge on a specific topic or theme
- Serves as a safe entry point for critical issues
- Integrates an intercultural perspective
- Provides opportunities for children to make local and global connections

The unit was divided into themes, and literature was purposefully selected for each theme. Drawing from suggested texts (Mathis 2012), my personal insight into literature, and other resources, we created a general list of books at the beginning; however, the students' responses assisted me in choosing literature as the unit unfolded.

Forced Journeys

The children's conversations and responses guided the planning and decision making for this unit on Forced Journeys. What literature do we use? What do we talk about? What do we write about? These decisions depend on the beliefs, interests, and curiosities that emerge in the classroom. Drawing from my list of possible literacy events, four components framed the planning: Local-to-Global Connections; Local-to-Global Perspectives;

Trying on New Perspectives; and Noticing, Understanding, and Influencing World Issues. For each, I created guiding questions. (See Figure 11.1.)

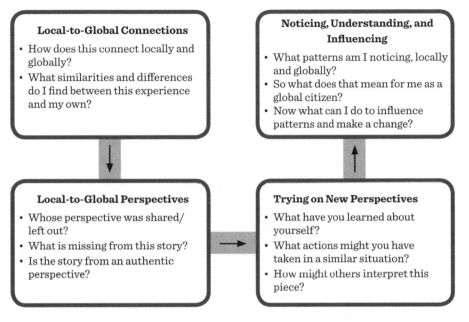

Figure 11.1 Four Components of the Forced Journeys Unit

Phase One: What Is a Journey?

Children want to see their lives reflected in the learning, which is why it was so important to understand the background knowledge children were bringing to the topic of journeys. In the first phase of the unit, we negotiated a shared understanding of the term *journeys*. The picturebooks used in this phase are shown in Figure 11.2.

TEXT	COUNTRY
Journey by Aaron Becker	USA
Where the Wild Things Are by Maurice Sendak	USA
Going Home by Eve Bunting. Illus. David Diaz	USA
A Storm Called Katrina by Myron Uhlberg. Illus. Colin Bootman	USA

Figure 11.2 Selected Texts for Phase One—What Is a Journey?

This phase remained semi-local, as all the books used were American. I began the unit with two imaginative books: *Journey* by Aaron Becker (2013) and *Where the Wild Things Are* by Maurice Sendak (1963). These books paired nicely because they both focus on a child "escaping" their situation at home, a feeling of concern to many nine- and ten-year-olds. During our classroom talks, many students discussed the adventure and emotion that can be involved in journeys. We agreed that the journeys reflected in these books were magical, imaginative, and chosen. Students shared times they wished they could have drawn a door on their wall or lived with the wild things in the jungle, escaping siblings, chores, and boredom.

We then took time to differentiate between forced and chosen journeys. As a class, we defined a forced journey as one that is not chosen by the person embarking on it and is typically initiated by an outside event or person. After our discussions each day, children completed a quick-write, defining a journey and describing the kind of journey they would like to go on. On the first day, I suggested, "Pretend you've met someone who's never heard the word *journey* before. Explain this word to them." I gave students seven minutes to brainstorm, draw, or write. This quick-write gave me a good starting point for our unit and let me know what understandings children were bringing to the topic. Some students had a very broad understanding of journey, whereas others connected the word to their own life and the journeys they hope to go on one day.

Some students understood that lessons can be learned from the journeys we undertake. Aniya discussed the beauty in journeys when you get to "explore the world and think about what you are going to be when you grow up." She, like most of the other children, saw journeys in a positive light. There were students who brought the term close to home, like Leila, who connected *journey* to the missions Mormons go on, an important part of her Tongan culture. Though our first encounter dealt with imaginative journeys, children saw beyond the magic, making local connections, recognizing overarching themes, and noticing that journeys can be very different, depending on the context.

Going Home by Eve Bunting (1998) was our next read-aloud. This picturebook opened a door for a conversation about the uncertainties within journeys and the way journeys can change our opinions. Zach said, "This is like the time I didn't want to go to my aunt's, but I did and ended up having a lot of fun. You never know how a journey is going to turn out unless you go on it." Tyrha was alarmed that the children in the book did not appreciate their Mexican heritage. In her quick-write after the discussion, she reflected on the way Carlos and his sisters, characters in the book, changed their perspective by becoming proud of their culture as they spent more time with their family.

At this point, many children saw journeys as positive and thrilling endeavors. Therefore, I brought in *A Storm Called Katrina* by Myron Uhlberg (2011) to start a conversation about other types of journeys, ones that may not be so predictable, exciting, or chosen. The tone changed when we got to this text. The students realized that journeys could be dangerous, emotional, and uncertain. The book sparked curiosity about Hurricane Katrina, and students were eager to learn more. I gave them some time to examine and discuss images from this historic event and encouraged them to think about how this journey was similar to and different from the others we had read so far. After their research, they drew their own pictures with captions and wrote short responses noting how this journey was different from the previous ones. The illustrations provided children with the opportunity to include objects or scenes they may not have included in a more formal written response (see Figure 11.3).

Figure 11.3 Student Image in Response to *A Storm Called Katrina*

From the prompted responses, it was obvious that these two read-alouds broadened students' understanding of journey by bringing in a new perspective. Most children noted that the journey in *A Storm Called Katrina* was forced, and some questioned why there were no white people in the illustrations of the book or in the images I provided. Bringing in *A Storm Called Katrina* not only shifted our thinking about journeys, but started a critical conversation about issues in the world, because the illustrations portray the primary victims of the storm as African American. Because we were left with curious and critical questions, we engaged in further research. One group read old news articles online, and another group read informational articles, graphs, and charts. After doing some online research, we learned that the elderly were affected the most, but African Americans had a higher fatality rate than whites because of their housing location, bringing up another important social issue.

The responses from children revealed that they were able to try out critical stances and explore curiosities pertaining to social issues. The critical stance came through initial responses to the literature, like Daniel's description of how the journey in *A Storm Called Katrina* differed from previous journeys in our readings. He felt the journeys were different "because there was a flood with no help. The white people had boats and shelter. The Black people had to walk in the alligator infested water with no help, no food, or no shelter." All of the written responses gave "attention to questions of power, diversity, access" (Janks et al. 2014, 5), and gave students the opportunity to analyze the design of the story and redesign it through their illustrations and writing.

Phase Two: Types of Journeys

After phase one, children were able to make a clear distinction between journeys of choice and forced journeys. To dive more deeply into the types of journeys experienced by people around the world, I paired six books for our next phase of read-alouds. These books brought in social, political, emotional, and historical issues, both local and global. The books chosen for this phase included one with a character facing an internal journey paired with an external journey, which allowed children to make personal connections to characters and outside connections to the contexts. The texts selected for this phase of the unit are listed in Figure 11.4.

TEXT	COUNTRY
I Know Here by Laurel Croza. Illus. Matt James	Canada
Migrant by Maxine Trottier. Illus. Isabelle Arsenault	Canada
A Place Where Sunflowers Grow by Amy Lee-Tai. Illus. Felicia Hoshino	USA/Japanese Perspective
My Name Is Sangoel by Karen Lynn Williams and Khadra Mohammed. Illus. Catherine Stock	USA/Sudanese perspective
I Am Thomas by Libby Gleeson. Illus. Armin Greder	Canada
Michael Rosen's Sad Book by Michael Rosen. Illus. Quentin Blake	England

Figure 11.4 **Selected Texts for Phase Two—Types of Journeys**

Beginning with the Canadian book *I Know Here* by Laurel Croza (2010), we examined the emotional journey a young girl in Canada begins as her family prepares to move once her father's work on a project is complete. I used this picturebook to invite the children to think, like the character in the book, about the things that they love. More than three quarters of the students could relate to the emotions of moving from one place to another and having to leave things they love behind. Students brainstormed additional life events that might send someone on a similar forced journey. Among the responses, children listed house fires, a death in a family, getting evicted, not being able to pay the bills, and too many family members living in a house.

These responses reflect some of the emotional journeys initiated by life events that these children had traveled. After our discussion, students reflected on what they love about their current location. In their quick-write responses, they drew images and wrote about one thing they would take with them if they were in the same position as the girl in *I Know Here*. Very few students wrote about a material item. Instead, they chose a person, pet, or place that they would take with them. I was surprised to see how many students drew and wrote about our school or classroom. Among those, Lexie responded, "I would want to take my school because it's special to me," and Tyler shared that he would take the classroom because it was where he had learned everything. Such responses remind us of the role we play in students' lives in making sure they are equipped with the tools to face the world.

The next text, *A Place Where Sunflowers Grow* by Amy Lee-Tai (2012), brought an opportunity to discuss political, historical, and cultural issues while also bringing in a Japanese perspective on the relocation and incarceration of Japanese Americans during World War II. The children were extremely thoughtful during this read-aloud. Naturally, they noticed the unjust treatment of Japanese Americans and were curious about why anyone would be treated a particular way based on race or ethnicity. As we read, I encouraged them to ask critical and curiosity-driven questions, to make connections to other texts we were reading, and to consider the power structures portrayed in the text. Their oral responses reflected understanding of the inequitable treatment of Japanese Americans during this historical event:

- "Why would someone of their own kind push them out?"
- "If they didn't do nothing, why would they make them live in those conditions?"
- "They were American citizens too, so why did they treat them like that?"
- "This is similar to *A Long Walk to Water* [a book some children read in literature circles] because they were both pushed out."

- "They were only picked to move because of their race."
- "The soldiers and government used guns to control the people."
- "This is like *A Long Walk to Water* because they both trapped people in camps with barbed-wire fences."

In their personal quick-writes, children evidenced taking on a critical stance, noticing power structures, and empathizing with the injustices those from backgrounds other than the mainstream faced. Engaging in critical literacy challenges the current status quo by questioning or juxtaposing contrasting viewpoints to uncover the way texts arrange individuals as global citizens (Leland, Ociepka, and Kuonen 2012; Luke and Freebody 1997). This critical perspective shows up in students' use of "pushed out" and "forced out" as well as their discussions and opinions on unjust treatment because of race and the frightening encounters children must have faced. Mark went as far as to write, "What happens if only the Americans were forced out? I just feel so mad!" Not only did they empathize with these people, but they were also using their voices to articulate their feelings about the mistreatment of Japanese Americans during World War II and to participate in the critical and complex conversation about equal rights for local and global citizens.

We continued our reading with *Migrant* by Maxine Trottier (2011) and discussed the physical and emotional journey Anna goes on as she migrates for farm work from Mexico to Canada, as well as Trottier's use of figurative language. This picturebook from Canada pairs nicely with the short stories in *Voices from the Fields*: *Children of Migrant Farmworkers Tell Their Story* by Beth Atkin (1993), an authentic perspective on migrant children in the United States. The images in this latter book brought the migrants' living conditions and everyday struggles close to home for the children. Both classes discussed how the emotions of migrant children are always changing as they progress through their journey. Children discussed similarities between this journey and those found in *Pancho Rabbit and the Coyote: A Migrant's Tale* by Duncan Tonatiuh (2013) and *A Day's Work* by Eve Bunting (1994). At the conclusion, they wrote their own figurative language, focusing on similes, metaphors, and hyperboles. A deep consideration of literature choice allowed for content standards to be naturally interwoven into themed units.

I Am Thomas by Libby Gleeson (2011), an Australian author, and *Michael Rosen's Sad Book* by Michael Rosen (2004), a British author, were paired back-to-back so we could dive more deeply into internal and emotional journeys. The conversations after each story were not long, because I wanted children to write narrative pieces that connected to the journeys Thomas and Michael went on in each of these books. When responding to

I Am Thomas, students connected to Thomas's internal journey and the theme of being true to yourself no matter what others may think. Responses to this text shared similar narratives of children struggling to be accepted by their peers.

The most personal narrative reflections came after reading *Michael Rosen's Sad Book* about the death of the author's son. After we finished the book, there were a few seconds of silence with both classes. When I finally asked, "What type of journey did Michael go on?" many quickly yelled, "Forced!" and "Emotional!" Before sending them off to write, I asked them to think for a minute about an emotional journey they had been on. Students wrote for the quietest nine minutes of our entire year. When the timer went off, many said they needed more time. As I read their responses that evening, I discovered a lot about the emotional challenges they encountered related to death and other life events as well as their connections to the life events of global characters.

By the time we got to *My Name Is Sangoel* by Karen Lynn Williams and Kahdra Moham-med (2009), students had started phase three of the unit. Phases two and three overlapped so that students looked at types of journeys as they explored a range of books. Phase three, described in the next section, involved students reading from a wide range of picturebooks. Each day, students would pick a picturebook, read it with a partner or in a small group, and respond to the text collaboratively. As a result, journeys from this range of reading started showing up in responses. For example, children reading *A Long Walk to Water* by Linda Sue Park (2011) in earlier literature circles connected Sangoel's journey to America with Salva's journey; both journeys were from Sudan. Many other students connected this book to other stories of characters adapting and responding to the cultural and language differ-ences they faced in a new country. This phase of read-alouds overlapped with students' personal inquiries into journeys and resulted in diverse connections and responses. The voices of children in the two classes became stronger and more connected to global issues, characters, and contexts during this phase. Children took on new perspectives and tried out critical stances collaboratively with peers and independently.

Phase Three: Exploring Journeys

Phase three was a time for children to engage in wide reading on the topic of forced journeys. By this time, children had a preference for the type of journey they wanted to explore, and those who didn't found books that looked interesting to them. The activities in this phase encouraged students to try out perspectives different from their own and put themselves in the shoes of characters they were reading about. The texts made avail-able to students during this phase are shown in Figure 11.5.

TEXT	COUNTRY
Run Far, Run Fast by Timothy Decker	USA/Set in Europe
Brothers in Hope by Mary Williams. Illus. R. Gregory Christie	USA/Set in Sudan
My Name Is Yoon by Helen Recorvits. Illus. Gabi Swiatkowska	USA/Korean perspective
Gleam and Glow by Eve Bunting. Illus.Peter Sylvada	USA
Big Red Lollipop by Rukhsana Khan. Illus. Sophie Blackall	Canada
Goodbye, Havana! Hola, New York! by Edie Colón. Illus. Raúl Colón	USA/Cuban Perspective
In English, of Course by Josephine Nobisso. Illus. Dasha Ziborova	USA/Italian perspective
Refugees by David Miller	Australia
The Memory Coat by Elvira Woodruff. Illus. Michael Dooling	USA
Hidden by Loic Dauvillier. Illus. Marc Lizano and Greg Salsedo	French
Jemmy Button by Jennifer Uman. Illus. Valerio Vidall	United Kingdom/set in Tierra del Fuego and London
Razia's Ray of Hope: One Girl's Dream of an Education by Elizabeth Suneby. Illus. Suana Verelst	Canada/set in Afghanistan
Line 135 by Germano Zullo	Switzerland
Azzi in Between by Sarah Garland	UK
A Day's Work by Eve Bunting. Illus. Ronald Himler	USA
Hannah Is My Name by Belle Yang	USA/Chinese Perspective
Fred Stays with Me by Nancy Coffelt. Illus. Tricia Tusa	USA
Pancho Rabbit and the Coyote: A Migrant's Tale by Duncan Tonatiuh	USA/Mexican Perspective
Apples to Oregon by Deborah Hopkinson. Illus. Nancy Carpenter	USA
The Butterfly by Patricia Polacco	USA
The Name Jar by Yangsook Choi	USA/Korean perspective
Paper Son: Lee's Journey to America by Helen Foster James and Virginia Shin-Mui Loh. Illus. Wilson Ong	USA/Chinese perspective
Ruby's Wish by Shirin Yim Bridges. Illus. Sophie Blackall	China
When I Get Older: The Story Behind "Wavin' Flag" by K'Naan and Sol Guy. Illus. Rudy Gutierrez	Africa
My Shoes and I by Rene Colato Lainez. Illus. Fabricio Vanden Broeck	El Salvador

Figure 11.5 Texts Chosen for Phase Three—Exploring Journeys

Each day, I set out fifteen books, rotating them so that children had a wide variety to choose from. All of the books carried the theme of Forced Journeys. By engaging in a wide reading of books on the same topic or theme, children could more easily make connections across texts, a mandated standard for which students on this campus were low performing in the previous year. During this unit, more global perspectives were integrated to broaden understandings of forced journeys and set conditions in which children could consider global issues.

On the first two days, students picked their first book and read them in groups of two or three. Children had an hour and a half to read, discuss, and respond to the text they chose. In their first response, they described their journey in six words, discussed a possible theme for the story, and wrote down something they learned from the character. This activity encouraged them to think deeply about what type of journey took place and the emotions the characters faced, and decide on traits that could define or describe the characters in the stories. Among the words generated to describe the diverse journeys were *poor, forced, sad, exciting, brave, adventurous, emotional, physical, hard, short, tiring,* and *dangerous*. During the next two days, students picked their second text. In their responses to it, they were prompted to make connections across texts.

To close the unit, students wrote a first-person journal entry from the perspective of a character in one of the texts they had read. The student example in Figure 11.6 shows how Kayla responded to *My Shoes and I* (Lainez 2010), an immigrant story from El Salvador.

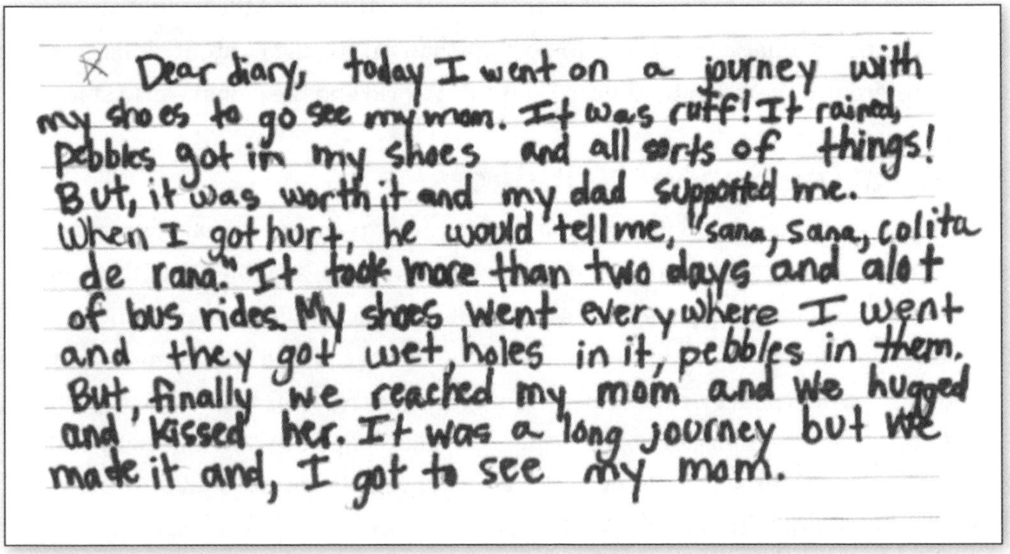

> ✗ Dear diary, today I went on a journey with my shoes to go see my mom. It was ruff! It rained, pebbles got in my shoes and all sorts of things! But, it was worth it and my dad supported me. When I got hurt, he would tell me, "sana, sana, colita de rana." It took more than two days and alot of bus rides. My shoes went everywhere I went and they got wet, holes in it, pebbles in them. But, finally we reached my mom and we hugged and kissed her. It was a long journey but we made it and, I got to see my mom.

Figure 11.6   Example of First-Person Journal Entry in Response to *My Shoes and I*

This activity was powerful because students were encouraged to think deeply about the characters and their internal and external journeys, as well as to put themselves in the characters' shoes. Some added details that were inferred from the text, whereas others stuck to the explicit details in the book. Either way, being able to take on the perspective of someone whose experiences are different from your own is an important trait for a global citizen.

By the time students read the third text of this phase, they were considering the point of view from which the story was told—insider or outsider—and how it might be different if told from another point of view. Many noted that the story would be very different if told from another perspective. Prompting children to think about the authors' points of view as insiders or outsiders also assisted them later in considering the authenticity of the text, something that is crucial when reading global and multicultural literature. Students then articulated three feelings they had while reading the texts to support their going beyond surface-level connections across texts.

This phase provided opportunities for students to choose books of personal interest and connect at local and global levels while attending to state-mandated skills. It was in this phase that students began taking interest in specific types of journeys, whether that of refugees, ones initiated by life events, or immigrant journeys, to name a few. They became interested in the real-world journeys of individuals far removed from their own world. The foreign became familiar. Their responses throughout this unit pointed to their ability to do more than connect with characters. It showed they could also rejoice and hurt with the characters. More important than mastering content skills, students built an intercultural understanding of their local world and the global world at large.

Negotiating School Mandates

My school district has tight mandates on content and the instructional approaches that make their way into classrooms. The curriculum is nonnegotiable. Luckily, I am at a district campus where the principal cares about meeting children's needs and granting children access to an education that connects them to the varied communities of which they are part. She trusts teachers and encourages us to dig deep, plan engaging learning experiences that are connected to the content standards, and do what is best for children. Administrators of this sort, although hard to find, not only get the standardized results they want but also position teachers and students to become lifelong learners.

When creating the unit, I made sure the state standards, the Texas Essential Knowledge and Skills, were authentically addressed in the order laid out in district scope and sequence charts. Doing so was my attempt to correlate my instructional approach to the district curriculum to avoid potential trouble if someone from the district noticed that my textbooks had not been pulled out, that the students were not taking the Friday multiple-choice assessments in the district curriculum, or that the curriculum being implemented in the classroom looked and sounded different from the one provided. I perceive that as teachers we are positioned to challenge people to come into our classrooms and see all the wonderful things that happen each and every day.

Final Reflections

Developing into a global citizen is not an easy task, as it requires us to act with courage and face uncertainties. Furthermore, knowledge of the world outside our own is of great importance to becoming an active global citizen. For this, the conditions we set in our classrooms have to open up safe entry points for children to make meaning of and position themselves on local and global issues. Whitney's focus on Forced Journeys gave students an opportunity to gain a better understanding of their own perspectives while taking on new and contrasting perspectives and connecting local and global issues through diverse literature and inquiry across global cultures. This unit points to the possibility of children engaging in authentic and relevant literacy experiences that provide opportunities to move beyond the local and into the global.

Recommended Books That Invite Global Perspectives

Croza, Laurel. 2010. *I Know Here*. Illus. Matt James. Toronto, ON: Groundwood.
In northeastern Saskatchewan, Canada, a young girl reflects on everything that is familiar to her and will soon be gone once her father finishes his work and the family moves to the city.

Gleeson, Libby. 2011. *I Am Thomas*. Illus. Armin Greder. Crows Nest, New South Wales, Australia: Allen and Unwin.
An adolescent struggles with being different. The outside pressures to be and act a certain way conflict with how Thomas feels internally.

Lee-Tai, Amy. 2012. *A Place Where Sunflowers Grow*. Illus. Felicia Hoshino. San Francisco, CA: Children's Book Press.

As conflict escalates during World War II, Mari and her family are sent to Topaz, an internment camp for Japanese Americans. Despite the difficulty of living in a place where nothing beautiful grows, Mari finds comfort in an art class that supports her journey from despair to hope.

Rosen, Michael. 2004. *Michael Rosen's Sad Book*. Illus. Quentin Blake. Cambridge, MA: Candlewick.

This powerful depiction of the long journey of grief and healing after a loss is based on the daily struggle Michael Rosen faced in dealing with his son's sudden death.

Uhlberg, Myron. 2011. *A Storm Called Katrina*. Illus. Colin Bootman. Atlanta, GA: Peachtree.

When Hurricane Katrina hits, Louis and his family are forced to evacuate their home in New Orleans's Ninth Ward, sending them on a journey through high waters full of critters, debris, and even bodies. Taking shelter in the Superdome, Louis realizes he must take action when his father is unable to find the family after they are separated.

References

Freire, Paulo. 1970. *Pedagogy of the Oppressed.* New York: Bloomsbury.

Gay, Geneva. 2002. "Preparing for Culturally Responsive Teaching." *Journal of Teacher Education* 55:106–116.

Janks, Hilary. 2012. "The Importance of Critical Literacy." *English Teaching: Practice and Critique* 11:150–163.

Janks, Hilary, Kerryn Dixon, Ana Ferreira, Stella Granville, and Denise Newfield. 2014. *Doing Critical Literacy: Texts and Activities for Students and Teachers.* New York: Routledge.

Kress, Gunther. 2010. *Multimodality: A Social Semiotic Approach to Contemporary Communication*. London: Routledge.

Leland, Christine, Anne Ociepka, and Kate Kuonen. 2012. "Reading from Different Interpretive Stances: In Search of a Critical Perspective." *Journal of Adolescent and Adult Literacy* 55:428–437.

Lewison, Mitzi, Christine Leland, and Jerome Harste. 2015. *Creating Critical Classrooms: K–8 Reading and Writing with an Edge*. 2nd ed. New York: Routledge.

Luke, Allan, and Peter Freebody. 1997. "Shaping the Social Practices of Reading." In *Constructing Critical Literacies*, ed. Sandy Muspratt, Allan Luke, and Peter Freebody, pp. 185–223. Cresskill, NJ: Hampton Press.

Mathis, Janelle. 2012. "Forced Journeys: A Conceptual Framework to Contemplate Migration." Paper presented at the biannual Congress of the International Board on Books for Young People, London, August.

Shannon, Patrick. 1995. *Text, Lies, and Videotape: Stories About Life, Literacy, and Learning*. Portsmouth, NH: Heinemann.

Short, Kathy G. 2009. "Critically Reading the Word and the World." *Bookbird* 2: 1–10.

Children's Books Cited

Atkin, S. Beth. 1993. *Voices from the Fields: Children of Migrant Farmworkers Tell Their Stories*. Boston: Joy Street Books.

Becker, Aaron. 2013. *Journey*. Somerville, MA: Candlewick.

Bridges, Shirin Yim. 2002. *Ruby's Wish*. Illus. Sophie Blackall. San Francisco, CA: Chronicle Books.

Bunting, Eve. 1994. *A Day's Work*. Illus. Ronald Himler. New York: Houghton Mifflin.

_____. 1998. *Going Home*. Illus. David Diaz. New York: HarperCollins.

_____. 2001. *Gleam and Glow*. Illus. Peter Sylvada. Orlando, FL: Harcourt.

Choi, Yangsook. 2001. *The Name Jar*. New York: Dragonfly.

Coffelt, Nancy. 2007. *Fred Stays with Me*. Illus. Tricia Tusa. New York: Little, Brown.

Colón, Edie. 2011. *Goodbye, Havana! Hola, New York!* Illus. Raúl Colón. New York: Simon and Schuster.

Croza, Laurel. 2010. *I Know Here*. Illus. Matt James. Toronto, ON: Groundwood.

Dauvillier, Loic. 2014. *Hidden*. Illus. Marc Lizano and Greg Salsedo. Translated by Alexis Siege. New York: First Second.

Decker, Timothy. 2007. *Run Far, Run Fast*. Honesdale, PA: Front Street.

Garland, Sarah. 2012. *Azzi in Between*. London: Frances Lincoln.

Gleeson, Libby. 2011. *I Am Thomas*. Illus. Armin Greder. Crows Nest, New South Wales, Australia: Allen and Unwin.

Hopkinson, Deborah. 2004. *Apples to Oregon*. Illus. Nancy Carpenter. New York: Aladdin.

James, Helen Foster, and Virginia Shin-Mui Loh. 2013. *Paper Son: Lee's Journey to America*. Illus. Wilson Ong. Ann Arbor, MI: Sleeping Bear.

Khan, Rukhsana. 2010. *Big Red Lollipop*. Illus. Sophie Blackall. New York: Viking.

K'Naan, and Sol Guy. 2012. *When I Get Older: The Story Behind "Wavin' Flag."* Illus. Rudy Gutierrez. Plattsburgh, NY: Tundra.

Lainez, Rene Colato. 2010. *My Shoes and I*. Illus. Fabricio Vanden Broeck. Honesdale, PA: Boyds Mills.

Lee-Tai, Amy. 2012. *A Place Where Sunflowers Grow*. Illus. Felicia Hoshino. San Francisco: Children's Book Press.

Miller, David. 2003. *Refugees*. Melbourne, Victoria, Australia: Lothian.

Nobisso, Josephine. 2002. *In English, of Course*. Illus. Dasha Ziborova. New York: Gingerbread House.

Park, Linda Sue. 2011. *A Long Walk to Water*. New York: Harcourt Houghton Mifflin.

Polacco, Patricia. 2009. *The Butterfly*. New York: Puffin.

Recorvits, Helen. 2003. *My Name Is Yoon*. Illus. Gabi Swiatkowska. New York: Frances Foster.

Rosen, Michael. 2004. *Michael Rosen's Sad Book*. Illus. Quentin Blake. Cambridge, MA: Candlewick.

Sendak, Maurice. 1963. *Where the Wild Things Are*. New York: HarperCollins.

Suneby, Elizabeth. 2013. *Razia's Ray of Hope: One Girl's Dream of an Education*. Illus. Suana Verelst. Toronto, ON: Kids Can Press.

Tonatiuh, Duncan. 2013. *Pancho Rabbit and the Coyote*: *A Migrant's Tale*. New York: Abrams.

Trottier, Maxine. 2011. *Migrant*. Illus. Isabelle Arsenault. Toronto, ON: Groundwood.

Uhlberg, Myron. 2011. *A Storm Called Katrina*. Illus. Colin Bootman. Atlanta, GA: Peachtree.

Uman, Jennifer. 2013. *Jemmy Button*. Illus. Valerio Vidali. London: Templar.

Williams, Karen Lynn, and Khadra Mohammed. 2005. *My Name Is Sangoel*. Illus. Catherine Stock. Grand Rapids, MI: Eerdmans.

Williams, Mary. 2005. *Brothers in Hope*. Illus. R. Gregory Christie. New York: Lee and Low.

Woodruff, Elvira. 1999. *The Memory Coat*. Illus. Michael Dooling. New York: Scholastic.

Yang, Belle. 2004. *Hannah Is My Name*. Somerville, MA: Candlewick.

Zullo, Germano. 2013. *Line 135*. Illus. Albertine. San Francisco, CA: Chronicle Books.

Chapter 12

Creating Intentional Space Through the Close Reading of Intercultural Perspectives

Jeanne Gilliam Fain

This chapter offers insight into the integration of global perspectives into classroom units and examines a range of cultural perspectives within the theme of the diversity of languages and stories in the world. These insights are based upon a yearlong action research project with eight teachers from an urban multilingual elementary school in middle Tennessee. The chapter focuses on lessons learned in a first-grade classroom where diverse languages and stories played a central role in the curriculum across the year. These experiences grew out of the challenge of integrating intercultural perspectives while balancing the demands of Common Core Standards, including close reading and a mandated basal curriculum.

Karen, a first-grade teacher, and I began our exploration of intercultural perspectives with basal texts (note that all names are pseudonyms). Teachers in this elementary school were mandated by district administrators to use a specific basal series as an integral part of the language arts block. One challenge with the basal was that it did not contain well-written stories and first graders couldn't easily see themselves or relate linguistically or culturally within a particular story. We knew that we had real obstacles to overcome as we thought about engaging first graders in meaningful ways with high-quality global literature, especially if our purpose was to highlight language and the power of story across global contexts in an authentic manner.

I am not a fan of basal texts. For me, they often do not honor the voices of students in the classroom and the writing is not usually of high quality. Karen felt very real administrative pressure to use basals as part of her literacy curriculum. After an initial lesson with a basal story that didn't critically engage first-grade learners, we took a step back from the basal and reflected collaboratively about how we could move toward creating intentional space within the classroom for the integration of global literature. I had selected high-quality global literature as part of the action research that included different cultural perspectives and issues of personal, local, and global relevance. I had also considered relevancy for different ages of children. Since I had received grant funding, school administrators had already agreed to allow us to use global literature that was not part of the basal series.

Karen and I read through the new collection of books and thought about which ones might build on first-grade children's rich linguistic and cultural resources. After deciding to shelve the basal as a read-aloud, we decided to start with *My Abuelita* (2009), written by Tony Johnston and illustrated by Yuyi Morales. Many children heard their language read aloud in first grade for the first time. The following day, we returned to the book a second time to discuss the central character and unravel the multiple layers of her cultural identity. We used a cultural x-ray (Short 2009) to critically examine the cultural identity of the *abuelita* (grandmother). The cultural x-ray was a tool to facilitate a close read of the text while also exploring the human experience of the grandmother and highlighting her voice as a storyteller (Short and Thomas 2011). Students used their prior experiences with family to help them document the cultural identity of the grandmother.

Based upon this first experience with a bilingual text, we developed a text set that integrated books from multiple global cultures around the theme of linguistic diversity. This text set provided children with multiple perspectives on language diversity and use across cultures. The books facilitated connections across languages and the uses of language as well as recognition of the resources offered by different languages. The text set not only encouraged intercultural understanding but also simultaneously provided a critical space for children to engage with standards from the Common Core as they made comparisons across texts and participated in close reading as a critical analysis of texts. Children considered and contended with multiple perspectives by making connections across books with a similar theme but in different global cultures.

According to Fisher and Frey (2012), close reading provides students with opportunities to think and learn about the various structures of a text. Students are asked to focus on textual information and not their own knowledge, because readers' experiences are viewed as interfering with examining the "four corners of the text." I found this definition problematic and so reframed *close reading* from this narrow definition to highlight the linguistic and cultural experiences of readers within a critical literacy framework.

We engaged with close reading as an intense reading of a text that draws upon experience, thought, memory, and interpretation of the reader (Beers and Probst 2012). This definition values the cultural and linguistic experiences of readers and is rooted in sociocultural theories of learning and literacy (Vygotsky 1978) and critical literacy as building intentional space for critical connections with texts (Vasquez, Tate, and Harste 2013).

Creating a Context for Global Literary and Informational Texts

Our inquiry unpacked the ways in which students construct multiple perspectives in literature through diverse global perspectives. In particular, we were interested in the role that students and teachers jointly play in close reading as critical analysis of texts within literacy instruction. Beers and Probst (2012) define close reading as "attention to the text; close attention to the relevant experience, thought, and memory of the reader; close attention to the responses and interpretations of other readers; and close attention to the interactions among those elements" (37). Reframing close reading emphasizes the power of the reader and the experiences he or she brings to the text. It is my aim to have students and teachers bring their critical perspectives to global texts and simultaneously examine the evidence of the text as connected to readers' interpretations.

With these voices in mind, I received a Tennessee Board of Regents Grant to bridge the gap between cognitive understandings of close reading and practical strategies of close reading. Through the grant, teachers and teacher educators reflected upon making intentional classroom space for authentic responses to texts of all types with a specific focus on global literary and informational texts and the inclusion of close reading strategies. Furthermore, time for reading and reflection on global literature, teaching practice, and feedback within the professional development cycle were crucial for meeting the needs of teachers. Collaborating through demonstrating lessons and coaching were cornerstones of supporting teachers in understanding and implementing close reading from critical global perspectives.

While examining responses to texts, I paid attention to texts and contexts that were culturally authentic and relevant to the contemporary and diverse audiences of learners in today's times (Street 2005). All learners need authentic literacy experiences and stories that facilitate knowing and an opportunity to collaboratively examine analytical texts that invite critical connections (Freire 1970).

School Context

Canyon Reed Elementary is a prekindergarten–fourth-grade Title I school in a large city in the southern United States. At the time of this study, this urban school had been open less than three years and had students with more than a hundred languages. This chapter shares experiences from a first-grade classroom, one of eight classrooms in which I worked. In this classroom, students spoke multiple languages, including Arabic, Spanish, and English. Karen and I worked with them to focus on close reading as critical analysis of texts within literacy instruction, specifically global texts on intercultural themes that reflected the multiple voices of the learners in the classroom. Teachers working with the grant had been given permission to use texts other than the basal.

All of the teachers in first grade, even those not participating in the grant, purposely elected to not use the mandatory basal. They tried using it in their rooms for several weeks and collectively decided to use global literary and informational literature instead for literacy instruction. Several were frustrated that the basal didn't have stories that connected to students' linguistic and cultural backgrounds, and others felt that the stories in the basal did not have strong plots. Because these teachers were recognized as effective teachers of literacy and their students traditionally demonstrated strong achievement in reading, they received permission to take this approach within the literacy block. Only two of the first-grade teachers were participating in the grant and had boxes of global and informational literature, and they shared the books across all seven first-grade classrooms. At other grade levels, however, teachers were directed to use the new basal with fidelity.

The classroom examples from first grade in this chapter highlight two read-aloud/literature discussions on the broad theme of diverse languages and stories of the world. These discussions focused on the linguistic knowledge (semantics, vocabulary, and directionality) of learners as they used their knowledge of language to make sense of the global literary and informational texts. Students powerfully took on the role of linguistic and cultural experts within these conversations to demonstrate confidence and linguistic competence across the sharing of global stories.

Book Selection

The grant project provided teachers with book bins filled with global literary and informational texts that were carefully selected around themes related to social justice. This chapter focuses on one particular intercultural text set around linguistic knowledge and diversity. Each grade level's bin included a different set of books, although a few texts were selected for every teacher, such as Woodson's (2012) *Each Kindness*. I attended to ethnicity, gender, culture, identity, and language in the book selection process. My goals were to share books that would (1) reflect students' cultures and (2) provide rich opportunities for critical discussion about multiple global perspectives. Themes included equity, overcoming adversity, multiple perspectives, discrimination, and unpacking stereotypes.

CRITIC Framework

We used the CRITIC framework developed from our action research to help us grapple with how to teach readers to think about intercultural perspectives through close reading. This framework in based on these processes:

1. **Choose a high-quality text with a global perspective to effectively integrate into the curriculum.** Children should see themselves in the texts and learn about the world they live in. The texts should be literary and informational and allow for the introduction of new perspectives for thinking about self and world.

2. **Read the text multiple times.** Readers need time to appreciate the story and the reading experience. Multiple reads without "killing the text" provide opportunities for creating purpose, constructing questions about the text, and developing predictions and inferences that the reader strives to confirm. There is a fine balance between overdoing a text and reading it multiple times on an as-needed basis. The emphasis is on multiple ways for students to unravel the layers of meaning within a text rather than requiring students to read it a certain number of times to gain evidence.

3. **Integrate intentional reading strategies into the close read.** Reader response strategies (Short 2004), signposts (Beers 2012), visible thinking strategies (Richhart, Church, and Morrison 2011), mini-lessons for analyzing

texts (Lehman and Roberts 2013), and dramatic approaches to texts (Medina and Campano 2006) assist readers in constructing multiple stances and informed perspectives from texts. Strategies should support the reader, instead of taking over meaning making. Strategies can serve as tools to assist readers in developing their own ideas, points of view, and stances toward texts.

4. **Talk about the text.** Students need time to share their understandings and viewpoints of the text in pairs through discussions in small- and large-group literature discussions. Talking facilitates meaning making. Readers need space that is designed to use their lived experiences to talk about text and real reasons to talk about global voices in texts.

5. **Investigate and look for connections across texts.** Readers investigate by digging deeply across texts to look for patterns and identify themes. This investigation includes thinking about the author's point of view and the big ideas (themes) as readers unravel the layers from multiple texts. The investigation extends beyond the superficial elements of the text and moves to the critical development of connections.

6. **Comprehend the text.** Readers use comprehension strategies, such as predicting, questioning, summarizing, determining meaning of vocabulary in context, and reflection. These strategies involve thinking about: What does the text say? What does it mean? What does it matter? (Gallagher 2004). Readers critically evaluate and analyze the text while simultaneously drawing upon their linguistic and cultural resources.

Diverse Languages and Stories in the World

The classroom teacher, Karen, and I brainstormed themes across the year that highlighted global literary and informational books and decided that one of those themes would be diversity in languages and stories around the world. This theme came from Karen's desire to highlight students' linguistic and cultural knowledge. Students brought their knowledge to every read-aloud and discussion, but she noticed that several students who knew Spanish and Arabic were rarely participating. Karen knew a few words in Spanish, and I have studied Spanish over several years. Neither of us knew Arabic.

The intercultural text set on Language and Stories consisted of these books:

- *The Heart's Language* (Lois-Ann Yamanka and Aaron Jasinski [illus.] 2005)
- *One Green Apple* (Eve Bunting and Ted Lewin [illus.] 2006)
- *Marianthe's Story: Painted Words and Spoken Memories* (Aliki 1998)
- *Chavela and the Magic Bubble* (Monica Brown and Magaly Morales [illus.] 2010)
- *Nasreddine* (Odilie Weulersse and Rebecca Dautremer [illus.] 2005)
- *This Is the Rope: A Story from the Great Migration* (Jacqueline Woodson and James Ransome [illus.] 2013)
- *The Librarian of Basra: A True Story from Iraq* (Jeanette Winter 2005)
- *Pancho Rabbit and the Coyote: A Migrant's Tale* (Duncan Tonatiuh 2013)

Two other books from this unit are highlighted in this chapter:

- *Dear Primo: A Letter to My Cousin* (Duncan Tonatiuh 2010)
- *Hands Around the Library: Protecting Egypt's Treasured Books* (Karen Leggett Abouraya and Susan L. Roth [illus.] 2012)

These two books use language in powerful ways. In *Dear Primo: A Letter to My Cousin,* a Pura Belpré Honor Book, Tonatiuh uses letters to effectively communicate the commonalities and differences between two cousins' homes in the United States and Mexico. The text is made up of the cousins' letters and drawings and includes sketches in the letters that are labeled in Spanish. The book includes a glossary of the Spanish words used in the text and an author's note where Tonatiuh discusses his personal story of migration from Mexico to Williamstown, Massachusetts. *Hands Around the Library: Protecting Egypt's Treasured Books* vividly retells the story of thousands of students, library workers, and protesters creating a human circle around the library in Alexandra, Egypt, to protect it from destruction. Susan Roth uses collage to bring the events to life. This book, an NCTE Orbis Pictus Nonfiction Recommended Book, is written in English, but the collages bring in many protest signs written in Arabic. The book ends with extensive notes on the ancient library in Alexandria and includes a few words from the protest signs in Arabic translated into English. Books that include multiple languages, such as these, can be intimidating for teachers who don't speak those languages to read aloud, but are also powerful demonstrations of the multiplicity of languages in the world.

Karen started the unit by creating a Venn diagram to chart languages known by first graders, languages used in the literature, and countries where the characters lived. This diagram set a tone for students as they considered language as a resource and language as a right (Ruiz 1984). Children freely shared their knowledge and learned from each other as they thought about the significance of language in the world.

Language Diversity as Strength

Dear Primo: A Letter to My Cousin (Tonatiuh 2010) was the first book that Karen read aloud in this unit. Typically, Karen sat in a large rocking chair and students were seated in front of her as she read. A whiteboard was near the chair, and the Venn diagram with the linguistic responses was on the other side of the chair. After reading aloud, Karen usually used a literature response strategy or close reading strategy. Students would turn to talk with partners as part of discussion or move into small groups to discuss their perspectives. They were used to having space and time to talk about books. Over time, they became accustomed to books that included languages other than English. This unit marked the first time that many had heard their first languages spoken or presented in a book.

As Karen read the title, *Dear Primo*, several students called out that *primo* means "cousin." Many students knew the Spanish words in this text, and several took on the role of linguistic experts. Across the reading, students continually negotiated the meanings of the words in Spanish, demonstrating their knowledge of *maiz* (corn) and *gallo* (rooster). They translated the words into English and defined them.

The first part of the read-aloud and discussion was more of a brainstorming session as they interacted with the text and teacher in a meaning-making discussion. This discussion seemed to encourage students to actively participate in the read-aloud. On the page about *fútbol* (soccer), students were eager to discuss the differences between soccer and football. Several shared about *fútbol* in Mexico. In one case, Karen started to look in the glossary to define *nopal* (cactus), but students immediately responded with the translation of the word in English. They used their linguistic knowledge from Spanish and inserted that knowledge into the discussion, helping peers make meaning from the text. At the end of the reading, students asked Karen to return to several pages, willingly revisiting parts of the text as a group on their own. In fact, it became a classroom norm that at the end of the reading, students would come up to the text and revisit and talk about pages that were important to them.

After the read-aloud and discussion, Karen asked students to think about what they had learned about the identities of the two cousins and to critically analyze the similarities and differences within the communities. Students were able to easily identify the cousins' similarities and contributed information from their backgrounds to explore those similarities. They had more difficulty thinking about the cousins' differences. Karen used additional think time and encouraged students to build off of each other as they carefully constructed their cultural perspectives regarding differences.

Children also made intertextual connections as they thought about how cousins live in different places, referring to *This Is the Rope: A Story from the Great Migration* (Woodson 2013) and *My Abuelita* (Johnston 2009). They connected to these stories in their struggle to create initial understandings about differences across cultures. Later, Karen and I realized that having this discussion about community first might have better supported students in finding differences. Karen took a risk with a book that she had not previously discussed with children and so was figuring out ways to thoughtfully move them into critical conversations around global issues without directing them too closely.

Linguistic Diversity as Protest

I took on the role of teacher in the discussion of *Hands Around the Library: Protecting Egypt's Treasured Books*. Before reading this book, we discussed our knowledge of the Arabic language. We did a quick poll of the languages known by students, and Arabic and Spanish were the most popular. Abdul started our conversation by saying that although he couldn't talk in Arabic, he knew it. After several class discussions, we discovered that Abdul had receptive knowledge of Arabic and could understand what someone said to him, but he couldn't always produce the correct words. He shared that his family reads many books in Arabic, including the Bible when they go to church. Abdul also commented that he really did recognize many words that he didn't understand, but he wanted to know more because he liked Arabic.

Since the illustrations created by Susan Roth were in collage, we talked about how collage is created within the publishing process of a book. Many students said that the people in the story looked "fake" in the illustrations. They preferred the actual photos that were placed at the end of the book.

As we moved into the discussion of the story, students immediately commented on the importance of the protest signs. We talked about why people use print to protest something that they care about deeply and the significance of taking action to protect cultural treasures like books in libraries.

Children connected this book to *The Librarian of Basra* (Winter 2005), critically comparing the issues in both books and talking about how bravery was required by the librarians and community members to protect books from serious harm and destruction. Another connection came when Jasmine asked, "Is this book like in the Martin Luther King book when they had those signs?" Her comment was connected to a read-aloud called *The Cart That Carried Martin* (Bunting 2013). Students linked the protest signs across the two texts by talking about the importance of standing up for what you believe even when it could be dangerous. They also talked about the role of peacekeepers and how signs can help people stand up for their rights.

Students moved into groups of two or three to discuss their thoughts about whether the library in Alexandria would ultimately be destroyed by violence. They were encouraged to think about the details in the story that guided them to their predictions. Chris said firmly, "People are going to destroy the library and make a huge mess." Jared said, "There is going to be some sort of violence that will occur to the library, but it will be okay because the place will be surrounded by guards." We discovered with additional reading that the library was saved because people joined together and saved the library by locking arms. No guards were ultimately needed. We were able to confirm a few theories about the library's safety.

We then returned to the discussion about the directionality of the text on the protest signs. Several thought that Arabic moved right to left. Abdul adamantly disagreed and was convinced that Arabic followed the pattern of English in moving left to right. Students also discussed differences between Arabic and Spanish.

Another conversation focused on the story as nonfiction, depicting real events in Egypt. In addition, we talked about how we would feel if someone tried to take our books. Chris indicated that he would say, "Back off. These are my books and don't take them away from me." After the discussions, students created protest signs in their writing journals.

Learning to Facilitate Critical Discussions Around Intercultural Perspectives

These discussions had times of intense discovery and exploration around intercultural perspectives such as protecting literature from harm in Iraq or Egypt. Students learned about these places and tried to place themselves in these contexts. Also, our conversations took turns into the linguistic differences in the print. For us, these turns were important as we moved to discussion of intercultural perspectives. These types of critical conversations take time and patience. Students rarely had the opportunity to share their thinking in the mandated curriculum, so they enthusiastically participated in these discussions.

The CRITIC framework assisted us in creating space for examining a range of intercultural perspectives. High-quality literature that offers global perspectives matters, and broadens our views and stances as learners. Multiple reads offer readers multiple times to try on critical stances and points of view. Intentional strategies offer readers real tools that they can use in the process of developing a stance. Talk creates a community of learners as they make meaning collaboratively around the text. Investigations allow readers to continue to unravel meaning from the texts. Comprehension engages readers in making meaning from global texts and working to expand their views about the world.

Negotiating School Mandates

Teachers live in a constant state of tension because of the language of the Common Core Standards, the implementation of these standards within schools, and the pressure of standardized testing. Karen said, "Teachers are constantly being told new methods to implement, but are rarely told how and when to implement them. I have heard the term *close reading* several times in my teaching career but never had a great understanding of what it really meant. Especially for me, a K–1 teacher, I thought close reading was a strategy primarily developed and used in the higher elementary grades and beyond. I thought close reading was only for nonfiction texts and only meant rereading."

There are many definitions of close reading that are quickly becoming part of educational jargon because of the Common Core Standards. For me, close reading is critically analyzing a text (Beers and Probst 2012). In this inquiry, we reframed and shaped the arguments about close reading to focus upon the creation of lifelong readers who explore global perspectives. We used the CRITIC framework to grapple with how we can teach readers to think about multiple perspectives on the world through close reading.

Karen is not alone in regard to the misalignment of standards and implementation. Teachers have a genuine concern about their loss of decision making about what texts are read aloud and how they are used within literacy instruction. In the case of this first grade, teachers decided as a group to use global literary and informational texts instead of the basal.

Teachers' joint decision making contributed toward their power in deciding which books to include within the curriculum. There was also a focused and intentional plan as a grade level to use the texts critically. Critical literacy is transformational when students shift roles and become co-investigators and problem posers (Freire 1970). Teachers can not only invite students to explore their understandings of the text through close reading but generate pivotal questions about issues of power across texts. Karen said, "I have tried to be more thoughtful about the texts I am choosing for read-aloud as well as those for shared reading. With carefully chosen literature, I am able to help my students grasp and achieve ELA Common Core Standards with texts they are interested in and push them to have critical discussions, written responses, and connections with their self, world, and other texts."

Final Reflections

The power of a global story read and discussed critically within a classroom cannot be underestimated. Students remember these stories throughout the year and use them as a frame for understanding new ideas about the world. The stories broaden their views and perspectives. As educators, we need to continue to make arguments for using powerful and thought-provoking units that involve incorporating a range of intercultural perspectives.

Teachers need time and space to think creatively and plan together to use global texts. This space is one where teachers make decisions based on their knowledge of the specific students in their classrooms. They know students' linguistic and cultural needs better than experts who write a scripted program for generic students. My goal is finding meaningful and intentional ways of exploring the integration of global voices.

Recommended Books That Invite Global Perspectives

Abouraya, Karen L. 2012. *Hands Around the Library: Protecting Egypt's Treasured Books*. Illus. Susan L. Roth. New York: Dial.
This true story depicts the actions of students, library workers, and protesters as they join hands to make a human chain, protecting the great library in Alexandria, Egypt, from destruction during mass demonstrations.

Tonatiuh, Duncan. 2010. *Dear Primo: A Letter to My Cousin*. New York: Abrams.
This book is a series of letters between Charlie and Carlitos, cousins who live in different countries. Their letters portray the similarities and differences between their lives in Mexico and the United States as well as the strong bond of family ties.

Winter, Jeanette. 2005. *The Librarian of Basra: A True Story from Iraq.* **San Diego, CA: Harcourt.**

This is the true story of Alia Muhammad Baker, a brave librarian who risks her life to save the library in Basra, Iraq, during bombing. She knows that her library is a meeting place for those who love books and that they will need books to come together as a community.

References

Beers, Kylene, and Robert Probst. 2012. *Notice and Note-Taking: Strategies for Close Reading.* Portsmouth, NH: Heinemann.

Bloome, David, and Ann Egan-Robertson. 1993. "The Social Construction of Intertextuality in Classroom Reading and Writing Lessons." *Reading Research Quarterly* 28:304–333.

Bloome, David, Stephanie Carter, Beth Christian, Sheila Otto, and Nora Shuart-Faris. 2005. *Discourse Analysis and the Study of Classroom Language and Literacy Events.* Mahwah, NJ: Erlbaum.

Fisher, Doug, and Nancy Frey. 2012. "Close Reading in Elementary Schools." *Reading Teacher* 66 (3): 179–188.

Freire, Paulo. 1970. *Pedagogy of the Oppressed.* New York: Continuum.

Gallagher, Kelly. 2004. *Deeper Reading: Comprehending Challenging Texts, 4–12.* Portland, ME: Stenhouse.

Gee, James. 1999. *An Introduction to Discourse Analysis.* New York: Routledge.

———. 2002. "A Sociocultural Perspective on Early Literacy Development." In *Handbook of Early Literacy Research*, ed. David Dickinson and Susan Newman, 30–42. New York: Guilford.

Lehman, Chris, and Kate Roberts. 2013. *Falling in Love with Close Reading: Lessons for Analyzing Texts and Life.* Portsmouth, NH: Heinemann.

Medina, Carmen, and Gerald Campano. 2006. "Performing Identities Through Drama and Teatro Practices in Multilingual Classrooms." *Language Arts* 83 (4): 332–341.

Richhart, Ron, Mark Church, and Karin Morrison. 2011. *Making Thinking Visible.* San Francisco, CA: Jossey Bass.

Ruiz, Richard. 1984. "Orientations in Language Planning." *NABE Journal* 8 (2): 15-34.

Short, Kathy G. 2004. *Literature Discussion Strategies.* https://www.coe.arizona.edu/short_strategies.

———. 2009. "Curriculum as Inquiry." In *International Perspectives on Inquiry Learning,* ed. S. Carber and S. Davidson, pp. 11-26. London: John Catt.

Short, Kathy G., and Lisa Thomas. 2011. "Developing Intercultural Understandings Through Global Children's Literature." *In Reclaiming Reading: Teachers, Students, and Researchers Regaining Spaces for Thinking and Action,* ed. R. Meyer and K. Whitmore, pp. 149-162. New York: Routledge.

Street, Brian. 2005. "Literacy, Technology, and Multimodality: Implications for Pedagogy and Curriculum." Paper presented at the fifty-fifth annual meeting of the National Reading Conference, Miami, FL, December.

Vasquez, Vivian, Stacie Tate, and Jerome Harste. 2013. *Negotiating Critical Literacies with Teachers.* Mahwah, NJ: Routledge.

Vygotsky, Lev. 1978. *Mind in Society.* Cambridge, MA: Harvard University Press.

Children's Books Cited

Abouraya, Karen. 2012. *Hands Around the Library: Protecting Egypt's Treasured Books.* Illus. Susan Roth. New York: Dial.

Aliki. 1998. *Marianthe's Story: Painted Words and Spoken Memories.* New York: Greenwillow.

Brown, Monica. 2010. *Chavela and the Magic Bubble.* Illus. Magaly Morales. New York: Houghton Mifflin.

Bunting, Eve. 2006. *One Green Apple.* Illus. Ted Lewin. New York: Clarion.

———. 2013. *The Cart That Carried Martin.* Illus. Don Tate. Watertown, MA: Charlesbridge.

Johnston, Tony. 2009. *My Abuelita.* Illus. Yuyi Morales. Boston: Harcourt.

Tonatiuh, Duncan. 2010. *Dear Primo: A Letter to My Cousin.* New York: Abrams.

———. 2013. *Pancho Rabbit and the Coyote: A Migrant's Tale.* New York: Abrams.

Weulersse, Odilie. 2005. *Nasreddine.* Illus. Rebecca Dautremer. Grand Rapids, MI: Eerdmans.

Winter, Jeanette. 2005. *The Librarian of Basra: A True Story from Iraq.* San Diego, CA: Harcourt.

Woodson, Jacqueline. 2012. *Each Kindness.* Illus. E. B. Lewis. New York: Nancy Paulsen Books.

———. 2013. *This Is the Rope: A Story from the Great Migration.* Illus. James Ransome. New York: Nancy Paulsen Books.

Yamanka, Lois-Ann. 2005. *The Heart's Language.* Illus. Aaron Jasinski. New York: Hyperion.

PART 5

Inquiries into Global Issues

Chapter 13

Global Children's Literature in Science: The Potential of Inquiry and Social Action

Jennifer Hart Davis and Tracy Smiles

Jennifer, an eighth-grade earth science teacher, had high hopes for her upcoming water unit. Having taught about water resources in years past, she knew that although students grasped the scientific content of the unit, they were not connecting personally with global issues surrounding water as some of the most urgent of their lifetimes. Jennifer saw an emphasis on teaching global environmental issues as imperative to her mission as a science teacher.

Jennifer reflects, "Water: we cannot live without it, yet few of us really understand or stop to consider our relationship with the natural resource that ties humanity together. Water is the very essence of life. While many of us in the developed world take our unlimited access to clean water supplies for granted, there is a water crisis in much of the world. What connection and responsibility do we have to our global neighbors with whom we share this resource? It was this globally unifying topic of water through which I sought to connect content and culture in my science classroom."

This impetus drove Jennifer to not only teach the scientific content associated with water resources, but to also build a connection for students through global literature. Jennifer wanted to better understand students' perspectives on their relationship with water, so she invited them to reflect on the following questions after they made observations about water use in their homes over a weekend:

• How do you use water in ways that allow you to survive (needs)?

- How do you use water in ways that allow you to make life healthier?
- How do you and your family use water in ways that you would consider a luxury and not a necessity (wants)?
- How do you waste water?
- Does your family ever use water in any type of ceremonial way? If so, how?
- Do you play in water? How? What kind?
- How valuable do you think water is as a natural resource in Corvallis? In the United States? In the world?

Jennifer's invitation yielded disappointing results. She observed, "Classroom discussions afterward centered on more obvious ideas, such as drinking water and using water to shower and brush their teeth. At this point in the lesson, students did not appear to be very engaged. I would summarize their attitude as, 'Yes, I use water just like everyone else. So what?'"

If the goal of a curriculum that is intercultural includes learners examining issues that have personal, local, and global relevance in order to demonstrate a responsibility for making a difference in the world and for developing an inquiry perspective on taking action, we wondered how intercultural understanding might play out in a science classroom. This chapter tells the story of the literacy and science content learning that unfolded through engagement with global children's and adolescent literature in Jennifer's earth science classroom at a suburban middle school in the central Willamette Valley.

Through the intentional use of children's and adolescent literature containing interesting stories about children and youth in other parts of the world and their relationships with water, Jennifer provided opportunities for students to connect scientific content about water cycling and global distribution to its social significance both globally and locally. This story demonstrates how, as a result of using literature concurrently with scientific inquiry into the water cycle, students identified significant issues related to water and thus changed their perspectives on a vital resource they had previously taken for granted.

Intercultural Understanding, Children's Literature, and the Science Classroom

Jennifer's experience is not unusual. Those of us who teach or work with adolescents know well that what excites us as teachers doesn't necessarily resonate with students.

The disconnect between what the teacher values and the adolescent deems important presents challenges for all members of the middle school community. For Jennifer, this challenge was felt in her deep, abiding concern for the environment and the future stewardship of the world's limited resources, such as water. Before becoming a middle school science teacher, she spent twenty years conducting research in soil and water quality; however, her perspectives changed when she discovered her passion for teaching.

Jennifer explains, "My background as a practicing scientist was grounded in the foundations of science—science being unequivocally technical and objective in nature. In my observation and attempted explanation of the natural world, I sought to remove the subjective nature of the human condition from my research and writings, thereby making the dissemination of scientific information as close to the 'truth' as possible. However, as I guide the next generation of citizen scientists, I found that I needed ways to integrate the objective nature of science with an understanding of how we, as a society, shape and are shaped by scientific information. Decisions and policies we create regarding natural resources are intricately woven into human placement of value on these resources."

Jennifer, through her friendship with Tracy, was invited to participate in the Willamette Valley Global Inquiry Community, a group of teachers and teacher educators who engaged in collaborative activities on the use of global children's and adolescent literature to develop intercultural understandings. This collaboration provided Jennifer an opportunity to explore how literature could enhance engagement with content and invite critical explorations into the relationship between scientific knowledge, cultural beliefs, and practices, and how such knowledge affects the preservation and ethical distribution of the planet's resources. Specifically, her goal in integrating global literature into the eighth-grade earth science curriculum was to give students an opportunity to not only access science content (water cycle, global climate, and weather patterns) but also to connect in a deeper way to the experiences and perspectives of young people in other cultures (cultural practices, adaptations). By making connections to their own and then other cultures, her hope was that students would be able to feel and develop respect for the common humanity that comes from the sharing and care of our natural resources.

Jennifer's intent in using literature within the context of an eighth-grade earth science classroom aligned with the broader goals of implementing a curriculum that is intercultural while simultaneously addressing challenges related to adolescent literacy. It has been well documented that as students move from elementary to secondary school, the expectations for reading to learn academic content increases significantly.

Specific kinds of skills are required to read discipline-specific texts that are written under the assumption that students have the background knowledge to learn from these texts (Lee and Spratley 2010). There lies the conundrum for adolescent learners. If students don't know the content, they will have problems understanding the text, and if they can't understand the text, "they are unlikely to learn content" (3).

On the other hand, reading complex literary texts provides opportunities for students to grapple not only with content, but with ethical dilemmas that foster empathetic and ethical reasoning (Lee and Spratley 2010). Similar to the challenges that face adolescent readers' comprehension of discipline-specific texts, literary texts require a great deal of prior knowledge, such as knowledge of text structures, experience with rhetorical tools employed by authors, and the ability to make intertextual connections between the reader's knowledge of the author, other authors, related texts, and so on (Lee and Spratley 2010). Therefore, current research on adolescent literacy calls for instructional planning that focuses on the construction of knowledge gradually, using easily accessible, high-interest texts and then increasing the complexity of such texts to develop adolescent readers' confidence as they engage in authentic, discipline-specific tasks (Moje and Dillon 2006).

Although few would question the obvious potential of global and cultural inquiry in social sciences, the connections to science were initially less obvious. However, Tracy and Jennifer learned that the study of nature and culture are, in fact, complementary lines of inquiry. Green Theory, a category within the broader field of literary and cultural studies, engages in analysis of literature and content through the insights of ecology (Coupe 2013, 154). Green Theory does not argue the complexity of culture and nature, but rather makes the case that human culture is a dimension of nature. The etymology of *culture* finds connections to *nature* in its original meanings, such as "inhabitation," "cultivation," and "worship" (Coupe 2013, 155). If our "views of the world are a web of interconnected stories, a distillation of all the stories we have shared," as Short (2012) contends, "this web of stories becomes our interpretive lens for new experiences so that story is our means of constructing the world—of world making" (10). Through collaborative inquiries into global issues through story, in this case water cycling and distributions, over time students can come to understand the local and global complexity of the issues and consider taking new actions in their own lives.

Integration of accessible, high-interest texts that presented students with powerful stories about people in other parts of the world and their relationships with water opened up opportunity for inquiry into global issues surrounding water. Jennifer wanted students to connect with content in a new, personal way. She explains, "I had been on a journey in my short tenure as an educator to gain a better understanding myself of what culture is and how I can marry that understanding with my passion for social justice. In order for my students to make socially responsible decisions, they must be able to step beyond their experiences and not only see how their decisions impact others, but to also empathize with those 'others.' Exposure to global literature was one pathway to make this possible. By exploring the value that global cultures place on water, my students would hopefully consider water resource issues from a global perspective."

Through her participation with the Willamette Valley Global Inquiry Community, Jennifer purchased literature to integrate into her science classroom. She had the resources and desire to use the literature effectively, but honestly admits, "The problem is that there is not always a clear pathway to the integration of culture into teaching science content."

Theory into Practice: Integrating Literature and Science

Jennifer began the water unit with an invitation for students to reflect on how they use water in their everyday lives. Based on their unperceptive responses to the guiding questions, she realized they had a difficult time reflecting on how their use of water might be considered a luxury or waste, and few responses referenced how they might use water in cultural or religious practices. Overall, it appeared students felt as though their use of water was relatively efficient and necessary to sustain their everyday way of life.

Jennifer introduced the science content through a number of hands-on activities, such as putting water into large zippered plastic bags with some air and putting the bags in the sun. Students made and recorded observations using key vocabulary words (*evaporation, condensation, collection, precipitation,* and so on) and then drew diagrams of the water cycle. Jennifer noted that students actually knew a lot about the water cycle because it was one of the few science content units in the elementary school curriculum.

Jennifer had students relate their models of the water cycle to real-world factors that affect global climate and distribution of water. To drive home the fact that most water (more than 99 percent) on Earth is not available for human uses such as drinking and crop irrigation, she had students do an activity where they first divided 100 milliliters (mL) of water into smaller containers to represent global supplies of salt water (98 mL) versus fresh water (2 mL). Most students were quite surprised at how much of Earth's water was salt water. Students were asked to pour two-thirds of the freshwater out to represent water that is tied up in the polar ice caps. Students were left with less than 1 mL of water, which represented the amount of Earth's water available for human use (0.37 percent of Earth's water) (Shiklomanov 1993).

Students also explored how freshwater supplies are unequally distributed across the globe using data maps. At this point, students understood just how limited freshwater was on Earth and that they lived in an area of no water scarcity while much of the world lives in areas of some water scarcity. Although students had been presented the staggering data, Jennifer felt that they were still not connected to these realizations on a personal level. That is when she decided to bring in literature.

The two books Jennifer selected for whole-class study were *A Long Walk to Water* by Linda Sue Park (2010) and *Our World of Water: Children and Water Around the World* by Beatrice Hollyer (2008). In *A Long Walk to Water*, students focused on the narrative of Nya, a young woman from Sudan who was solely responsible for supplying her family with water, at times walking eight hours a day through the desert. *Our World of Water* contained individual chapters that presented the reader with an in-depth look at the life of a child from one of several countries: Peru, Mauritania, Bangladesh, Ethiopia, Tajikistan, and the United States. Jennifer felt that these high-quality texts explored more than the superficial "tourist perspective" of people living in other parts of the world. Instead, they presented rich and realistic descriptions of the everyday lives of children and their relationships with water. Jennifer was somewhat surprised by students' excitement about the text selections. These literature choices were notably different from the science texts, such as articles and scientific reports, they were used to reading in her class, and she observed how these personal narratives grabbed her students' attention and provided opportunities to personally connect with the text. This was an exciting discovery.

Content-area teachers are challenged by a schedule that allows for limited time with students. Often, within the span of forty-five minutes content-area teachers are charged with covering a vast amount of material, and Jennifer's situation was no different. Her process for integrating literature was to have students read the texts or selections within the texts in small groups. She asked them to answer the same questions they had answered for themselves about water use at the beginning of the unit, only this time from the perspective of the child about whom they read. Students identified similarities and differences between themselves and their counterparts' according to their relationships with water through graphic representations of their observations, connections, surprises, and questions (Heffernan 2004). Not only did the visual representations of their interpretations of the literature and content foster poignant discussions about cultural and global issues related to water use and availability, but the integration of literature from diverse cultures provided opportunities for students to integrate global perspectives through exploration of global environmental issues around water. Furthermore, Jennifer found the use of student-led activities such as literature circles and sketch to stretch were not only efficient and engaging, but produced more genuine and diverse responses that expanded and enriched other students' perspectives when reflections were shared in small- and whole-group settings (Short, Harste, and Burke 1996).

Jennifer observed high levels of engagement as students worked through the science activities and books. She overheard discussions that excited her, and also demonstrated deep shifts in thinking about water issues as well as increased interest in people living in other parts of the world and respect for their resourcefulness in acquiring and preserving life-sustaining water. She repeatedly heard comments such as these:

"All I have to do is walk to the sink to get water; they have to work so hard!"

"Can you believe she has to walk all that way without shoes?"

"Yeah, and then she had to take her little sister with her!"

"I can't imagine not being able to take a shower whenever I wanted!"

"They are so careful with water, they even use the leftovers to wash themselves."

Jennifer noted that these comments indicated that students were really stepping into the lives of children living in other regions of the world.

Adding Global Literature to the Water Unit: Inquiries on Global Issues

A key aspect of a curriculum that is intercultural is inquiries that focus on specific global issues that highlight challenging political, social, and environmental topics and lead to some type of action. Jennifer, on her own journey of developing intercultural understanding, recognized that these students' social class could affect the way they interpreted literature. She was concerned that when students encountered narratives from children who had access to fewer resources, they might pity them rather than feel connected to and develop a respect for humans' ability to adapt to their natural environments. She also suspected that it would be easier for students to identify differences between themselves and their counterparts rather than similarities when they began inquiries into global issues around water. Neither of these concerns were evidenced by student work or commentary, which she attributed to a curricular framework that guided her in making thoughtful instructional decisions.

The framework offered pathways for how, through engagement with global literature, students might explore diverse cultural perspectives and complex global issues. The student-created products revealed expanded perspectives on students' cultural relationships with water, diverging from initial, more superficial observations. Broader implications for how water is used and perceived globally were evident in the artistic and written reflections on the science content and literature study. For example, students initially focused on water for drinking to survive, but by the end of their global inquiry into water issues, they had demonstrated a clearer understanding of other uses of water, such as for religious purposes and celebrations.

Jennifer also observed students categorizing their discussions of personal water use as "wants" and "needs." The biggest change in their thinking was seen in their realization that their use of water would, to the rest of the world, be considered a luxury. Swimming in a pool, taking showers every day, watering lawns, and having access to clean water are luxuries that many around the world do not enjoy. Students better understood the high cultural value placed on water and admired children in the narratives who used water with careful attention and yet led fulfilling, rich lives. Learning about the care and value that children and youth in other cultures give to water use gave students a new perspective on what wasting water in their own lives looked like.

Eighth-grader Matt reflected, "Doing this project has really changed my perspective on how we use water. For example, I didn't realize how valuable it is to people in Ethiopia. They have to walk long ways just to find small ponds, while we can access it by turning on our sinks. I also realized that we take water for granted. We sometimes leave the sink running while we brush our teeth or take a long shower. So this project has made me think twice when I use water and think if I need to use it or not."

Randal made similar observations, noting, "In the water unit I learned that water in some countries is so scarce that people fight over it. While in the U.S., you can take a few steps to the sink and have water pour out of the spout; as much as you want. To most people in the U.S., water doesn't seem very valuable."

Jennifer was delighted to see how literature provided opportunities for students to discover interesting commonalities with the characters in the texts. For example, Jacob, a student with autism who had difficulty making personal connections, recognized that he and Saran of Bangladesh use water for religious ceremonies (see Figure 13.1).

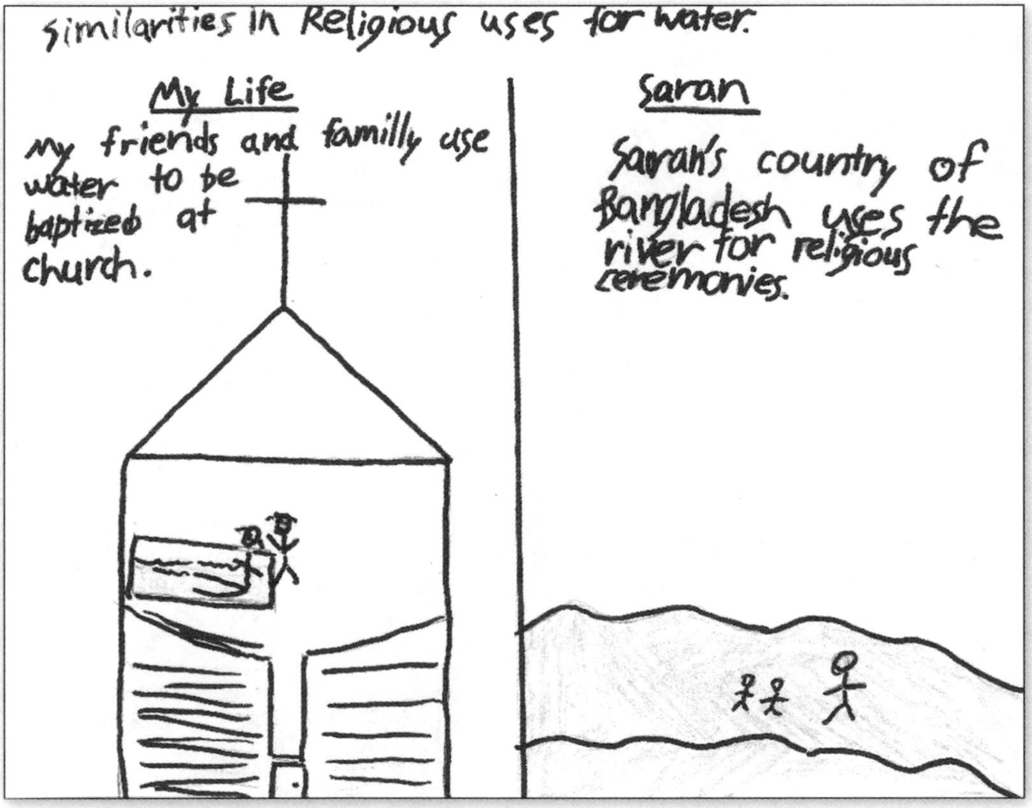

Figure 13.1 **Jacob's Illustration Comparing How Saran of Bangladesh and Jacob's Family Use Water for Religious Ceremonies**

In Figure 13.2, Jossi added that in Khadija's culture of Mauritania, they use water to wash rams for ceremonial purposes.

Jossi was able to envision Khadija's very different relationship with water. The depth of Jossi's new perspective as represented in her drawing and text was summed up in this comment: "Learning about Khadija and her family really opened my eyes. It is amazing how one person can learn to cope with as little as she does. She is incredible and I would not be able to live with the little water she has."

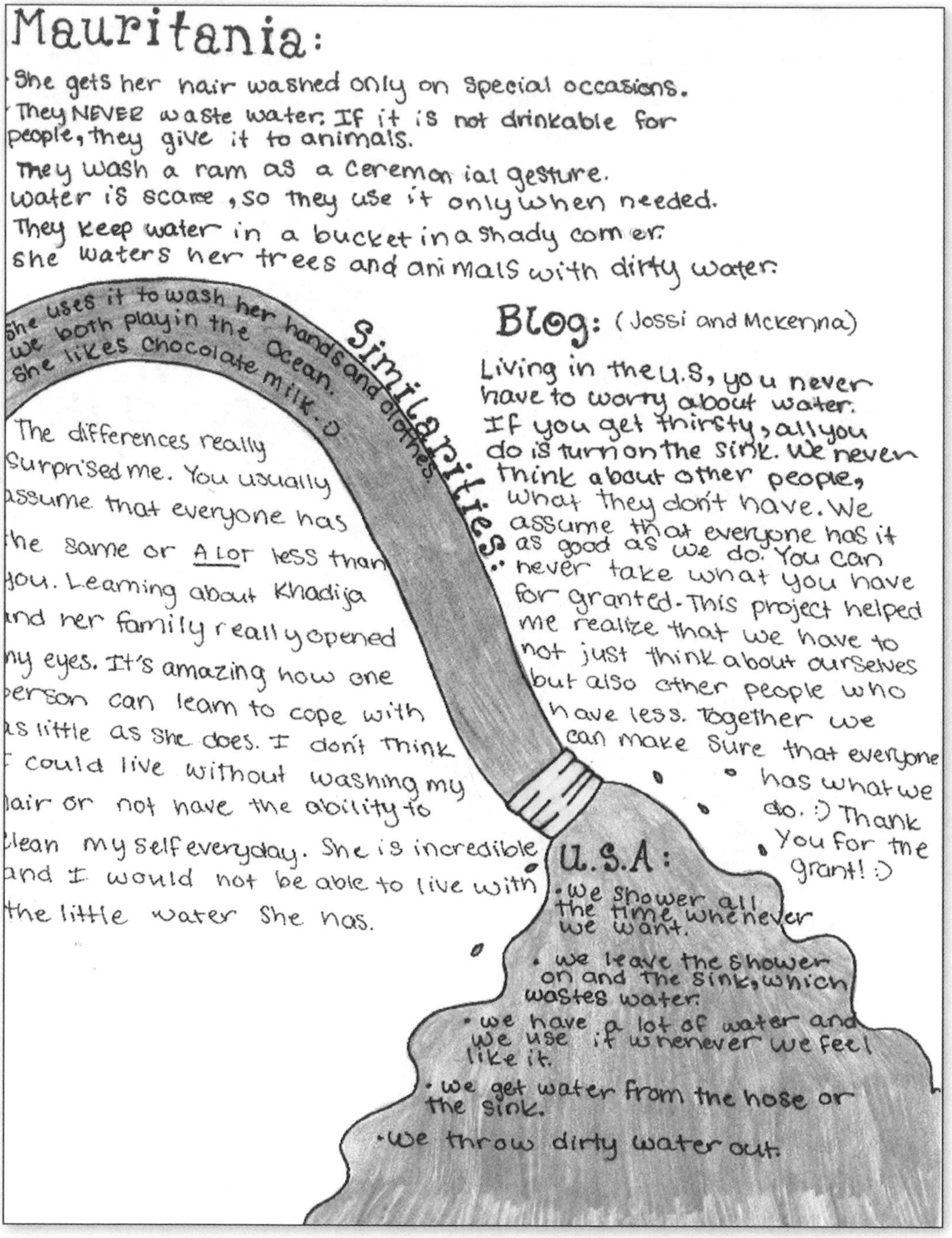

Mauritania:

- She gets her hair washed only on special occasions.
- They NEVER waste water. If it is not drinkable for people, they give it to animals.
- They wash a ram as a ceremonial gesture.
- Water is scarce, so they use it only when needed.
- They keep water in a bucket in a shady corner.
- She waters her trees and animals with dirty water.

Similarities
- She uses it to wash her hands and clothes.
- We both play in the ocean.
- She likes chocolate milk. :)

The differences really surprised me. You usually assume that everyone has the same or A LOT less than you. Learning about Khadija and her family really opened my eyes. It's amazing how one person can learn to cope with as little as she does. I don't think I could live without washing my hair or not have the ability to clean myself everyday. She is incredible and I would not be able to live with the little water she has.

Blog: (Jossi and Mckenna)

Living in the U.S, you never have to worry about water. If you get thirsty, all you do is turn on the sink. We never think about other people, what they don't have. We assume that everyone has it as good as we do. You can never take what you have for granted. This project helped me realize that we have to not just think about ourselves but also other people who have less. Together we can make sure that everyone has what we do. :) Thank you for the grant! :)

U.S.A:
- We shower all the time, whenever we want.
- We leave the shower on and the sink, which wastes water.
- We have a lot of water and we use it whenever we feel like it.
- We get water from the hose or the sink.
- We throw dirty water out.

Figure 13.2 Jossi's Illustration Depicting Similarities and Differences in Her Water Use Compared to Khadija's Family

Beverly found connection in Khadija's narrative, noticing that she and Khadija love to play in the ocean and both use water to prepare their food (see Figure 13.3).

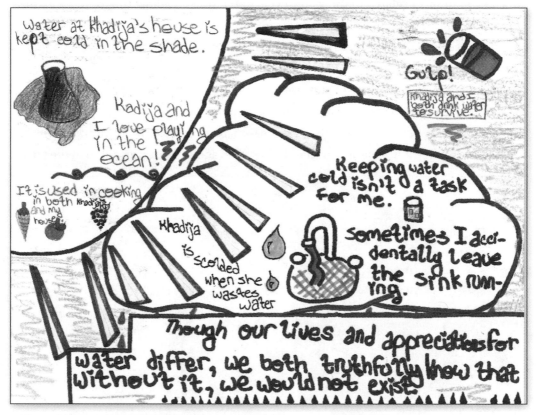

Figure 13.3 Beverly's Illustration Reflecting How Resourceful Khadija Was with Water, and How Beverly as a US Citizen Tended to Take Water for Granted

Bev concluded, "This book opened my eyes to the fact that I take water for granted when I should really treasure it for keeping me alive."

Another surprising outcome of the water unit literature study came from Chaeun, a Korean student learning English who often remained quiet during class discussions. Chaeun's vivid illustration powerfully expressed the similarities and differences between her Korean culture and that of Sudan (see Figure 13.4). Chaeun used this opportunity to discuss how her relationship with water in Korea was very similar to her relationship with it in the United States and how they were both different from a person's in Sudan.

Jennifer's first use of authentic global literature in the science classroom yielded powerful results for both her and her students. She experienced firsthand how, through the development of conceptual understandings of global issues surrounding water, students' views and attitudes toward water were significantly affected, moving beyond familiar regurgitation of facts related to the water cycle to really seeing how the forces of nature, coupled with issues of power, oppression, and social justice, make the access to natural resources difficult for a large part of the world's population. She'd not only met her primary instructional goal that students learn and explore science content while developing a deeper understanding of cultural and global issues related to natural resources, but also recognized that the two are inextricably intertwined. Using high-quality global literature clearly provided students with meaningful access to the content, gaining an understanding and appreciation for the children and adolescents presented in the books.

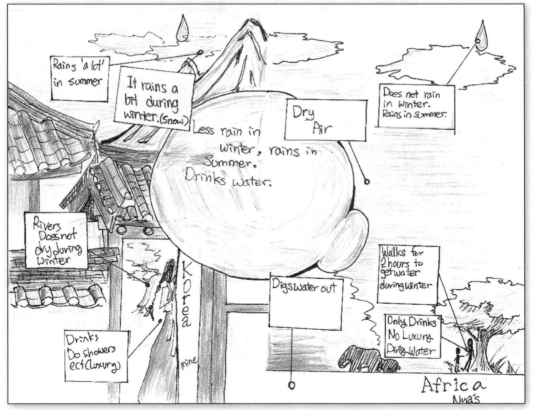

Figure 13.4 Chaeun's Illustration Expressing Difference Between Her Native Culture of Korea and That of Nya's in Sudan

It was more difficult to determine whether the goal of social action had been reached and the unit led to a change in habits. The unit was implemented at the very end of the year, with students moving to high school the following year. However, students' comments seem to indicate that they were considering thoughtful small and large changes in their actions. What is more obvious is that the curricular framework offers content-area teachers new avenues for engaging adolescent learners with content and facilitates critical explorations of that content, whether in science, math, social studies, or language arts.

Negotiating School Mandates

Oregon adopted the Common Core State Standards (CCSS) for English Language Arts and Mathematics in 2010, and the Next Generation Science Standards (NGSS) in 2014. With the changes in the state's content standards came new assessments, changes in curricular scope and sequence at each grade level, and the continued pressure to ensure that students perform well on these high-stakes assessments. In addition to the changes in standards and assessments, the state of Oregon passed into law a proficiency-based assessment mandate. Jennifer is responsible for supporting students in navigating discipline-specific texts as outlined in the CCSS, preparing them for the OAKS science exam and the Smarter Balanced ELA test, and evaluating student work samples to measure proficiency with the standards.

Given these challenges, Jennifer's work in the classroom is built on the premise that students should be "immersed in life and living as problem posers and problem-solvers" in the fullest sense (Siu-Runyan 1999, 5). Jennifer sees the scope and sequence of standards as offering guideposts for selecting themes and content, but the needs and interests of students ultimately influence the kinds of engagements and texts she implements in her classroom. For her, the tension between standards and student needs need not be an either/or proposition. Rather, Jennifer sees literacy as a "tool for students to construct their understanding of the world, others, and themselves" (Short 2012, 8).

Jennifer's beliefs are shaped by her experiences as a scientist and grounded in her hopes for raising awareness in students about the extraordinary planet where they live and the importance of caring for that precious place. The biggest challenge she faces is time. Excessive assessments and content coupled with limited contact with students could easily push her to the limits of fatigue and frustration. However, guided by her core beliefs coupled with collaborative relationships such as the inquiry that led to the instructional project described in this chapter gives Jennifer the energy to teach.

Final Reflections

Jennifer feels she is just beginning to see and enact her vision of using children's and adolescent literature throughout her science curriculum to develop intercultural understandings and have these understandings permeate her curriculum. Developing a sense of curriculum and frameworks for enacting that curriculum in a way that makes sense is probably one of the greatest challenges teachers face. The framework for a curriculum that is intercultural provided a way to open up explorations of content and engage in inquiries into global issues. Global literature opened avenues for Jennifer to integrate content in ways meaningful to the adolescent learners in her care, and to understand that the availability of water clearly shapes culture.

Beatrice Hollyer (2008), author of *Our World of Water*, says, "We have a funny human habit of valuing only what seems rare to us, things like masterpieces of art or diamonds. We think that water is so very common that we needn't value it so highly" (6). For Jennifer, this passage set the stage for students to consider both how and on what we and others place value. This inquiry created an opportunity for eighth graders living in the Willamette Valley of Oregon, where water scarcity is not of great concern, to see the interconnectedness of their lives with others around the world and consciously consider that anyone anywhere *can* experience water scarcity as global warming continues to proceed, ignored by most.

Recommended Books That Invite Global Perspectives

Hollyer, Beatrice. 2008. *Our World of Water: Children and Water Around the World*. New York: Henry Holt.

This informational book explores water usage around the world by following the everyday lives of children in a variety of global communities. Each chapter contains an in-depth look at the life of a child in Peru, Mauritania, Bangladesh, Ethiopia, Tajikistan, and the United States.

Park, Linda Sue. 2010. *A Long Walk to Water.* New York: Clarion Books. This novel in two voices tells the alternating stories about two eleven-year-olds living in Sudan at different times. Present-day Nya walks eight hours a day through the desert to provide her family with water, and Salva became a refugee during civil war in 1985, walking across the continent to find his family and safety. Their stories eventually converge in a surprising way.

References

Coupe, Laurence. 2013. "Green Theory." In *The Routledge Companion to Critical and Cultural Theory*, 2nd ed., ed. Simon Malpas and Paul Wake, 154–166. Mahwah, NJ: Routledge.

Heffernan, Lee. 2004. *Critical Literacy and the Writer's Workshop: Bringing Purpose and Passion to Student Writing*. Newark, DE: International Reading Association.

Lee, Carol, and Anika Spratley. 2010. *Reading in the Disciplines: The Challenges of Adolescent Literacy*. New York: Carnegie Corporation.

Moje, Elizabeth, and Deborah Dillon. 2006. "Adolescent Identities as Demanded by Science Classroom Discourse Communities." In *Reconceptualizing the Literacies in Adolescents' Lives*, 2nd ed., ed. Donna Alvermann, Kathleen A. Hinchman, David Moore, Stephen Phelps, and Diane Waff, 85–166. Mahwah, NJ: Erlbaum.

Shiklomanov, Igor. 1993. "World Fresh Water Resources." In *Water in Crisis: A Guide to the World's Fresh Water Resources*, ed. Peter H. Gleick, 13–24. New York: Oxford University Press.

Short, Kathy G. 2012. "Story as World Making." *Language Arts* 90 (1): 9–17.

Short, Kathy G., and Carolyn Burke. 1991. *Creating Curriculum: Teachers and Students Creating Communities of Learners*. Portsmouth, NH: Heinemann.

Short, Kathy G., and Jerome Harste, with Carolyn Burke. 1996. *Creating Classrooms for Authors and Inquirers*. Portsmouth, NH: Heinemann.

Siu-Runyan, Yvonne. 1999. "Inquiry, Curriculum, and Standards: A Conversation with Kathy Short." *The Colorado Communicator*, February, 4–17.

UNICEF/WHO. 2008. *Progress on Drinking Water and Sanitation: Special Focus on Sanitation*. http://www.wssinfo.org/fileadmin/user_upload/resources/1251794333-JMP_08_en.pdf.

Children's Books Cited

Hollyer, Beatrice. 2008. *Our World of Water: Children and Water Around the World.* New York: Henry Holt.

Park, Linda Sue. 2010. *A Long Walk to Water.* New York: Clarion Books.

Chapter 14

Children Taking Action on Global Issues

Kathy G. Short with Lisa Thomas

The willingness to take action in order to create social change is essential to developing intercultural understanding and becoming a global citizen. Moving from a commitment to social justice into a curriculum that supports young children in taking action that is meaningful and not adult-imposed is much more difficult. This struggle to encourage authentic action was a tension we explored within a four-year school-based inquiry on building intercultural understanding through engagements around global literature (Short 2009). We were uncertain how to invite children to engage in action through inquiries into global issues, so we developed schoolwide inquiries on human rights and hunger. These inquiries provided a space to explore how to create instructional contexts that encourage children to act. Our focus was on ways of taking action that were significant to children and that went beyond charity and adult-directed action to children identifying and acting on the issues underlying global problems.

Freire (1970) argues that action must grow out of stances of critique and hope to lead to social change. Children had engaged in critical discussions around literature where they examined issues of discrimination and oppression, questioning "what is" to challenge the status quo. Their discussions also included talk about "what if" and the possibilities for change to create a better world. Less frequent was talk that leads to meaningful action. We realized that, although dialogue about literature engages children as critical thinkers, this talk often goes no further. To complicate the issue, many of the actions that do occur in elementary schools are isolated projects to raise money for a cause, such as natural-disaster relief, and are not child-initiated, with a focus on charity, not social change. Our tension was how to encourage authentic action that was collaborative and co-planned with children from an inquiry stance.

We engaged in inquiries with children on human rights and hunger and read professional literature on service learning and critical pedagogy to inform us as educators. These experiences led to developing a set of principles to consider in creating inquiries with the potential to engage children in authentic and meaningful action. This chapter describes each of these principles along with the theoretical perspectives that support each one and examples of how they played out in classroom practice. Before focusing on the principles, we provide a brief description of the instructional context and an overview of the two inquiry units from which the classroom examples are excerpted.

Situating Our Inquiry Within the School Context

The context for our work was a small K–5 public school of two hundred students within a large urban district with a culturally and linguistically diverse population in a middle-class/working-class neighborhood. Lisa Thomas, the curriculum coordinator, established a learning lab as an alternative approach to professional development. Lisa and the teachers decided on a schoolwide focus, and each teacher brought children to this lab for an hour once a week for experiences around the focus. In this case, our focus was on global inquiry and intercultural understanding, specifically on taking action. Instruction in the lab grew out of intense teacher study and collaboration facilitated by a study group that met after school twice a month. The ideas discussed within the study group were pursued within the learning lab, providing teachers with an opportunity to closely observe and document student learning. In the study group, teachers shared their observations, critiqued instruction, and examined student work to inform instruction for the next lab session. Teachers also explored these ideas in their classrooms based on their goals and classroom units. Participation in the lab and study group included all grade levels and was voluntary. My role was as a university collaborator who came to the school once a week to work in the lab, meet with teachers in the study group, and help plan instruction.

Within these contexts, we gathered teaching journals, field notes of lab sessions, and audiotapes and videotapes of literature discussions. Teachers analyzed this data and wrote classroom vignettes about critical incidents in a summer writing group. These vignettes were published in an online journal, *WOW Stories*, over a three-year period (2007–2009, wowlit.org). Specific descriptions of the literature engagements and examples of children's responses in the human rights and hunger inquiries are published in this journal.

An Inquiry on Human Rights and Taking Action

The framework of a Curriculum That Is Intercultural was significant in enacting our theoretical beliefs and organizing instruction at the school. This framework led us to develop inquiries around global issues, specifically human rights and hunger. These two units are briefly described here with more detailed examples included in the discussion of authentic action.

During our second year, we developed an inquiry into human rights, planning to consider fairness within children's lives to develop the concept of rights and then move into a broad exploration of human rights around the world. We assumed that children would select a specific human right to explore in greater depth for investigation, either as a whole class or within small groups. The children, however, took the inquiry in a different direction.

We started with the concept of fairness to ground the inquiry in children's lives and help them create a conceptual understanding of rights. Children frequently complain about something being unfair, so we asked them to create maps of the school to document unfair events. After sharing their maps, we defined rights as what is violated when something feels unfair, and children met in small groups to develop lists of what they believed were their rights in school.

The children then moved into literature experiences with text sets organized around global human rights to expand their perspectives and explore a possible focus for in-depth investigation around issues such as child labor, education, freedom, discrimination, violence, basic needs, and the environment. Children also met in literature circles around novels such as *Iqbal* (D'Adamo 2003), the true story of a twelve-year-old boy who led the child labor movement in Pakistan. They were surprised by the accounts of children taking action, because they viewed action as the responsibility of adults. The idea that *children* could make a difference in the world became a compelling tension.

We returned to the text sets, selecting books in which children took action, and looked carefully at their strategies for action. Several books on global issues familiar to our city, such as homeless people and undocumented immigrants, were used for drama in role playing. After reading *The Lady in the Box* (McGovern 1997), children split into pairs, with one taking on the role of a child advocating for a homeless woman, trying to persuade another child, acting as a store owner, to allow her to sleep on the grate in front of the store. In another drama, we read *Friends from the Other Side* (Anzaldúa 1997) in which a young girl hides an undocumented boy and his mother from the Border Patrol. Half of the children became newspaper reporters, and the other half selected a person from the book to role-play as they broke into pairs to do interviews about incidents related to the border.

Students' compelling interest in how children take action made it clear that they were more interested in human rights issues in their own school than in global issues. Each class went back to their "unfair" maps and lists of rights to create a web of possible issues, and selected one they considered significant to investigate. These issues included rules on the playground, choices at recess time, trash on the playground, and the types of food provided for school lunch. Their research included interviewing adults at the school to get different perspectives on the issues and field notes of observations in particular areas of the school. They took different types of action based on their research, many of which involved identifying the adults who could make a change and developing a strategy for effectively advocating to that person or group. These action projects were engaging for the children and involved a high commitment to action, even though the action they took was often not what they initially expected before their research.

An Inquiry into Power and Hunger

After observing the annual canned-food drive at Thanksgiving the following fall, we developed an inquiry around hunger, beginning with a broad focus on power to connect to children's lives and to frame the inquiry around the interconnections of power and hunger. Children considered who had power in their lives through examining the decisions they made at school and at home and the decisions adults made for them. Children also explored power and shifts in power in familiar pieces of literature. After each experience or read-aloud, students listed issues related to power on a chart.

We transitioned into hunger by exploring "tight times" to connect with the economic crisis in our community, using the picturebook *Tight Times* (Hazen 1983) as a touchstone text. Our goal was to understand that any family can have "tight times" but that the nature of those difficulties varies from delaying a trip to Disneyland to not having enough food on the table. This discussion led to examining the difference between needs and wants in tight times. Students also kept food journals to record their own food intake and explored the kinds of food eaten in countries around the world.

The main focus of the inquiry was on uncovering the root causes of hunger locally and globally through fiction and nonfiction, films, guest speakers, and a global banquet. The global banquet (Oxfam) involved dividing students into three groups and giving them food according to the world population, with 15 percent receiving more than they could eat as pizzas, 60 percent receiving just enough to eat as rice and beans, and 25 percent receiving not enough to eat as one small shared bowl of rice. Read-aloud novels, such as *Nory Ryan's Song* (Giff 2000), provided insights into personal experiences of hunger. A community food bank volunteer helped children understand the difference between sustainability (teaching someone to garden) and charity (offering a food box). Another guest, Abraham, who had come to Tucson as a Sudanese refugee as one of the "lost boys," told his compelling story.

After examining root causes of hunger, each class identified ways they wanted to take action on hunger and worked through how to effectively engage in that action. These projects ranged from helping a classmate's family who faced tragedy and possible homelessness to working with the community garden project at the food bank to identifying global organizations that provide animals to families in countries within Africa. We were particularly struck that children wanted to work with community and global organizations that focus on sustainability where those receiving a gift use it to take responsibility for their own action instead of being dependent on others. This inquiry involved children in taking action both locally and globally.

Authentic Approaches to Taking Action

As we reflected on these two inquiries, we developed a set of principles to consider in constructing a learning environment that supports authentic action. We continuously moved between analyzing these experiences and immersing ourselves in the professional literature to challenge our interpretations and develop our understandings. These principles are criteria we consider in developing action projects that are authentic and meaningful for children. They are used in this chapter to reflect on the two inquiries. More detailed examples from these units are included within each of the principles.

Develops Through Inquiry and Experience

When action is grounded in children's lives, experiences, and knowledge, that action grows out of inquiry and understanding instead of functioning as an isolated project. Kaye (2003) argues that meaningful action must be combined with academic content so that the content children are exploring through inquiry informs the action and the action drives further learning and inquiry. Action goes beyond volunteering to collect trash in a stream, for example, to analyzing that trash, figuring out the sources, and working with the community to reduce pollution. Students need time for reflection and inquiry and for learning strategies and content.

The action taken by students in the two inquiries was carefully grounded in their lives, beginning with their life experiences and following their interests, tensions, and understandings about local and global issues. In the human rights inquiry, children documented unfair events at the school to develop conceptual understandings about rights. Literature played a key role through read-alouds about unfair events in schools. In their discussion of *A Fine, Fine School* (Creech 2001), fourth graders noted that the principal was well intentioned and "wanted kids to learn as much as possible," but was unfair because "everyone needs a break once in a while" and "you have to have time to play with your friends and have family time." A fifth grader argued, "School is important for your brain, but not that important," and a first grader declared, "He is torturing the kids and they must be tired every day." Although adults see the book as humorous, children were agitated and vocal, saying the principal's decisions to extend school were unfair. Their strong feelings led to a discussion of unfair events at their school. To further explore this issue, children drew maps from a bird's-eye view of the school and labeled places where unfair events had occurred (Figure 14.1).

Figure 14.1 Unfair School Maps: Matt, Age Six

The hunger study began with using literature to explore times of difficulty in families and community. These books helped children realize that tight times force some families to do without things they want and others without things they need such as food and shelter. In their discussion of *A Shelter in Our Car* (Gunning 2004), they decided the homeless family in the car needed food and shelter, compared with the boy who wanted special shoes his grandmother could not afford in *Those Shoes* (Boelts 2007). They saw different levels of wants and needs, arguing that the family's desire for a new chair after their home burned in *A Chair for My Mother* (Williams 1984) was a more significant "want" than the desire for popular shoes. We continued reading picturebooks about families in tight times, creating a continuum of levels of wants and needs. These books provided a way for children to access difficult issues in their community and created a bridge for connecting to these issues on a global level.

Meets Genuine Needs

Action involves the recognition that a real need exists and is viewed as such by children. Children need time to research and to understand the issue from multiple perspectives by investigating whether a need actually exists and the nature of that need (Vasquez 2004). Second graders thought that trash on the playground came from the local landfill and planned to write a letter of protest to the owners. Their research revealed that chil-

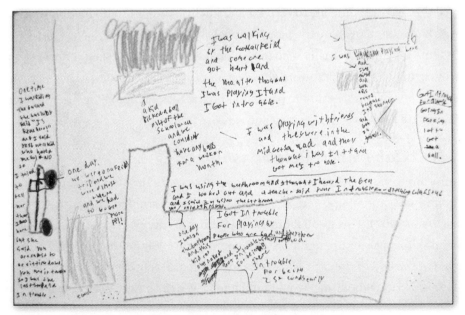

Figure 14.1 (continued) Unfair School Maps: Breanna, Age Ten

dren were the source of the trash and the problem was the location of the trash barrel at the far end of the playground. First graders were shocked to learn from the community food bank volunteer that children and the elderly constitute the major groups who go hungry, not the homeless. Students believed hunger was the result of not enough food in the world until our reading of nonfiction books such as *Famine* (Bennett 1998) and experiences in the global banquet led to the realization that enough food does exist and the issue is unequal distribution.

Determining a need is not enough—children also must view that need as significant. Visits by a refugee from Sudan and a local food bank volunteer created a sense of urgency for children to take action on hunger. Hunger was a problem that was remote and removed from their lives until it became personal with real faces and people.

An understanding of need can also be developed through literature, as occurred when fourth-grade students made a strong connection with children in refugee camps. In discussing *Brothers in Hope* (Williams 2005), students worried about how one boy could possibly care for another without adults to help. They were concerned about these refugees and wanted to know what happened to them after the book ended. They tried to put themselves in the situation and could not imagine how they would survive, but seemed to gain comfort from the fact that the boys had each other. They also connected with the relationship between two girls in *Four Feet, Two Sandals* (Williams and Mohammed 2007), recognizing that their friendship helped them cope with the horrors of war. They believed that having someone to care for and having someone care for you was reflected in the girls' decision to share the pair of sandals.

Students may intellectually recognize global needs, but they do not always develop a sense of caring or empathy toward those issues. Literature provides the opportunity to make an emotional connection to particular characters, bringing together the heart and mind to create a sense of connection and a desire for action.

Builds Collaborative Relationships

Reaching out to work *with* others by developing partnerships and sharing responsibility with community members, parents, organizations, and students is critical to authentic action (Wade 2007). These collaborative relationships involve learning about each other and gaining respect, understanding, and appreciation. Since the human rights inquiry occurred at the end of the fifth graders' final year in the school, they wondered why they should take action when they would not benefit. When they realized they had a unique perspective because of their knowledge of the school, they took responsibility for help-ing fourth graders consider ways to work with adults in developing playground rules. Fourth graders made a shift when they interviewed the playground monitor to find out who made the rules and the reasons behind the rules. The monitor's nervousness and concern for their safety led them to realize that she was not their enemy, but someone to think with about rules. Students realized that they could take more effective action by collaborating with others.

Literature such as *Subway Sparrow* (Torres 1993) and *Sami and the Time of the Trou-bles* (Heide and Gilliland 1992) provided examples of collaboration that challenged children's assumptions that individuals act alone. These books show children who act with adults or their peers on important issues in their worlds. Individualism is a strong value in American culture and often leads to depictions of one person acting alone. Kohl (1995) points out that the Rosa Parks myth depicts her acting alone as a tired anony-mous seamstress rather than as a longstanding activist against segregation within an organized movement. He argues that not everyone can see themselves acting alone as a national hero, but everyone can imagine themselves participating in a community effort against injustice.

Results in Mutual Exchanges

Many action projects in schools take the form of charity—"give a handout to the poor and unfortunate." Students raise money to send away to those experiencing hardship. The giving goes in one direction, and students remain distanced from those whom they are helping (Cowhey 2006). Authentic action occurs when there is a mutual exchange of ideas, information, and skills among *all* participants. Each person sees the others as having something to share, and everyone gains from the experience. By taking action on human rights within the school context before examining global issues, students directly interacted with those involved with the action and recognized how much they were gain-ing from the experience.

Literature can be a tool for envisioning a mutual exchange even when children do not have direct interaction with recipients. Fourth graders raised money for refugee chil-dren in Darfur because they felt that they had learned so much from the characters in books about courage and perseverance in the face of tremendous hardship. They want-ed to give something in return. Their action came out of respect rather than pity. Their concerns about Sudanese refugees led them into further research on the boys as well as on refugee camps and helped them understand the reasons for violence that results in people fleeing their homes and living in difficult circumstances. Eventually, they came across an organization that focused on children making a difference for refugees in Darfur and created several projects to earn money to purchase goats that could be used for milk in the camps.

Includes Action and Reflection

Authentic action is based on children having responsibility throughout the process, including witnessing the outcome of their action when possible. A continuous cycle of action and reflection spirals throughout the process: identifying a problem, researching to understand it, planning, anticipating consequences of the action, taking action, observing what happens, reflecting on what occurs, accepting responsibility for consequences, and then acting again. Dewey (1938) argues that when learners do not have time to reflect on action, they lose much of the learning potential from an experience. A balance of action and reflection allows children to be aware of the effect of their work on their thinking and life as well as on others, an understanding that is essential to mutual exchanges.

Students may move across more than one type of action within a project (Terry and Bohnenberger 2007). In the hunger inquiry, students engaged in *research for action* to determine the needs and the organizations that take action on hunger. Fifth graders engaged in *direct action* to raise money for a classmate whose family was facing hunger and eviction after the sudden death of the father and the mother's loss of her job. First graders engaged in *indirect action* as they raised money for seeds to support a community garden project at the local food bank. Third graders took *indirect action* by raising money for global projects that involved sustainability. First graders engaged in *advocacy for action* by creating posters about the ways that gardens could allow a family to support themselves, influenced by books such as *The Good Garden* (Milway 2010). As students acted and reflected, they developed a range of perspectives and problem-solving strategies to carry into new situations.

The focus on sustainability became significant to third graders through their discussions of *Beatrice's Goat* (McBrier 2001) and *One Hen* (Milway 2008), set in Uganda and Ghana. The students talked about how Beatrice had to work for the gift of the goat by planting food, building a barn, and caring for the goat. They were excited to see how the gift of one goat changed the life of an entire family by providing milk and baby goats that could be sold. *One Hen* is the story of a boy who receives a loan to buy one hen that he grows into a large poultry business. Students noted that if someone had just given food to Kojo's family, that gift would have lasted for a meal and they would have been hungry again. They realized that giving a goat or chicken provided agency for families in making their lives better and decided to raise money for sustainable changes. They did not want to make just a one-time difference, but a change that "keeps on giving." This same focus on sustainability led first graders to focus on the community garden project at the local food bank instead of just gathering canned food for food boxes.

Invites Student Voice and Choice

Too often, action projects in schools are conceived and directed by adults, with little room for student voice or choice. Rosenblatt (1938) argues for students and teachers living together as equals in classrooms based on democratic social relationships, not in hierarchies of power where a few decide for all. Students have the right to participate meaningfully in the decisions that affect their lives and in the "behind the scenes" thinking that leads to determining those choices. The valuing of individual voices is balanced with recognition of group responsibility. Through dialogue, students learn to have conviction and courage about their views while keeping an open mind to the views and needs of others. Freire (1970) argues that dialogue provides the most potential for transformation, so we worked to encourage thoughtful in-depth dialogue around issues students found significant.

The younger children felt they did not have responsibility because they did not believe they could take action—action was what adults did *for* them. They initially thought that if an adult told them what to do, their "right" was to do what adults demanded. They did not see rights as choices they could make in their lives that have consequences. Their lack of agency in making decisions and considering their actions concerned us. We read picturebooks such as *Fred Stays with Me* (Coffelt 2007), *Daddy Is a Monster Sometimes* (Steptoe 1983) and *Evan's Corner* (Hill 1993) to help them realize they negotiate with, and sometimes manipulate, their parents and are not powerless. *Daddy Is a Monster Sometimes* was a compelling book for first graders. They peered closely at the illustrations and talked about whether the father had a right to be angry when his children used manipulation to get another ice cream cone. Some argued that "the kids have a right to be mad when the dad is mean," whereas others said that "dad had a right to be mad because they made noise and did things they weren't supposed to do." This discussion led children to talk about how they manipulate their parents and to demonstrate the faces they use to get their way. In discussing *Fred Stays with Me*, they commented that the girl stood up to her divorced parents and that her parents did not have the right to decide whether the dog went with her as she moved between the two homes.

As first and second graders came to realize that they do have agency, we encouraged them to consider their agency on broader world issues. They cared about others in the world, but saw themselves as powerless, leaving the responsibility for adults. In an inquiry on environmental issues, they read books in which characters take action, such as *Aani and the Tree Huggers* (Atkins 1995) and *Just a Dream* (Van Allsburg 1990), and charted the choices made by the characters, the consequences of each choice, the right that each choice influenced, and the action that was taken. When they later considered issues on their rights in school, their strong feelings about the actions they could take indicated that they had moved beyond a passive acceptance of adults making decisions for them.

The first response of fourth and fifth graders to human rights was a sense of entitlement to use this power for their own benefit. Fourth graders wanted to determine the playground rules without input from other classrooms, and a fifth grader argued he should be able to do his math work whenever he wanted without considering the teacher and other students. Their immersion in global literature in which children take action for others, often at great expense, such as *The Carpet Boy's Gift* (Shea 2003) and *Rebel* (Baille 1994), shifted their perspectives away from individual benefit to group responsibility. As they discussed *The Carpet Boy's Gift*, fourth and fifth graders were concerned about parents selling their children to work in the Pakistani carpet mills and the lack of enforcement of laws against child labor. They were upset that children did not have adults acting on their behalf and were too scared to defend themselves. Their initial talk was judgmental until they realized the dire poverty and desperation that led to children becoming indentured laborers because of parents' debts. They moved beyond blaming families to condemning a system that benefited from child labor.

Iqbal's willingness as a twelve-year-old boy to lead the movement against child labor surprised students. They expected him to run away to save himself, not come back and lead protests to free other children at the risk of his own life. A fifth grader commented, "It seems that whenever someone fights for the rights of others, most of the time someone gets hurt or dies." Students questioned whether they would be willing to risk their lives for others, but the fact that a real boy their own age had done just that and been killed was unsettling. They were so interested in Iqbal that teachers read aloud the novel *Iqbal* (D'Adamo 2003). They connected with Iqbal as a character, coming to care about him and admire his willingness to take on such a huge responsibility. This novel led them to talk about their responsibility for making a difference, given Iqbal's willingness to take such huge risks.

Miguel's sketch (Figure 14.2) in response to this book indicated his understanding of Iqbal's action, saying, "The chain is empty to show that Iqbal is free and the top part is dark and red to show he is angry because it was wrong to be chained and forced to work. I made it white behind the loom to show that Iqbal knew he and the other children could be free and he was going to make it happen. He knew that child labor was wrong and was brave enough to stand up for himself and the other children." Miguel saw the chain as a symbol of strength and action, not despair.

Figure 14.2 Sketch to Stretch in Response to *Iqbal* (D'Adamo 2003) by Miguel (Age Nine)

A participation model by Hart (1992) addresses children's involvement in decision making, pointing out that the focus of power and control usually remains with adults who work *for* children rather than *with* children. Hart's Ladder of Participation emphasizes the effect of different types of adult/child interactions on the distribution of power and control. At the lower levels, students are not genuinely involved in decisions; adults make decisions and manipulate children into agreeing with these decisions. At the top of the ladder, children have the most power and control over decisions, with adults providing support and guidance as needed.

Involves Civic/Global Responsibility for Social Justice

Civic engagement is often viewed as being a good citizen by voting, volunteering, and engaging in political activities that do not involve challenging the status quo (Banks 2004). Taking civic or global responsibility from a social justice perspective (Freire 1970) puts the focus on issues of power and on challenging domination and oppression by looking at the social conditions within local and global communities in the following ways:

- Critique—questioning what is—not just accepting problems as the way things are, but asking *why* problems exist and identifying the underlying issues and who benefits.
- Hope—imagining "what if" and considering alternative ways of living to develop a vision of equity and justice.
- Action—taking action to work for social justice and change. This action grows out of critique and hope, questions and vision.

Civic responsibility goes below the surface of a problem to get at root causes, social contexts, beliefs, and consequences of a problem. Children learn to problematize by questioning what is assumed to be "normal" by society and developing critical consciousness. They do not just serve lunch in a soup kitchen; they also analyze the reasons for poverty in the community. They may visit seniors in a nursing home, but they also explore why the elderly are isolated in our society. The canned-food drives in many US schools reinforce stereotypes of the poor, oversimplify problems and solutions, and fail to teach an understanding of the causes of poverty (Cowhey 2006). By challenging stereotypes of those who live in poverty, developing an understanding of the complex causes of poverty, introducing activists who work at these causes, and removing the stigma of poverty, students take a social justice stance.

Our study of hunger explored the multiple causes of hunger, in both the United States and the world, through fiction and nonfiction books and resources. We found that nonfiction books, such as *Famine* (Bennett 1998), provided definitions, terminology, and facts that made the problem real and sent a message that this issue was actually happening in the world and not just an interesting story. Fiction, such as *A Shelter in Our Car* (Gunning 2004), humanized those facts and helped children feel empathy for those who experience ongoing hunger.

This experience helped us realize that we were using too much fiction. We valued the role of fiction in humanizing global issues and providing emotional connections to characters and issues, but needed to integrate more nonfiction resources to make the issues real. We used nonfiction books on hunger and famine, fact cards on hunger and child mortality rates in specific countries, a science film on food production, the real stories of people experiencing hunger told by visitors to the classroom, and a fabulous book called *What the World Eats* (D'Aluisio 2008) that uses photographs to show a week's worth of food in different countries. These nonfiction resources helped develop an understanding of the extent of the problem and the wide range of reasons people go hungry.

We balanced nonfiction with fiction to create understandings of human struggles and emotions. The fiction texts included picturebooks and novels in which characters experience hunger as well as excerpts from a movie of a family struggling with hunger and a drama text created at the global banquet. The use of such a wide range of texts provided multiple perspectives about the causes of hunger. Only near the end of the inquiry did students consider actions they might want to take, given those causes.

Reading aloud *Nory Ryan's Song* (Giff 2000) was significant for fourth graders in thinking about power as the root cause of hunger. They noticed that "some people have power over land like the English having power over Ireland. They had power over streams and didn't let the Irish fish." Another student noted, "And they had power over land because they collected rent and kicked people out of homes if they couldn't pay. They even had power over people's things because they took their animals if someone was late with rent." "Yeah," added a student, "when they lost their animals, they lost their food, like eggs, and so were even more hungry."

Civic engagement goes beyond an emphasis on local or global needs to asking questions about prevailing practices and developing ideas for making the world a better place. The goal is social change, not just filling a gap in services or donating money, but questioning the conditions in society that create a need and seeking to alter those conditions. Instead of charity, the focus is promoting change and transformative practices (Wade 2007).

In the human rights inquiry, children raised issues about prevailing practices in which adults make rules for the playground without providing space for children's voices. Fourth graders gradually realized the need to work with adults and other children to develop rules that work for everyone. They suggested a system where class representatives met with the principal and playground monitors on a regular basis to discuss the playground rules. They moved from blaming adults for problems and asking adults to make changes for them to taking responsibility for challenging injustice and working for change.

In the hunger inquiry, students became aware that enough food exists in the world to feed everyone and critically examined the issues of power that lead to unequal distribution of that food. Elise's sketch to stretch of the meaning of taking action indicates her understandings of these issues (Figure 14.3). She said that her sketch showed the need to help the hungry and that "everyone in the world has to help." The lightbulb signified "the need to know about hunger and what causes hunger to figure out how to help others." The heart signified that "people have to want to do it by caring and making a choice to help." Elise's understandings of the need to connect the heart and mind and to hold everyone responsible indicate her ability to see the larger picture and her willingness to work with others to make change in the world.

Figure 14.3 Sketch to Stretch on the Meaning of Taking Action (Elise, Age Nine)

Negotiating School Mandates

The major tension for teachers in this school context was around the high-stakes state tests at the end of the school year. The first year we immersed students in a global curriculum, we hoped that increasing the amount of time they were reading books and engaged in critical thinking around literature and global issues would be reflected in their test scores. When the test scores did not show growth, we realized that the issue was not students' ability to think and read, but their lack of experience in doing "test tasks" and in understanding directions for those tasks. Teachers were no longer using worksheets and isolated test exercises, so children were unsure of the tasks on the test, even though they had the knowledge and skills to do those tasks.

The next year, we provided time during the month before the test for students to study tests as a genre, inquiring into the types of reading passages and tasks they would encounter and figuring out what they were being asked to do. They took sample tests, not to practice skills, but to engage in problem solving around different strategies for how to approach sections of the test (Santman 2002). Not surprisingly, their test scores rose dramatically.

Final Reflections

Children are constructing themselves as human beings by developing the ways in which they think about and take action within their lives and their world. Our challenge is to build on children's lived experiences to move toward multiple perspectives and action. Our research indicates the complexity of the difficult issues that must be addressed within schools to go beyond talk *about* global issues into authentic and meaningful action *for* social change.

A key factor in making this shift is *time and opportunity*—time to research root causes of global and local problems, explore multiple perspectives on those problems, and critique and hope, and then act and reflect on that action. Taking action runs counter to the individualistic and materialistic nature of American society and to adult views of children as needing protection. Many children do not have opportunities to engage meaningfully in making decisions that affect their lives. Adults determine their choices and protect children instead of engaging them in experiences where they gain new perspectives and strategies for problem posing and problem solving. Children need perspective, not protection.

Dialogue about literature can play a key role in supporting this process. Books can help children reflect on and connect to their life experiences, immerse them in the lives and thinking of global cultures, offer new perspectives by taking them beyond their life experiences and challenging their views of the world, and provide demonstrations of ways they might work with others to take action. The lives of children in books provide a demonstration that children's voices can make a difference and that there are multiple ways in which children can take action. They are able to try on perspectives and actions beyond their own by living in the story world of the characters whom they have come to care about. Through engagements with global literature, children can develop complex understandings about global issues, engage in critical inquiries about themselves and the world, and take action to create a better and more just world. The significance of these experiences is that children move from a position of powerlessness to a position of possibility.

Recommended Books That Invite Global Perspectives

D'Aluisio, Fatih. 2008. *What the World Eats.* **Illus. Peter Menzel. New York: Tricycle.**
Readers visit twenty-five families in twenty-one countries through full-color photographs of each family posed around the foods they typically eat in a week. The authors use the photographs to investigate different cultures' diets and standards of living as well as the effect of globalization and each family's hopes and struggles. A wealth of supporting information is available in recipes, maps, sidebars, and charts.

Milway, Kate Smith. 2008. *One Hen.* **Illus. Eugenie Fernandes. Toronto, ON: Kids Can Press.**
A boy from Ghana turns a small loan to buy a hen into a thriving farm that provides support for him and his village. The book is part of CitizenKid, a collection that informs kids about global citizenship and ways to take action in the world—in this case, the microloan system.

Shea, Pegi D. 2003. *The Carpet Boy's Gift.* **Illus. Leane Morin. Gardiner, ME: Tilbury House.**

This fictional picturebook is based on the legacy of Iqbal Masih, a real boy from Pakistan who escaped from a carpet factory but returned to liberate other child workers. The book includes information on child labor and on companies involved in social action.

Torres, Leyla. 1993. *Subway Sparrow.* **New York: Farrar, Straus and Giroux.**

Three strangers, all speaking different languages, work together to free a sparrow trapped in their subway car. Set in New York City and written by a Colombian author/illustrator.

References

Banks, James. 2004. *Diversity and Citizenship Education.* New York: Wiley.

Cowhey, Mary. 2006. *Black Ants and Buddhists.* Portland, ME: Stenhouse.

Dewey, John. 1938. *Education and Experience.* New York: Collier.

Freire, Paulo. 1970. *Pedagogy of the Oppressed.* South Hadley, MA: Bergin and Garvey.

Hart, Roger. 1992. *Children's Participation: From Tokenism to Citizenship.* Florence, Italy: UNICEF.

Kaye, Catherine. 2003. *The Complete Guide to Service Learning.* Minneapolis, MN: Free Spirit.

Kohl, Herbert. 1995. *Should We Burn Babar? Essays on Children's Literature and the Power of Stories.* New York: New Press.

Lewison, Mitzi, Chris Leland, and Jerome Harste. 2008. *Creating Critical Classrooms.* Mahwah, NJ: Erlbaum.

Oxfam. Oxfam Global Hunger Banquet. https://www.oxfam.org/en/countries/oxfam-america-hunger-banquetr.

Rosenblatt, Louise. 1938. *Literature as Exploration.* Chicago, IL: Modern Language Association.

Santman, Donna. 2002. "Teaching to the Test?: Test Preparation in the Reading Workshop." *Language Arts* 79 (3): 203–211.

Short, Kathy G. 2009. "Critically Reading the Word and the World." *Bookbird* 47 (2): 1–10.

Terry, Alice, and Jan Bohnenberger. 2007. *Service-Learning . . . by Degrees.* Portsmouth, NH: Heinemann.

Vasquez, Vivian. 2004. *Negotiating Critical Literacies with Young Children*. Mahwah, NJ: Erlbaum.

Wade, Rahima. 2007. *Social Studies for Social Justice*. New York: Teachers College Press.

Children's Books Cited

Anzaldúa, Gloria. 1997. *Friends from the Other Side*/Amigos del otro lado. Illus. Conseulo Mendez. San Francisco, CA: Children's Book Press.

Atkins, Jeannine. 1995. *Aani and the Tree Huggers*. New York: Lee and Low.

Baille, Allan. 1994. *Rebel*. Illus. Di Wu. Boston: Houghton Mifflin.

Bennett, Paul. 1998. *Famine: The World Reacts*. Mankato, MN: Smart Apple.

Boelts, Maribeth. 2007. *Those Shoes*. Illus. Norah Jones. New York: Walker.

Coffelt, Nancy. 2007. *Fred Stays with Me*. Illus. Tricia Tusa. Boston: Little, Brown.

Creech, Sharon. 2001. *A Fine, Fine School*. Illus. Harry Bliss. New York: HarperCollins.

D'Adamo, Francesco. 2003. *Iqbal*. New York: Aladdin.

D'Aluisio, Fatih. 2008. *What the World Eats*. Illus. Peter Menzel. New York: Tricycle.

Giff, Patricia Reilly. 2000. *Nory Ryan's Song*. New York: Scholastic.

Gunning, Monica. 2004. *A Shelter in Our Car*. Illus. Elaine. Pedlar. San Francisco, CA: Children's Book Press.

Hazen, Barbara. 1983. *Tight Times*. Illus. Trina. S. Hyman. New York: Viking.

Heide, Florence, and Judith Heide Gilliland. 1992. *Sami and the Time of the Troubles*. Illus. Ted Lewin. New York: Clarion Books.

Hill, Elizabeth. 1993. *Evan's Corner*. Illus. Sandra Speidel. New York: Puffin.

McBrier, Page. 2001. *Beatrice's Goat*. Illus. Lori Lohstoeter. New York: Simon and Schuster.

McGovern, Ann. 1997. *The Lady in the Box*. Illus. Marni Backer. Turtle Books.

Milway, Kate Smith. 2008. *One Hen*. Illus. Eugenie Fernandes. Toronto, ON: Kids Can Press.

_____ . 2010. *The Good Garden*. Illus. Sylvie Daigneault. Toronto, ON: Kids Can Press.

Shea, Pegi D. 2003. *The Carpet Boy's Gift*. Illus. Leane Morin. Gardiner, ME: Tilbury House.

Steptoe, John. 1983. *Daddy Is a Monster Sometimes*. New York: HarperCollins.

Torres, Leyla. 1993. *Subway Sparrow*. New York: Farrar, Straus and Giroux.

Van Allsburg, Chris. 1990. *Just a Dream*. Boston: Houghton Mifflin.

Williams, Karen Lynn, and Khadra Mohammed. 2007. *Four Feet, Two Sandals*. Illus. Doug Chayka. Grand Rapids, MI: Eerdmans.

Williams, Mary. 2005. *Brothers in Hope*. Illus. Gregory Christie. New York: Lee and Low.

Williams, Vera. 1984. *A Chair for My Mother*. New York: Greenwillow.

PART 6

So What? Explorations of Intercultural Understanding

Chapter 15

The Importance of Global Literature Experiences for Young Children

Prisca Martens and Ray Martens with Michelle Hassay Doyle, Jenna Loomis, Laura Fuhrman, Elizabeth Soper, Robbie Stout, and Christie Furnari

Kids in India and the U.S. are both kind. We're happy. We're from a country. I think they're the same as us ... We're different because they're from India. They speak different languages and have different clothing and different holidays.

Seven-year-old Alisha made this comment toward the end of a cross-cultural study of India in her first-grade classroom. For several weeks she and her classmates had read fiction and nonfiction literature about the people, children, culture and traditions, art, land and resources, cities and villages, and daily life in India. In an interview, Alisha was invited to share how she thought kids in India were similar to and different from kids in America. Her comment revealed her growing awareness of commonalities in human experience that permeate all cultures (for example, kind, happy, live in a country) and simultaneous respect for and appreciation of cultural differences (such as language, clothing, holidays). Through the cross-cultural study and other experiences with global literature, Alisha and the other first graders developed intercultural understandings and perspectives about themselves and others.

Comments like Alisha's strengthened our commitment and that of six prekindergarten, kindergarten, and first-grade teachers to integrate global literature and reframe the curriculum. Through experiences with global literature we daily saw children's curiosity and excitement, heard their questions and inquiries about what they were reading, observed and supported the critical stances and thinking they demonstrated, and witnessed their learning and the intercultural understandings they were developing.

Choo (2013) supports the importance of literature in developing intercultural understandings. She contends that through experiences with literature, students develop rich understandings of what it means to be human. In Choo's words, literature promotes a "hospitable imagination" (159) through which we engage with, prioritize, and are accountable to others in the world.

The need for intercultural understandings that respect and value those who live, believe, and think differently is essential. Banks (2004) argues the need for thoughtful and moral literate citizens in our global world. He sees the major issue humans face not as the inability to read and write but as our allowing differences in race, culture, and religion to prevent us from working together to solve problems. Our goal was for children to understand and respect the diverse aspects and significance of culture in their own and others' lives (Pattnaik 2003). Global literature experiences were the primary means of attaining that goal.

Because global literature was not central to the district curriculum, teachers worked with us for several years to reframe instruction around a curriculum that was intercultural. In this chapter we share the learnings children demonstrated in these reframed curriculums. We argue that global literature matters. Our findings show that by immersing children in story worlds, global literature supported them in conceptualizing culture and themselves as cultural beings, appreciating the range of ways they are both similar to and different from other children, and identifying themselves as citizens with responsibilities for making their communities and the world a better place.

Contextualizing Our Work

Our literacy community included six public school teachers in two schools in the Baltimore metropolitan area on the East Coast. The metropolitan area school was 62 percent children of color with 41 percent free/reduced meals. At this school Christie Furnari taught prekindergarten, Liz (Elizabeth) Soper and Robbie Stout kindergarten, and Laura Fuhrman and Michelle Doyle first grade. Twenty miles away was the rural school with 12 percent children of color and 11 percent free/reduced meals. Jenna Loomis taught first grade at this school.

The differences in the two school communities highlighted the need and importance of global literature. In the metropolitan school, classrooms typically included students who were born in another country (such as Nigeria, India, Nepal, South Africa, Trinidad, Zambia, Sri Lanka, Korea, Cuba); several who were born in the United States but whose families had immigrated within the previous twenty years; and numerous students who spoke languages other than English at home (such as Greek, Nepali, Telugu, Punjabi, Spanish, Bemba, Kikuyu, Korean, Chinese, Hindi, Afrikaans, Yoruba, Tagalog, Swahili). These children lived and breathed diversity daily. Global literature provided opportunities to deepen children's understandings of their rich community and strengthen the bonds of respect, appreciation, and friendship already forming. The rural school had less ethnic and socioeconomic diversity, with most children having grown up and lived in the area or the United States their entire lives. Global literature invited these children to experience "living through" other kinds of diversity through story (Rosenblatt 1978).

For all of the children, global literature served as both a mirror in which they saw themselves and human experience—including their feelings, emotions, hopes, and dreams—reflected and a window through which they learned about other people, places, situations, and cultures they had not yet encountered (Sims 1982).

District Curriculum

For three years, supported by a Global Literacy Communities grant from Worlds of Words, we worked to reframe the district curriculum (Martens and Martens 2011, 2013a, 2013b). Although the curriculum included some intercultural literature, the content was sequenced and controlled and focused on teaching skills. The teachers knew the expectations in their district curriculum and often addressed those standards/skills with global literature. Sometimes, though, they taught the district lessons and included global literature experiences during other parts of the day.

Reframing Our Curriculum

Using the curriculum framework on intercultural understanding, we created experiences with global literature for exploration in four areas: (1) personal cultural identities, (2) ways people live in specific global cultures, (3) different cultural perspectives in any unit of study, and (4) global issues that lead to opportunities for taking action. To enact the curriculum we developed text sets for the area of focus at a particular time and used engagements such as read-alouds, literature discussions, writing workshop, independent reading, partner reading, and inquiry studies, to bring the curriculum to life. (A sampling of books from our different text sets is found in Figure 15.1.) To contextualize our work and findings, we briefly share a few key experiences in each area.

CULTURAL IDENTITY
Ajmera, Maya, Sheila Kinkade, and Cynthia Pon. 2010. *Our Grandparents: A Global Album*. Watertown, MA: Charlesbridge.
Brown, Peter. 2013. *Mr. Tiger Goes Wild*. New York: Little, Brown.
Chen, Chih-Yuan. 2006. *The Featherless Chicken.* Alhambra, CA: Heryin Books.
Diggs, Taye. 2011. *Chocolate Me!* Illus. Shane W. Evans. New York: Feiwel and Friends.
Knowles, Sheena. 1998. *Edward the Emu*. Illus. Rod Clement. New York: Harper Collins.
Pellegrini, Nina. 1991. *Families Are Different*. New York: Holiday House.
CROSS-CULTURAL STUDIES: MEXICO
Ada, Alma Flor. 2002. *I Love Saturdays y Domingos*. Illus. Elivia Savadier. New York: Atheneum.
Amado, Elisa. 2011. *What Are You Doing?* Illus. Manuel Monroy. Toronto, ON: Groundwood.
Cohn, Diana. 2002. *Dream Carver.* Illus. Amy Cordova. San Francisco, CA: Chronicle Books.
Garza, Carmen Lomas. 1990. *Family Pictures; Cuadros de Familia.* San Francisco, CA: Children's Book Press.
Mora, Pat. 2009. *Gracias/Thanks.* Illus. John Parra. New York: Lee and Low Books.
Tonatiuh, Duncan. 2010. *Dear Primo: A Letter to My Cousin*. New York: Abrams Books.

Figure 15.1 **A Sampling of Global Literature in Different Text Sets**

CROSS-CULTURAL STUDIES: INDIA

Das, Prodeepta. 2010. *Geeta's Day: From Dawn to Dusk in an Indian Village.* London: Frances Lincoln.

Heine, Theresa. 2004. *Elephant Dance: A Journey to India.* Illus. Sheila Moxley. Cambridge, MA: Barefoot Books.

Krishnaswami, Uma. 2003. *Monsoon.* Illus. Jamel Akib. New York: Farrar, Straus and Giroux.

Lewin, Ted. 1995. *Sacred River: The Ganges of India.* New York: Clarion Books.

Makhijani, Pooja. 2007. *Mama's Saris.* Illus. Elena Gomez. Boston: Little, Brown.

Smith, Jeremy. 2003. *Lily's Garden of India.* Illus. Rob Hefferan. Tunbridge Wells, Kent: Ticktock.

TAKING ACTION

Boelts, Maribeth. 2009. *Those Shoes.* Illus. Noah Jones. Somerville, MA: Candlewick.

Cole, Henry. 2012. *Unspoken: A Story from the Underground Railroad.* New York: Scholastic.

Foreman, Michael. 2009. *A Child's Garden: A Story of Hope.* Somerville, MA: Candlewick.

Park, Linda Sue. 2004. *The Firekeeper's Son.* Illus. Julie Downing. New York: Clarion Books.

Pinkney, Andrea Davis. 2010. *Sit-In: How Four Friends Stood Up by Sitting Down.* Illus. Brian Pinkney. New York: Little, Brown.

Roth, Susan, and Cindy Trumbore. 2011. *The Mangrove Tree: Planting Trees to Feed Families.* New York: Lee and Low Books.

Figure 15.1 A Sampling of Global Literature in Different Text Sets (continued)

Personal Cultural Identities

Understanding self as a cultural being is at the core of the curriculum, and through our work we've come to appreciate its importance and significance in all areas of curriculum and life. We wanted learners to understand culture as shared beliefs and ways of living (i.e., religion, gender, geographical regions, language, class, and family structure), not merely as ethnicity (Geertz 1973). As they developed that understanding, children began to appreciate how their backgrounds and cultural experiences influenced their personal perspectives, an understanding foundational to their intercultural perspectives.

Our focus on personal identities included a variety of experiences that helped children think about who they were as cultural beings. These included explorations of their families and family histories and different aspects of their identities that make them unique. Details about these explorations are found in Chapter 3 of this book.

Ways People Live in Specific Global Cultures

Cultural identity is not just knowing ourselves; it involves a global perspective and seeing ourselves as part of the world community (Banks 2011). Crossing cultural borders broadens learners' perspectives about the world and their place in it (Cai 2002; Short and Thomas 2011).

Stories, both fiction and nonfiction, immersed children in the lives of others and invited them to experience another aspect of life (Rosenblatt 1978; Short 2012). The kindergarten children participated in cross-cultural studies of Mexico and the first graders in studies of India (Martens et al. in press). The economic and political differences between the United States and those countries complicated comparisons that arose, and teachers wove discussions of such inequalities into the studies to support children's understandings. Teachers read books aloud and also provided browsing times for children to transact with the books independently or with partners. Kindergartners and first graders took graffiti notes (see Appendix D) to document points they wanted to remember over the weeks of their studies. To reflect on their learnings, kindergartners painted pictures and wrote stories about something they learned about Mexico, and first graders wrote and illustrated books about India.

Different Cultural Perspectives in Any Unit of Study

Global literature needs to be woven throughout the curriculum to support the connections children make in their learning and their developing intercultural understandings.

Rather than using global literature only during reading, integrating these books into all subject areas highlights respect for diverse cultures and perspectives in our global world. Teachers read global literature throughout the day. When first graders studied endangered plants in Maryland, teachers broadened the discussion to endangered plants and animals around the world through global literature.

Global Issues That Lead to Opportunities for Taking Action

A critical aspect of cultural identity is for learners to see themselves as integral members of their communities (home, school, neighborhood, and beyond) who assume responsibilities and question "what is," imagine "what if," and take action for social change (Banks 2004; Freire 1970; Short 2011).

We began discussions of what it means to assume responsibility and take action on the first day of school (Martens et al. 2015). These discussions focused on such topics as being responsible for yourself and your possessions, being a good friend, and being a helpful member of the classroom and school communities, and often grew naturally out of conversations around books in the cultural identity and cross-cultural studies text sets. What kind of person am I? What do my actions show about who I am? The discussions continued throughout the year, and children took action in various ways in their classrooms, schools, and homes. Global literature in the taking-action text set extended the importance of identifying problems and taking action to solve them beyond the local communities.

Our Work Together

We met as a team with teachers to discuss readings and develop our own understandings about intercultural learning, global picturebooks, and art; share what was happening related to global literature in our classrooms; look at examples of children's written and artistic responses to the literature; and brainstorm ideas to move us forward. We documented children's responses to literature and in research journals, collected their writing and art, took photographs, and made audio/video recordings. Analyzing this data by coding for patterns, we identified three significant learnings for the children: their understandings of their own personal cultural identities; their appreciation of and respect for the ways they are both similar to and different from others; and their identification of themselves as responsible citizens of their communities and the world who take action to address problems. We discuss these next.

Learnings of Young Children Through Experiences with Global Literature

We share our learnings by contextualizing them in data and experiences with global literature.

Children developed an understanding of culture and their own personal cultural identities.

Through experiences with global literature, children developed initial understandings of culture, its complexity, and its role in their own and others' lives. They came to realize that their background, beliefs, values, ways of living, family, and so on were parts of their own and others' cultural identities. Evidence that the children developed these understandings appeared in our discussions of families and cultural identities.

Learning About Families

The children developed an appreciation for the countless ways in which families are different, including who was in their families, where they lived, what jobs family members did, and how they celebrated different occasions. The world maps on which children plotted where their families originated helped to generate discussions and understandings about the unique aspects of families. Children often initially struggled with the concept that their families began someplace else. Comments like, "But I was born in Baltimore" were common at first. Through discussions in school around literature such as *My Name Is Sangoel* (Williams and Mohammed 2009) as well as discussions with their families at home, children gradually came to understand their place in the history of their families. First grader Ki was one who persistently insisted he was from Baltimore. After several days, though, he proudly came in one morning and announced to his teacher Michelle, "My mom said my family started in Africa. Now I get it!" (Martens and Martens 2011).

Exploring Cultural Identities

Data on children's responses to global literature also revealed that children explored the complexity of cultural identity, including inner beliefs and values as well as physical characteristics. Skin color was one topic that emerged in discussions of cultural identity. When Liz and Robbie read *Shades of People* (Rotner and Kelly 2010) in kindergarten, children immediately began comparing their skin colors with each other and commenting about differences. This led to discussions of how skin color doesn't define a person, and the importance of respecting everyone.

World maps also led to discussions of skin color. During one of Jenna's map discussions with her first graders, Mandisa and Alice both plotted their families' origins in Kenya (Martens and Martens 2011). Joe asked, "If Mandisa and Alice are both from Kenya, why do they have different-colored skin?" Jenna explained that both of Mandisa's parents were from Kenya, whereas one of Alice's parents was from Kenya and the other from Europe. This opened the door to discussions related to identity. Jenna later read *Am I a Color Too?* (Cole and Vogl 2005) and invited children to write "I Am" poems that highlighted aspects they believed were special about their cultural identities. Dawn wrote, "I am not a color. I am a writer. I am a sister. I am a singer. I am a friend. I am gymnastics. I am Dawn." Michael wrote, "I am not a color. I am football. I am riding my bike. I am surfing. I am soccer. I am a helper. I am Michael."

Evidence of the children's understandings of their cultural identities also appeared in their cultural x-rays (see Appendix D). Independently the children wrote and drew what others could observe about them around the outside of the figure and what they valued as important inside their hearts. After completing her cultural x-ray, Avery explained the outside of the figure first, saying, "I like to wear unique clothes so I wrote, 'I am unique.' I do a sport, which is yoga. I'm seven and a half. I have white skin. I have blue-green eyes. My hair is the color dirty blond. I am a girl and I am from France and England and Scotland. Inside my heart I am happy, brave, helpful, smart, loving, and thoughtful. And, I love my family. I used bright colors for my x-ray because I'm happy, and I made myself outside because I like to be out in nature. I drawed [sic] a flower, some grass, a squirrel, and some butterflies, and the sun, and the sky." The cultural x-rays demonstrated that the children were developing an understanding of the complexities in their own and others' cultural identities. (Other evidence of first graders' understandings of themselves and their cultural identities appear in their "All About Me" books. Examples are found at http://wowlit.org/on-line-publications/stories/storiesiv7a/3/.)

Christie Furnari (2013a, 2013b) had prekindergarten children construct adapted cultural x-rays over the course of several weeks to help them think about their identities. Each week she read literature that highlighted different parts of the body, such as *Shoes, Shoes, Shoes* (Morris 1998) for the feet, and children created that part and wrote and drew about it (see Figure 15.2). After they had completed the x-rays, Christie interviewed the children. Allison said, "I want to be an animal doctor for animals . . . I like to help my mom with my hands and I clean my room and watch my brother . . . I am amazing . . . We help our friends and pick ourselves up and eat breakfast and get bigger and bigger." The interviews provided evidence of the children's developing perceptions of themselves as cultural beings.

Figure 15.2 Examples of Cultural X-Rays in Prekindergarten

Through reading and responding to global literature, children grew in their understandings of culture and their own personal cultural identities. They began to understand that who they are as people is complex, involving both external and internal characteristics. These understandings were foundational to living, learning, being, and relating to others in our global world.

Children appreciated and respected the ways they were both similar to and different from others.

Through in-depth cross-cultural studies, children developed understandings and respect for the ways different cultural peoples live, believe, and think around the world. Drawing on their understandings of their own cultural identities, they also recognized and appreciated the commonalities they share with others. Evidence that children developed respect and appreciation for the ways they are similar to and different from others was clear in kindergartners' study of Mexican culture and first graders' study of India.

The kindergarten study of Mexican culture lasted about three weeks. Through books such as *In My Family/En Mi Familia* (Garza 2000) children learned about families and everyday life. Stories like this generated lots of discussions and questions that Robbie and Liz (Stout and Soper 2013) extended. The kindergarten children liked hearing about piñatas, and the teachers used those curiosities to also talk about how different cultures have varying ways of celebrating birthdays. The children were surprised to hear that some people in Mexico ate cacti, which led to discussions of food sources. While Liz and Robbie tried to weave more critical aspects of their Mexican inquiry into the discussions, children's stories and art reflected personal connections they made. The critical discussions, however, laid the foundation for more in-depth learning as children grew.

Children painted and wrote stories about something they learned. Ryan painted a birthday party with children and a piñata at a house similar to houses in America, because he'd noticed and commented on that similarity in some book illustrations. For his story he wrote, "In Mexico we eat fish and cactus and did you know that [you] have to take off the prickers [needles]? In Mexico they have drums. In Mexico they have bull fighting." Other themes that emerged in the children's writings and art included families doing things together and celebrations such as Day of the Dead and Cinco de Mayo.

First graders studied India for six to eight weeks, and Jenna, Michelle, and Laura (Doyle 2013a; Fuhrman 2013) worked to highlight the complexities of this rich culture. *Same, Same but Different* (Kostecki-Shaw 2011) compared the lives of two pen pals: an American boy living in the city and an Indian boy living in a rural area. Although the book has strengths, it can leave the impression that India has no cities and America has no rural areas. Teachers addressed this through text sets (on the themes of People, Land/Resources, Cities/Villages) of books that explored each theme from a range of perspectives. The depth of children's thinking was evident in the questions they raised about such topics as cows wandering the streets because they were considered holy, and tigers and elephants being killed for profit that led to them becoming endangered. Their questions and comments opened opportunities for conversations about economics, environmental issues, and different beliefs and ways of living and communicating, which everyone around the world has rights to that we respect. (Information on the India studies with examples of the children's work and books is available at wowlit.org/on-line-publications/stories/iv5/6/; wowlit.org/on-line-publications/stories/iv5/7/; and wowlit.org/on-line-publications/stories/storiesiv7a/6/.)

First graders wrote books about what they learned, using the graffiti notes they took for each text set as a resource for ideas (Doyle 2013a; Fuhrman 2013). The books included two cultural x-rays also. One was of themselves, created several months after their first, and the other was of a child in India. Since thinking of a general Indian child would be difficult for children, teachers gave them the option of thinking about a character in one of the books they'd read. Many used Geeta, the young girl in *Geeta's Day: From Dawn to Dusk in an Indian Village* (Das 2010) for their Indian child.

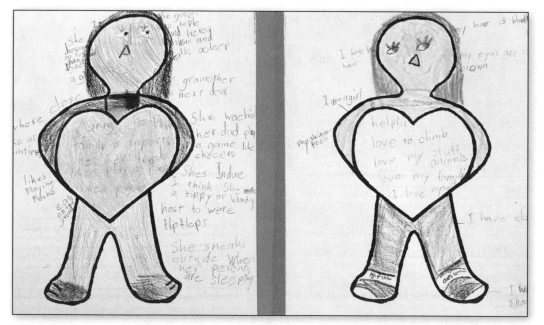

Figure 15.3 **First Grader Lauren's Cultural X-Rays of Geeta, an Indian Girl (left), and Herself (right)**

We interviewed children about their cultural x-rays to understand their perspectives of themselves and Indian children. Lauren's two x-rays are in Figure 15.3. Her comments about her own x-ray included having long blond hair, brown eyes, skin that's peach, and, inside her heart writing "helpful, love to climb, love my stuffed animals, love my family, and love myself." Her description of Geeta's x-ray included the fact that she's a girl, goes to temple, likes playing, is Hindu, and wears a bindi. For Geeta's heart she wrote "caring, helpful, family is important, likes her friends, and likes playing." When asked how children in India and in America are similar and different, Lauren responded, "[We're similar because] we both have clothes, we play, we are helpful and caring. [We're different because] India people . . . have more things to eat and we have different clothes." Lauren's responses showed that she recognized that although there were external differences between American and Indian children, there were also similarities that included wearing clothes, playing, and being helpful and caring.

Other children's comments about the similarities and differences between Indian and American children demonstrated similar perspectives. Carly said, "Kids in India and me are the same because we're both pretty and helpful and like rainbow clothes. And we're good at playing and learning . . . We're different because . . . they have black hair and I have yellow hair . . . And, they live in India and I live in the USA." Cory shared, "In our hearts we're the same by being happy, caring, nice, and learning things. We're different because here kids wear different clothes and [there] they wear Saris." Alisha's response at the opening of this chapter is another example.

Immersing children in cross-cultural studies developed an appreciation of the complexities of culture as well as commonalities across humanity. They didn't perceive people and their ways of living and believing as strange, but valued and were eager to learn more about them. As Lehman, Freeman, and Scharer (2010) say, "Children's ability to understand, value, and celebrate diversity evolves from recognizing their places and their particular experiences as part of the universal whole of humanity" (19).

Children began to see themselves as citizens of their communities and the world with responsibilities to take action to solve problems.

Through global literature experiences, children identified themselves with others as citizens of our global world. They recognized the importance of assuming responsibility for making the world a better place, beginning in their local home and school communities. Evidence that the children understood their responsibilities for taking action in the world was documented in their responses to the literature and stories or posters they created.

As the children understood their own and respected others' cultural identities through global literature, they developed a sense of their citizenship in our world. With citizenship comes responsibilities to help and take care of this world. Discussions of being responsible citizens began the first days of school in relation to self and personal belongings, what it meant to be a good friend, and taking care of the environment. In prekindergarten, Christie Furnari (2013a) used *I Like Me* (Carlson 1990) to think with children about what it means to be responsible for yourself. In kindergarten Robbie and Liz (Stout and Soper 2013) read *Listen to the Wind: The Story of Dr. Greg and Three Cups of Tea* (Mortenson and Roth 2009) to generate discussions of how friends take action to help each other, and children wrote their own stories about being a friend.

The metropolitan school is a "Green School" with a meadow, a rain garden, a trail of native trees, a Bayscape garden filled with plants native to the area, and a bluebird trail on the school grounds. Michelle Doyle (2013b) and her first graders assumed responsibility each year for taking care of the Bayscape and enlisting the help of other classes in the school. Michelle found that "by talking about erosion, studying the native plants, mulching, and pulling weeds, the children realized that their actions matter. They developed a respect and sense of protectiveness for this area." Books like *The Curious Garden* (Brown 2009) also helped children reflect on the importance of caring for the environment.

Reading and discussing global literature in the taking-action text set connected responsibilities for self and local communities to a global perspective, developed the concept of taking action, and showed the range of ways children can make a difference in the world. The teachers read and discussed the stories, considering the problem characters identified, what made it a problem, the action characters took, and the result. They related this to which traits inside the characters' hearts prompted them to take action.

Sketch to stretch responses to literature provided evidence that the children understood their responsibilities for taking action. *One Child* (Cheng 2000) is the story of a girl who surveys the environment and is saddened by the pollution, trash, and fighting, and works to make the world a better place. In her sketch to stretch (see Figure 15.4) Kayla drew the girl crying on the left in response to the environmental problems, and smiling on the right after she took action to clean up the environment. Kayla wrote, "Try your best to help the earth." For her sketch to stretch Claire wrote, "PROTECT the EARTH!!!

Figure 15.4 First Grader Kayla's Sketch to Stretch for *One Child* (Oreng 2000)

My own suggestion is turn the lights off if you don't need it. Walk if you can. Plant a seed. Throw away trash." Khyree's response to the story was, "One girl's world was gray and she realized that if you stop littering and start planting you can make a difference in the world. If you can IMAGINE, anything can happen."

Teachers read literature and had rich discussions around global issues and how others in parts of the world take action, such as cleaning oil spills (Grindley 1995), bringing electricity to an African village (Kamkwamba and Mealer 2012), or planting trees (Codell 2012). When the children generated their own ideas for taking action, however, they focused on their personal lives with topics related to their families, friends, and the environment. Children wrote books or made posters about donating clothes or toys to others in need, helping their parents, standing up for their friends, building bird houses, and protecting trees for birds and animals and to clean the air. Examples of the children's work are available at wowlit.org/on-line-publications/stories/storiesiv7a/7/ and wowlit.org/on-line-publications/stories/storiesiv7a/8/.

Children connected to taking action on a personal and local level at this point in their lives because that was the world they related to most closely. These "local" actions, though, began to develop in them a sense of agency and responsibility for themselves and their world that will grow as they get older. Teachers wanted children to understand that their actions now do matter. When Jenna read *Ordinary Mary's Extraordinary Deed* (Pearson 2002), her first graders noticed that it wasn't like other books in the text set (Martens et al. 2015). Marty said, "This is like *Because Amelia Smiled* [Stein 2012]. They take action in little ways, not big ways like in other books." To demonstrate that "little ways" matter, Jenna printed 3-by-8-inch slips of paper that read, "Ordinary students are taking action! How extraordinary! ____ took action by ____ when ____." Over the next few days, children filled in slips with ways they took action. Kaylee took action by "helping my grandma clean the dishes when grandma had too much cleaning to do"; Marie by "helping my dad make his coffee when he had two lunches to pack"; and Jakob by "fixing the broken headphones in the Listening Center." At the end of the week children worked together to make a chain by looping a strip through the "ring" of another and gluing it into another ring. When they finished, children measured their chain at eighteen feet. Jenna commented, "The children were *amazed*! They quickly realized that their little actions *do* make a difference!"

Final Reflections: Why Global Literature Matters

The children's questions, comments, writings, and drawings revealed the power of global literature in the context of a curriculum that is intercultural. Through experiences with text sets focused on personal cultural identities, cross-cultural studies, and issues that lead to responsible citizenship and taking action, as well as integrating global literature throughout the day, children grew in their intercultural understandings, convincing us that global literature matters in the lives of children and classrooms.

Global literature matters because it is story. Story is how humans make sense of their lives and the world (Short 2012). Christie found this with prekindergarten children. She commented, "Through listening to and responding to global literature stories, my children grew in their appreciation of themselves and others, explored their imaginations, and learned that they too have stories to tell. Everybody has a story!"

Story also immerses learners in diverse cultures, situations, and perspectives they may or may not yet have experienced. It allows them to consider how those different from them live, and understand the beliefs and experiences they both share (Short 2012). We found this to be true in our cross-cultural studies. After Michelle's study of India with her first graders ended, she reflected, "By immersing ourselves in Indian culture over time through stories, the children moved beyond knowing surface characteristics of the culture to understanding beliefs, values, perspectives, and diversity that exist within it." The questions, curiosities, and critical thinking global literature presents invite learners to wrestle with complex ideas that build on and develop open-mindedness, respect, and appreciation for multiple perspectives of the world.

Global literature matters because it speaks to young learners and enhances their understandings of themselves, others, and the world. In reflecting on stories she read to her kindergarten children, Robbie said, "Stories celebrate diversity and individuality and offer opportunities to talk about similarities and differences and accepting others." Children are always eager to listen to and talk about stories. Stories feed their curiosities about the world and spark critical discussions as well as imaginations. Liz remarked, "Through stories like *A Circle of Friends* [Carmi 2003] and *The Sandwich Swap* [Rania and DiPucchio 2010] my kindergartners made connections to their lives and learned different ways they can be a friend to others."

Although parents or teachers may hesitate to read literature about unfamiliar cultures or situations to young children, we have found young children respectful and eager to listen to and discuss stories about such topics as religious beliefs, war, discrimination, and environmental issues. In our experience, even if our four-to-seven-year-olds could not initially relate to the setting or situation, they connected to the characters in the story. They had not been in a refugee camp like Lina and Feroza in *Four Feet, Two Sandals* (Williams and Mohammed 2007), but they related to Lina and Feroza because they understood what it meant to make friends, share, and have to say good-bye. In reflecting across *First Come the Zebra* (Barasch 2009), *One Child* (Cheng 2000), and *The Mangrove Tree: Planting Trees to Feed Families* (Roth and Trumbore 2011), six-year-old Rami said, "In each story the character made the world a better place." Because the children identified with and cared about the characters, they were concerned and wanted to know about the situations. We agree with Stan (2014) that "the more culturally specific a story is, the more universal it becomes . . . A well-written story enables readers to connect with the main character at the core and bring their own experiences into the mix" (19). Young children, we have found, have not yet developed deep biases toward others and situations. Experiences with global literature build on the open-mindedness many children already possess and broaden their respect and appreciation of multiple perspectives in the world.

Global literature matters because it provides hope in a chaotic world. Experiences with global literature offer opportunities for children to see how intercultural understandings build peace in the midst of misunderstandings and conflict. In considering first graders' comments and writings after experiences with *The Invisible Boy* (Ludwig 2013), Laura said, "By reflecting on times someone's actions made *them* feel invisible, the children become aware of how their actions affect others . . . and consider their identity as a friend." After her reading and discussion of *A Child's Garden: A Story of Hope* (Foreman 2009) with her first graders, Jenna commented, "The children's responses and insights demonstrated their understanding that as the boy took responsibility for tending to the vine, he brought hope to his broken community that before was surrounded by hate. They learned that actions have important results." Laura's and Jenna's experiences support Choo (2013), who argues that literature promotes hospitable imaginations that encourage us to value others, make ourselves accountable to them, and open ourselves to them, which leads to reconciliation and harmony.

As four-to-seven-year-olds, our young learners are only on the threshold of developing intercultural understandings and hospitable imaginations. The foundation is laid, though, on which they can continue to develop richer understandings of themselves as complex cultural beings, a deeper appreciation of others and diverse perspectives, and their agency and willingness to be responsible citizens who take action to solve problems in the world.

Recommended Books That Invite Global Perspectives

Cheng, Christopher. 2000. *One Child*. Illus. Steven Woolman. New York: Interlink.
A young girl watching television is saddened by the destruction, pollution, and harm to animals. She decides to take action and works to reverse the damage by planting trees, cleaning the yard, walking, and speaking out.

Cole, Heidi, and Nancy Vogl. 2005. *Am I a Color Too?* Illus. Gerald Purnell. Kirkland, WA: Illumination Arts.
Tyler wonders why people label themselves and others by the color of their skin when regardless of color, everyone smiles, dances, and dreams. He recognizes that the essence of a person includes, but is deeper than, skin color.

Kerley, Barbara. 2005. *You and Me Together: Moms, Dads, and Kids Around the World.* **Washington, DC: National Geographic.**

Striking color photographs accompanied by brief phrases show children and their families from around the world involved in activities such as dancing, fishing, taking a walk, holding hands, napping, or taking a ride. Back matter includes a world map, brief information on each photo, and a message from Marian Wright Edelman.

Pearson, Emily. 2002. *Ordinary Mary's Extraordinary Deed.* **Illus. Fumi Kosaka. Layton, UT: Gibbs Smith.**

Ordinary Mary is on her way to her ordinary home from her ordinary school when she finds some ordinary blueberries. She gives them to her neighbor, who makes muffins and gives them to her paperboy and others, starting a chain of acts of kindness that extends around the world and back to Mary.

Williams, Karen Lynn, and Khadra Mohammed. 2007. *Four Feet, Two Sandals.* **Illus. Doug Chayka. Grand Rapids, MI: Eerdmans.**

Two young girls from Afghanistan, Lina and Feroza, meet in a refugee camp in Pakistan. They both reach for sandals thrown from a truck by relief workers, and each ends up with one. They find a way to share the sandals and become friends.

References

Banks, James. 2004. "Teaching for Social Justice, Diversity, and Citizenship in a Global World." *The Educational Forum* 68:296–305.

_____. 2011. "Educating Citizens in Diverse Societies." *Intercultural Education* 22 (4): 243–251.

Cai, Mingshui. 2002. *Multicultural Literature for Children and Young Adults.* Westport, CT: Greenwood.

Choo, Suzanne. 2013. *Reading the World, the Globe, the Cosmos: Approaches to Teaching Literature for the Twenty-First Century.* New York: Peter Lang.

Doyle, Michelle Hassay. 2013a. "Empowering Young Writers as Authors and Illustrators Through a Study of India." *WOW Stories* 4: (5). http://wowlit.org/on-line-publications/stories/iv5/7/.

———. 2013b. "First Graders Taking Action in Their Part of the World." *WOW Stories* 4: (7a). http://wowlit.org/on-line-publications/stories/storiesiv7a/7/.

Freire, Paulo. 1970. *Pedagogy of the Oppressed*. South Hadley, MA: Bergin and Garvey.

Fuhrman, Laura. 2013. "Crossing Cultural Borders More Deeply: Integrating a Study of India Throughout the Curriculum." *WOW Stories* 4: (7a). http://wowlit.org/on-line-publications/stories/storiesiv7a/6/.

Furnari, Christie. 2013a. "A New Focus: Understanding Ourselves Through Global Picturebooks." *WOW Stories* 4: (5). http://wowlit.org/on-line-publications/stories/iv5/4/#1.

———. 2013b. "Everybody Has a Story: Telling Our Stories in Pre-Kindergarten." *WOW Stories* 4: (7a). http://wowlit.org/on-line-publications/stories/storiesiv7a/4/.

Geertz, Clifford. 1973. *The Interpretation of Cultures*. New York: Basic Books.

Lehman, Barbara, Evelyn Freeman, and Patricia Scharer. 2010. *Reading Globally, K–8: Connecting Students to the World Through Literature*. Thousand Oaks, CA: Corwin.

Martens, Prisca, and Ray Martens. 2011. "Building Intercultural Connections Through Literacy: Community Explorations of Global and Multicultural Literature." *WOW Stories* 4: (1). http://wowlit.org/on-line-publications/stories/storiesiv1/.

———. 2013a. "Learning About Ourselves and Others Through Global Literature." *WOW Stories* 4: (5). http//wowlit.org/on-line-publications/stories/iv5/.

———. 2013b. "Artists Reading and Thinking: Developing Intercultural Understandings Through Global Literature." *WOW Stories* 4: (7a). http://wowlit.org/on-line-publications/stories/storiesiv7a/.

Martens, Prisca, Ray Martens, Michelle Hassay Doyle, Jenna Loomis, Laura Fuhrman, Christie Furnari, Elizabeth Soper, and Robbie Stout. 2015. "Building Intercultural Understandings Through Global Literature." *The Reading Teacher* 68 (8): 609–617.

———. In press. "Reclaiming Early Literacies by Learning About Self and Others Through Global Literature and Art." In *Reclaiming Early Childhood Literacies: Narratives of Hope, Power, and Vision*, ed. Richard Meyer and Kathryn Whitmore. New York: Routledge/Taylor and Francis.

Pattnaik, Jyotsna. 2003. "Learning About the 'Other': Building a Case for Intercultural Understanding Among Minority Children." *Childhood Education* 79 (4): 204–211.

Rosenblatt, Louise. 1978. *The Reader, the Text, the Poem*. Carbondale, IL: Southern Illinois University Press.

Short, Kathy G. 2011. "Children Taking Action Within Global Inquiries." *The Dragon Lode* 29 (2): 50–59.

———. 2012. "Story as World Making." *Language Arts* 90 (1): 9–17.

Short, Kathy G., and Lisa Thomas. 2011. "Developing Intercultural Understandings Through Global Children's Literature." In *Reclaiming Reading*, ed. Richard Meyer and Kathryn Whitmore. New York: Routledge.

Sims, Rudine. 1982. *Shadow and Substance: Afro-American Experience in Contemporary Children's Fiction*. Urbana, IL: National Council of Teachers of English.

Stan, Susan. 2014. *Global Voices: Picture Books from Around the World*. Chicago, IL: American Library Association.

Stout, Robbie, and Elizabeth Soper. 2013. "Developing Art, Language, and Writing Through Discussions of Friendship and Culture in Kindergarten." *WOW Stories* 4: (7a). http://wowlit.org/on-line-publications/stories/storiesiv7a/5/.

Children's Books Cited

Barasch, Lynne. 2009. *First Come the Zebra*. New York: Lee and Low Books.

Brown, Peter. 2009. *The Curious Garden*. New York: Little, Brown.

Carlson, Nancy. 1990. *I Like Me*. New York: Puffin.

Carmi, Giora. 2003. *A Circle of Friends*. New York: Star Bright Books.

Cheng, Christopher. 2000. *One Child*. Illus. Steven Woolman. New York: Interlink.

Codell, Esme Raji. 2012. *Seed by Seed: The Legend and Legacy of John "Appleseed" Chapman*. Illus. Lynne Rae Perkins. New York: HarperCollins.

Cole, Heidi, and Nancy Vogl. 2005. *Am I a Color Too?* Illus. Gerald Purnell. Kirkland, WA: Illumination Arts.

Das, Prodeepta. 2010. *Geeta's Day: From Dawn to Dusk in an Indian Village*. London: Frances Lincoln.

Foreman, Michael. 2009. *A Child's Garden: A Story of Hope*. Somerville, MA: Candlewick.

Garza, Carmen Lomas. 2000. *In My Family/En Mi Familia*. San Francisco, CA: Children's Book Press.

Grindley, Sally. 1995. *Peter's Place*. Illus. Michael Foreman. New York: Harcourt Brace.

Kamkwamba, William, and Bryan Mealer. 2012. *The Boy Who Harnessed the Wind*. Illus. E. Zunon. New York: Dial.

Kostecki-Shaw, Jenny Sue. 2011. *Same, Same but Different*. New York: Henry Holt.

Ludwig, Trudy. 2013. *The Invisible Boy*. Illus. P. Barton. New York: Knopf.

Morris, Ann. 1998. *Shoes, Shoes, Shoes*. New York: Harper Collins.

Mortenson, Greg, and Susan Roth. 2009. *Listen to the Wind: The Story of Dr. Greg and* Three Cups of Tea. New York: Dial.

Pearson, Emily. 2002. *Ordinary Mary's Extraordinary Deed*. Illus. Fumi Kosaka. Layton, UT: Gibbs Smith.

Rania, Queen, Consort of Abdullah II, King of Jordan, and Kelly DiPucchio. 2010. *The Sandwich Swap*. Illus. Tricia Tusa. New York: Disney Hyperion.

Roth, Susan, and Cindy Trumbore. 2011. *The Mangrove Tree: Planting Trees to Feed Families*. New York: Lee and Low Books.

Rotner, Shelley, and Sheila Kelly. 2010. *Shades of People*. New York: Holiday House.

Stein, David Ezra. 2012. *Because Amelia Smiled*. Somerville, MA: Candlewick.

Williams, Karen Lynn, and Khadra Mohammed. 2007. *Four Feet, Two Sandals*. Illus. Doug Chayka. Grand Rapids, MI: Eerdmans.

_____. 2009. *My Name Is Sangoel*. Illus. Catherine Stock. Grand Rapids, MI: Eerdmans.

Chapter 16

Developing Intercultural Understanding Through Global Children's Literature

Kathy G. Short with Jaquetta Alexander, Amy Edwards, Jennifer Griffith, and Lisa Thomas

We were excited to begin our collaborative inquiry with children around encouraging intercultural understanding through global literature. Our plans centered on explorations of culture and global issues, with the eventual goal of children engaging in social action. Those plans were adjusted, however, once we engaged in the first literature discussion. Lisa read aloud a short story to children and invited them to share their connections. Most children took turns, making a short comment and then sitting back, satisfied that they had accomplished what was expected. When Lisa encouraged them to talk with each other and not worry about raising their hands, they talked over one another, quickly descending from turn taking into chaos. Many told stories about their own lives that were only peripherally related to the book, and some appeared to be making up stories to gain status with peers.

Clearly, we had a long way to go to move toward intercultural understanding and global perspectives when we could not even facilitate dialogue around a familiar book. Four years later, we met to examine transcripts from children's discussions of global literature, celebrating the ways in which children talked thoughtfully and respectfully with each other about substantive global and local issues. During those four years, we learned a lot about how to invite dialogue around global literature and deepened our insights into intercultural understanding, particularly what those understandings looked and sounded like in children's dialogue.

Our focus on intercultural understanding grew out of the realization that although children live in a global world, their experiences can occur within the confines of limited worldviews, resulting in judging and finding deficient those whose cultural ways of living and thinking differ from their own. This way of thinking shuts down future opportunities in personal and professional relationships and the richness of the lives they construct. Judging cultures beyond their own as "strange" positions their culture as the norm against which any other way of thinking or living is evaluated. If, instead, they approach the world with openness to global cultures as multiple ways of living in the world, as alternatives rather than right or wrong, opportunities open up instead of closing down.

Our work was based in the belief that thoughtful interactions around global children's literature are one means of encouraging children to develop more open-minded perspectives. Literature provides an opportunity for children to "live through" and experience many ways of thinking and living in the world. Valuing the role that global literature can play, however, is quite different from actually successfully offering these opportunities in the classroom. Although we had gained many insights into constructing curricular experiences, we wanted to be able to assess children's intercultural understandings to better shape the curriculum in response to their inquiries. This chapter shares our work in identifying the types of intercultural understandings that children evidenced in their talk within literature circles. These types gave us deeper insights into intercultural understanding as educators so that we could better support children as global learners.

Our School Context

The context for our inquiry was a small K–5 public school in a large urban district with a culturally and linguistically diverse population from a working-class neighborhood. Because of our location in the Southwest, many students were Latino, but there were also Asian American, African American, and American Indian students. A total of 45 percent qualified for free or reduced lunch. Teachers identified global inquiry through literature and the arts as their school focus, and we explored critical and conceptual thinking through an inquiry-based approach using literacy engagements with global literature. My role was a collaborative one within the learning lab and study group as a university educator and researcher. Teachers met with the curriculum coordinator, Lisa Thomas, in a biweekly study group to discuss curriculum development around global literature, and she taught a one-hour lesson in the lab for each classroom once a week that was then discussed in the study group. Jaquetta, Amy, and Jennifer were classroom teachers in the school who met with Lisa and me in the summer to look at the transcripts from their students.

During our fourth year of working together, we wanted to examine the influence of engagements with global literature on children's intercultural understandings. Our goal was to identify the types of intercultural understandings evident in children's talk about global literature. Those understandings would inform classroom instruction as well as serve as the basis for a set of categories that we and others could use to examine and evaluate intercultural understanding.

Theoretical Frame

Research and theory on intercultural understanding, learning, and competence supported us in looking at the children's talk. As mentioned in Chapter 1, we defined intercultural understanding as "a stance of openness to multiple ways of thinking and being in the world and to differences as resources for our shared humanity and responsibility in working together to create a better and more just world." To examine children's talk, however, we needed more specific descriptions of this stance.

Researchers and global organizations have produced taxonomies and rubrics to consider in developing measures of interculturalism (Byram 1997; Merryfield 2002; Bennett 2004; Oxfam 2006; Mansilla and Jackson 2011; Kramsch 2011). Most recently, Kenneth Cushner (2015) has reviewed existing assessment tools for intercultural competence and provided useful analyses related to their strengths and limitations. The theorists we found most useful were Helmut Fennes and Karen Hapgood (1997) and Roland Case (1991).

Fennes and Hapgood (1997) identify an intercultural learning continuum based on the work of Hoopes (1979) that moves from *ethnocentricism* to *awareness* that something different from one's own culture exists (see Figure 16.1). This awareness can lead to *understanding* through developing a concept of culture and of cultural differences. Understanding provides the basis for an awareness of prejudice and stereotypes and leads to *acceptance and respect* through recognizing the validity of cultural differences without judging that culture based on one's own cultural norms and respecting differences that contradict elements of one's own culture. *Appreciation and valuing* involve seeing cultural diversity as a resource for growth and development, not a problem. This perspective leads to *change* where one integrates attitudes and behaviors from other cultures into one's own views and actions, thus resulting in *intercultural competence.*

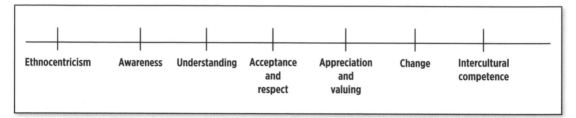

Figure 16.1 Continuum of Intercultural Learning (Fennes and Hapgood 1997)

The work of Case (1991) on a global perspective as consisting of both substantive and perceptual dimensions was particularly useful in informing our analysis. The substantive dimension refers to the knowledge of various features of the world and how it works, including knowledge of cultural values and practices, global interconnections, present concerns and conditions, historic origins and past patterns, and alternative and future directions. The perception dimension consists of the orientations, values, and attitudes that establish the lens through which students perceive the world. This lens includes open-mindedness, anticipation of complexity, resistance to stereotyping, inclination to empathize, and nonchauvinism. These attitudes of mind are viewed as fundamental to a global perspective.

Action Research

Our question was how the curriculum we had developed was influencing intercultural understanding. We were excited about the curriculum innovations and the critical thinking of students, but we had not closely examined their intercultural understandings. Our perception was that they were thinking globally, but we needed to engage in careful data collection and analysis to ensure that we went beyond impressions.

We planned literature discussions in each classroom in May around four types of books that connected to our curricular framework. We decided to do intensive audio- and videotaping in late spring so that students were comfortable with the discussion process. Small groups in each classroom met to discuss four books that reflected the four areas of our curriculum framework. Figure 16.2 lists the books that were options for the literature circles, with each teacher selecting one book from each area based on which seemed most appropriate for her students.

PERSONAL CULTURAL IDENTITY	
Ada, Alma Flor. 2002. *I Love Saturdays y domingos*. Illus. Elivia Savadier. Atheneum.	A biracial child visits her English-speaking and Spanish-speaking grandparents (United States).
Altman, Linda Jacobs. 1993. *Amelia's Road*. Illus. Enrique Sanchez. Lee and Low Books.	A young migrant girl is tired of moving from place to place (United States).
Mandelbaum, Pili. 1990. *You Be Me, I'll Be You*. Kane/Miller.	A biracial child explores her skin color and identity (Belgium).
Shin, Sun Yung. 2004. *Cooper's Lesson*. Illus. Kim Cogan. Children's Book Press.	A Korean American boy struggles with learning to speak Korean (United States).
CROSS-CULTURAL STUDIES	
Garay, Luis. 1997. *Pedrito's Day*. Orchard.	Pedrito replaces money that he lost while playing (Nicaragua).
Skarmeta, Antonio. 1998. *The Composition*. Illus. Alfonso Ruano. Groundwood.	Pedro must decide between soccer and his family in a military dictatorship (Chile).
Williams, Karen Lynn. 1990. *Galimoto*. Illus. Catherine Stock. Lothrop.	A young boy finds materials to make a special toy (Malawi).
Winter, Jeanette. 2009. *Nasreen's Secret School*. Simon and Schuster.	A young girl is able to go to a secret school for girls (Afghanistan).
INTEGRATION OF INTERCULTURAL PERSPECTIVES	
Ajmera, Maya, and John Ivanko. 2000. *To Be a Kid*. Charlesbridge.	Photos from around the world show activities that children have in common (Global).
Kerley, Barbara. 2009. *One World, One Day*. National Geographic.	Photos follow the course of one day in our world (Global).
McDonald, Megan. 1996. *My House Has Stars*. Illus. Peter Catalanotto. Orchard.	Children describe the homes they live in around the world (Global).
INQUIRIES INTO GLOBAL ISSUES	
Brown, Peter. 2009. *The Curious Garden*. Little Brown.	A boy carefully tends a secret garden that spreads color (United States).
Cowley, Joy. 1999. *The Video Shop Sparrow*. Illus. Gavin Bishop. Boyds Mills.	Two children find a sparrow trapped in a closed store (New Zealand).
Foreman, Michael. 2009. *A Child's Garden: A Story of Hope*. Candlewick.	A boy in a war-torn country is separated by a fence from the land he loves (England).

Figure 16.2 Global Literature Used in Literature Circles

The tapes of the literature discussions were transcribed, and the five of us met for intensive data analysis. We initially read through the transcripts, making notes of our observations and considering the professional literature on intercultural understanding. Based on this initial analysis, we engaged in constant comparative analysis (Strauss and Corbin 1998) to group the themes and topics that had been identified into categories. These categories were tried out on three transcripts of different books and age levels to develop a final set of categories that were then used to code all of the transcripts. We analyzed them together as well as separately.

Intercultural Understanding as Knowledge, Perspective, and Action

When we began the analysis, our expectation was that we would identify a set of perspectives and attitudes that create intercultural understanding. Our analysis, however, quickly revealed that students need some knowledge about the world and specific cultures and events. We were impressed with the comments of students, but even more so with the ways in which they talked with each other. As we thought about the chaos of their talk and disregard for each other during our first year, we realized that intercultural understanding goes beyond perspective and knowledge to action. In this case, because we were examining literature discussion transcripts, that action was evident in how students interacted with each other.

This chapter is organized around intercultural understanding as knowledge, perspective, and action with examples from the student talk. The subcategories that we identified reflect our particular students and sociocultural context. As teachers, we need to know what this talk sounds and looks like to be able to evaluate children's intercultural understandings and to design instruction that will encourage their continued growth as intercultural learners. There is no endpoint in intercultural understanding, since it is an orientation to thinking about the world that continues to develop throughout a person's lifetime and across different contexts. (See Figure 16.3.)

Intercultural Understanding as Knowledge

Intercultural understanding as knowledge focuses on knowledge about the world and how it works, including people, events, places, issues, and societal systems. Although perspectives receive the most emphasis in intercultural understanding, some knowledge about the world is necessary for students to talk with each other, make connections

INTERCULTURAL UNDERSTANDING AS KNOWLEDGE	
(knowledge about the world and how the world works, including people, events, places, issues, and societal systems)	
Global Knowledge	global-to-global, global-to-local, or local-to-global connections; historical context of knowledge
Cultural Awareness	awareness of societal norms, understandings of language learning processes, values of kid culture
Conceptual Understanding	symbolic thinking, theme statements
INTERCULTURAL UNDERSTANDING AS PERSPECTIVE	
(values and attitudes that students bring as part of their orientation or world view to the discussion)	
Anticipation of Complexity	explore multiple explanations, examine interaction of multiple factors, recognition of connection and difference, exploration of more than one answer or interpretation
Need to Understand a Situation	clarify details, seek to understand by investigating and questioning, struggle to understand, testing understanding against experience, explore multiple reasons for an action
Challenging the Ordinary	recognize the need for change, resistance to stereotypes, questioning popular beliefs, noticing a difference without judgment
Capacity to Empathize with Others	empathize with characters, authors, peers, or adults; work to understand the why of a person's actions; use of personal experience to connect with a character; stepping into a character's view
INTERCULTURAL UNDERSTANDING AS ACTION	
(the ways in which students talk to and interact with one another in daily life)	
Willingness to Reconsider	listening to the perspectives of others, considering other's views, changing your interpretations, collaboratively thinking with others

Figure 16.3 **Intercultural Understanding as Knowledge, Perspective, and Action**

across contexts, and develop deep understandings from literature.

Global educators from the field of social studies have identified what they consider the content of global understanding, often citing two main sources. Kniep (1986) identifies content as including studies of universal human values; economic, political, ecological, and technological systems; global issues and problems; and global history. Hanvey (2004) includes knowledge of current world conditions and events; the diverse values, ideas, and practices of global cultures; the dynamics of global systems; and alternatives to the ways that the world currently works. Case (1991) synthesized various sources to suggest that a substantive dimension to a global perspective includes universal and cultural values and practices; global interconnections; present worldwide concerns and conditions; origins and past patterns of worldwide affairs; and alternative future directions of worldwide affairs.

In our analysis of children's talk across grade levels, the major areas of knowledge that we noted were global knowledge of events, practices, and history; cultural awareness of societal norms and practices; and conceptual understandings. Mateo, a kindergarten child, talked about the importance of learning about the world, saying, "It makes the world a little more important when you know more, and it gets more and more important."

Global knowledge includes instances where children worked to understand an event or character by using their knowledge of current or past events and cultures to make connections across cultures. Children made *global-to-global connections* when they connected one culture to another, as when Connor, a fifth grader, connected the building of fences to separate people in a current war in Eastern Europe with the Holocaust as the group struggled to understand the role of the fence in *A Child's Garden* (Foreman 2009). In discussing *The Composition* (Skarmeta 1998), Joey connected the book's portrayal of a dictator in Chile with Castro in Cuba, saying, "Dictators are violent, and if you want to stay alive, you actually have to listen to a dictator sometimes."

Global-to-local connections involved children connecting a global event with their own context, as when the fifth graders discussing *A Child's Garden* linked the need for presidents of warring countries to meet and negotiate a peace treaty with their own need to have a peace picnic with the fourth-grade class to resolve a basketball controversy. Maria, a third grader, connected Afghanistan and the United States, saying, "It's like we live on the nice side where people aren't allowed to come and do war, but they're on the side having the war."

Knowledge as **cultural awareness** occurred in several kinds of talk. One was *awareness of societal norms,* such as when kindergartners talked about the biracial child in *You Be Me, I'll Be You* (Mandelbaum 1990) and made a connection to societal values related to skin color. Michael commented, "Because if you don't like other people's skin color, they will be mad or sad." The children were aware of societal norms around skin color and how those norms affect feelings.

Another type of cultural awareness was *language learning*. Many students came from families for whom Spanish was a first language, so they had personal experiences with learning a second language. They had also experienced going to Mexico and being teased when they could not speak their heritage language fluently. Third graders used this knowledge in discussing *Cooper's Lesson* (Shin 2004) in which a Korean American boy attempts to learn his heritage language of Korean. Anthony commented, "People want to say something, but it won't come out like, like you stutter and you can't say it." Ysa added, "Yeah, other people speak Korean, and they're trying to make fun of you because you can't speak Korean. And when he actually speaks it, it doesn't come out right."

Cultural awareness was also present in children's talk about a generational culture, *kid culture*, which they shared with each other, not adults. In discussing *Pedrito's Day* (Garay 1997), kindergartners used that knowledge to explain why Pedrito stopped to play marbles, saying, "The older boys invited Pedrito to play with them." JJ added, "The older boys caused the little boy peace when the big boys asked him to play." The children made it clear that they did not think Pedrito was neglecting his duty when he stopped to play, because an older child asking a younger child to play took precedence over anything else.

We also noted that global knowledge grew out of books and life experiences to enable children to reach a deep level of **conceptual understanding** of values and beliefs. Sometimes children's discussions moved to *symbolic thinking* about those values, such as when fifth graders talked about *A Child's Garden* in which a vine covers the fence separating the two communities. Zach said, "The vine kind of symbolized hope for everybody in that town, not only people inside the fence but those who were outside of the fence." Stanley added, "It can also symbolize bringing people together, working together because the two vines grow together. I think it means no matter how hard things get, never lose hope." Other times, the conceptual thinking was obvious in *theme statements*, such as when first graders discussed *You Be Me, I'll Be You*. Isaac said that "the author was trying to tell us that nobody's perfect." He was worried that the biracial child didn't think she was good because her skin color was not like her mother's or her father's but noted that she discovers that "we are fine as we are."

Older students have greater and more detailed sources of global knowledge to draw upon, but these examples show the ways in which young children use knowledge about the world and cultures to explore cross-cultural connections. This knowledge allowed them to work at figuring out the reasons that characters might engage in particular practices or hold certain beliefs—to explore the "why" behind actions instead of considering them strange or weird. Global knowledge facilitated the making of connections across cultures to identify shared values and practices and to feel a sense of connection, despite differences, at a human level.

Intercultural Understanding as Perspective

Many scholars have identified the values and attitudes that they consider significant in determining what people notice in the world and how they think about those observations, particularly whether they are accepting and respectful of diversity. These values and attitudes are often seen as an orientation that the individual brings to interactions and determines the point of view or lens through which to view experiences and events (Sleeter 1991). Fennes and Hapgood (1977) argue that this orientation can range from an ethnocentric view based in a narrow, self-absorbed, and judgmental perspective to an open-minded view from which to make sense of the world. These attitudes are not pieces of information about the world or skills that students need to do or practice, but a lens that determines what students notice and accept and whether they formulate opinions based on open-minded inquiry or unexamined biased assumptions (Case 1991).

Asia Society and EdSteps (Mansilla and Jackson 2011) developed a global competence matrix to evaluate the capacity and disposition of students to understand and act on issues of global significance. The four areas that they identify combine perspectives and skills to include investigating the world beyond students' immediate environment, recognizing their own and others' perspectives, communicating ideas effectively to diverse audiences, and translating their ideas into appropriate actions to improve conditions.

Open-mindedness, the willingness to assess our views and thoughtfully consider alternative positions and values, is clearly at the heart of an intercultural orientation. We examined children's talk to identify perspectives that seemed essential to their becoming more open-minded and noted children's inclination to anticipate and embrace complexity instead of searching for a simple single answer, their perseverance in trying to understand a situation instead of immediately judging from their experiences, their willingness to challenge the ordinary and status quo as the way things should be, and their capacity to empathize with others. These perspectives came together to create an open-mindedness that permeated children's willingness to suspend judgment and to consider diverse ways of thinking and living in the world, particularly when they chose not to impose their cultural beliefs and practices as the norm against which to judge other cultures.

The **anticipation of complexity** was evident when children looked beyond simple explanations for complex issues and recognized that multiple factors interact within a situation. One way they recognized complexity was to *explore multiple explanations for or perspectives on* a situation. Third graders were discussing *To Be a Kid* (Ajmera and Ivanko 2000), a global book with photographs of things that kids do around the world, which led them to the issue of parents trusting their children. They were quite vocal about their rights as children and resentful of adult restrictions, so we were surprised to hear them consider multiple explanations for their parents' behaviors. Leilany said, "You've got to trust us to give us freedom" and that led the group to explore different reasons for their parents setting up restrictions. She pointed out, "If you were to go out with another adult that you know but your parents don't know, your parents would have to know that person for a really long time to have trust in that person. Your kid is very important to an adult, because that's your daughter or son, but you have to have a little bit of trust in that person that is your child." Ysa added, "It's mostly about protection because your mom doesn't want you to get kidnapped."

Kyle provided another example: "When I go to California, we go outside with my friends, and they trust us because we play football and we are near a huge wall that is nice and glassy." This discussion showed their willingness to *examine the interaction of multiple factors* and their *exploration of more than one answer or interpretation* of a situation. In particular, they explored the differences between parents wanting to both protect and control them as well as parents not remembering what it's like to be frustrated as a child and to want some freedom.

The *simultaneous recognition of connection and difference* was another way children anticipated complexity. It's much easier to focus on universals across all people, but that can lead to color blindness and an emphasis on harmony at the expense of recognizing what makes each person unique. On the other hand, a focus on difference at the expense of connection can lead to seeing difference as a problem, as what separates and divides us from others or makes others "weird" or "exotic." To move between connection and difference at the same time is a more complex perspective. Fifth graders engaged in this talk as they explored *One World, One Day* (Kerley 2009), a nonfiction book that goes across one day in the lives of children around the world. Joey commented that "kids across the world have a lot of the same duties for work and we have to do our daily chores, but there are differences in the things you do as work." Stanley replied, "But no matter what culture you are, you could still find a day where you have fun and can be with your friends, just in different ways." Connor said, "It's your day," to which Stanley added, "Yeah, and no one can ruin it." Their talk inferred that adults are the ones who typically try to ruin the day for kids, a connection that was probably not intended by the author. Seth, a first grader talking about this book, commented, "All the places have different things, but all the places have a lot of things the same too."

A second major perspective in children's talk was their **need to understand a situation**. They worked hard to *clarify details* and to *seek to understand a situation by investigating and questioning*. First graders' discussion of *A Child's Garden* included a search to understand why the guards cut down the vines and would not allow them to grow. They considered many possibilities, including a historical connection between the book and the civil rights movement in the United States when fences and laws kept people apart because of the color of their skin. Nahid commented, "The guards were trying to cut down the vines like they don't want the city to be pretty or to grow. Why couldn't they let the vines grow?" Her comment took them back into the book to keep investigating and considering why the guards were so opposed to vines growing on the fence and why the fence had been built to separate people in the first place.

Children also worked to understand a situation by *testing their understanding against experience*. After reading *Nasreen's Secret School* (Winter 2009), third graders were puzzled by why girls in Afghanistan were not allowed to go to school, whereas boys were. Kyle commented on one possible reason: "Some people say that boys are stronger than girls. I think the soldiers were thinking girls won't defend themselves and the boys could, so they didn't let the girls go to school." María agreed that the soldiers were treating girls like babies, but she went on to point out, "You know, girls can be powerful like Ysa. She's a girl and she's really strong and can defend herself really easy—like she doesn't have to give up strong, she can just do it." The other children agreed because they were quite familiar with Ysa's ability to control her classmates, male or female, and so felt that this reason was not valid as an explanation, and continued searching. They explored *multiple reasons for the actions* of the soldiers, including protecting the girls, believing that boys deserve more, and not wanting girls to learn so they could control them.

A third major perspective was **challenging the ordinary**, children's willingness to not just accept the ways things are normally done—the status quo—as the way things need to continue to be done. Challenging the ordinary can begin with awareness that your perspective is not the norm, as occurred when first graders discussed *One World,*

One Day. Carah pointed out that "our language seems pretty normal and the Chinese language and Spanish language seem different to us, but our language sounds weird to them." Carah's willingness to not impose her culture as the superior one is particularly striking given the English-Only legislation in our state.

Challenging the ordinary included their *recognition of the need for change*. In third graders' discussion of how parents view kids in *To Be a Kid*, Leilany pointed out that "parents might see kids as a different point of view, but their childhood might have been different from our childhood." She went on to argue that things have changed since adults were children, but they don't recognize that and let their children "have some kind of freedom, and it gets kids frustrated about their parents trying to control them." María added, "It's kind of hard to be a kid because sometimes you don't get to do stuff that you want to do." She and other children gave examples of unfair situations where parents made decisions that gave freedom to other members of the family but did not recognize their rights. They provided possible explanations for parents' behaviors, including their inability to remember what they had felt as children, but also argued for the need for change in those perspectives.

Challenging the ordinary includes *resistance to stereotypes and questioning popular beliefs* instead of going along with common societal practices or views. When first graders talked about the biracial child in *You Be Me, I'll Be You*, they made a connection to members of their family who are treated differently because of skin color. Danny talked about his family, saying, "My family is Mexican, and my aunt is the only one that's darker in my family, and people aren't nice to her. There's nothing bad with your skin." Their talk indicated their questioning of discrimination related to skin color. They loved their family members and did not want them treated differently. This resistance to stereotypes also involved the absence of "we-they" dualisms, condescending views toward people in developing countries, and emphasis on exotic features of a situation or group of people—comments that marginalize and dehumanize.

Children were able to *notice difference without making a judgment* that compared those differences with societal norms. As fifth graders discussed *One World, One Day,* they talked about children being asked to do chores by adults. They talked about their chores as "taking out trash and cleaning the bathroom," whereas in countries like Sudan, children are "milking cows and given guns and told to keep their families safe." Joey commented in a nonjudgmental way, "They have their own responsibilities to do for their family, and we have our chores to do."

A fourth perspective was **the capacity to empathize with others**, the willingness to place themselves in the role or situation of others and to imagine issues from others' perspectives. Sometimes children expressed *empathy for the characters, author, peers, or adults* in their lives. Kindergartners empathized with the feelings of the main character of *You Be Me, I'll Be You* as they tried to figure out why Anna did not want people to look at her, with Lily saying, "She thinks her face and her hair look ugly, but she changed her mind." We also found talk where children *stepped into a character's role* and talked as that person and where children drew on personal experiences to connect to a character's feelings and actions.

Children explored empathy as they worked to *understand the why of a person's actions*. In discussing *The Composition* (Skarmeta 1998) about a boy in Chile who has to hide his family's activities from the government, fifth graders struggled to understand why the boy's parents were not more open with him about their beliefs and activities. Connor said he thought "his parents were kind of putting him down because they said that children are just children and can't take a stand." Zach pointed out that "they were protecting him and didn't want him to get involved." Joey agreed, adding, "They keep quiet because they don't want him to get scared and because everyone was scared when Daniel's father was taken away. They just want to protect him." Stanley provided another possibility, saying, "I would disagree with Joey because they were telling him that he is just a kid and doesn't know if he's against the government or not." But, Connor countered, "Most kids are not involved with the government until they are older, so the parents didn't realize that he had an opinion." Their concern with why the character's parents behaved in a particular way reflected not only empathy but willingness to consider multiple perspectives even though their first inclination was to view these parents as another example of adults not trusting kids.

Students can learn more about global cultures and peoples, gaining *knowledge about* without necessarily gaining *understanding of*. Both are important to an intercultural perspective but play different roles in reaching toward an open-minded view of the world. Understanding does not necessarily mean acceptance of particular views or practices as your own, but does involve the willingness to suspend judgment based on your own values and beliefs to understand another person's reasons for engaging in those practices.

One aspect of perspective that we did not consider in this analysis is the recent work by Choo (2013) on hospitable imagination and whether students were able to fully be open to the other without limits in order to imagine their experiences and viewpoints.

We did see evidence that students were developing a sense of responsibility as readers and bringing a critical lens to their reading, but Choo pushes this further to perceiving the world through the other's eyes, not our own. We saw glimpses of the fifth graders moving beyond self to otherness to responsibly engage with the other, but this was not a characteristic of their thinking or even our own.

Intercultural Understanding as Action

If intercultural understanding has become deeply embedded within a person's view of the world, this understanding goes beyond knowledge and perspective to action. Since we were examining transcripts of literature discussions, evidence of action was not visible except in the ways students interacted with each other. We had vivid memories of our initial literature discussions where students either took turns or talked on top of each other. As we analyzed the transcripts, we were impressed with the shift in how students listened to and built from each other, especially the fifth graders who had been in the school for the four years of our inquiry.

In particular, students were **willing to reconsider** their views. Sometimes their talk indicated their willingness to *listen to the perspectives of others,* which is what occurred when first graders were discussing *One World, One Day.* Seth and several other children shared personal connections to a page that showed a boy interacting with his family. Isaac shared next and started his comment with, "I agree with Nahid, Danny, and Seth because I watch TV with my sister and brother" and then went on to share his own personal experience, making it clear that he had listened carefully to the sharing about family from the other students.

Listening to the perspectives of others can cause one to *consider others' views* and even *change one's interpretation.* In discussing *Amelia's Road* (Altman 1993), the story of a migrant child who is tired of moving with the crops from place to place, fifth grader Connor said, "I think that the dad liked his crops more than his daughter." Alyssa agreed with him, saying, "I know—that's so sad," and Stanley added, "He likes money more than his daughter." Connor then offered a different interpretation of the father's behavior, saying, "Yeah, I wonder if it's because he wants to feed the family or if it's for money." Joey suggested, "It might be both." What struck us about this exchange was the way in which the fifth graders listened to each other and built from what others were saying in addition to changing their interpretations through their talk.

This willingness to *think collaboratively with others* was also evident when third graders discussed *A Child's Garden* (Foreman 2009). Kyle said that he believed that "they need to stop all these wars" and the "leader of the group should make more peace, because killing people just makes them madder." Leilany suggested that "every leader should all go together and have a peace treaty" and went on to describe people "getting together to sign a contract saying they won't fight no more." Jason disagreed, saying, "You know how people get mad at each other and they really want to beat each other up?" Kyle argued, "They could talk it out." But Jason said, "Not really. Like if they talk it out, they'll just keep fighting and fighting. Like pretend it was us when we had the basketball war with fourth grade. They tried to talk it out to us and we were so mad, and then we started battling each other." Leilany countered by pointing out that another person could help the two sides by getting them together and saying, "This person has a good idea and that person has a good idea, and so they can see what their issues are with each other and they have a chance to be with each other and learn why each other is always mad."

"They need to talk it out although you might have to cuff the soldiers together to get them to sit and talk and not hurt each other," added Kyle. Their collaborative talk involved listening to each other's perspectives and considering their views instead of quickly settling into a particular point of view or students expressing opinions without listening to each other.

Final Reflections

Our initial focus around intercultural understanding was on students' perspectives and orientations, but children's talk indicated the significance of knowledge and peer relationships interacting with perspectives. In addition, we noted that the fifth-grade students, who had been part of the global inquiry curriculum for four years, demonstrated sophisticated intercultural knowledge, perspectives, and action. In addition, we identified types of emerging intercultural knowledge, perspectives, and action among young children.

This analysis led us to a more complex definition of intercultural understanding that involves the interweaving of global knowledge, critical perspectives, and collaborative action. Students do need knowledge about local and global events, social norms, their own identities, and global cultures as a base from which to consider critical perspectives and connections. They also need critical perspectives as reflected in their willingness to question the status quo and not accept current practice as "just the way the world is." Their perspectives involve anticipating complexity, struggling to understand the reasons for a particular action or situation, challenging stereotypes and popular beliefs, valuing difference as a resource, and working to understand the ways in which others think and act. Finally, their intercultural understanding goes beyond talk to action, particularly in how they relate to others in their classrooms and choose to take action in the world. The ways in which they do or do not work with peers and teachers to listen to alternative perspectives, reconsider their own views, and collaboratively think with others indicates whether interculturalism has become internalized into their ways of thinking and acting in the world.

Knowledge without perspective can lead to little or no change in students' actions or thinking as they notice inequity but do not challenge that inequity. Perspective without knowledge means that students may be open-minded without understanding the complex factors that are the root causes of global issues and so are unable to take action thoughtfully. Action indicates whether students are actually living their understandings in how they interact in their daily lives.

These categories of intercultural understandings provide the basis for developing evaluation measures to use in our work with global inquiry. They provide a way for teachers to listen to and evaluate children's talk in global engagements and to know what they are listening for related to intercultural understanding. The insights teachers can gain about students and the curriculum serve as the basis for evaluation measures and for identifying areas that need further development in work on global inquiry.

In-depth insights into intercultural understanding also provide a way to evaluate our instructional strategies around global literature. We recognize the danger of using strategies that are tangential, or even in opposition, to the goals of global education, through focusing on "we-they" dualisms or superficial features of cultural lifestyles that reinforce stereotypes. Simply having students read more about the world can lead to stereotypes and negatively influence the development of intercultural understandings. Looking at students' talk within an engagement around these categories provides a way to evaluate our teaching. Our goal is transformation, not reification, of the worldviews of students and of ourselves.

Recommended Books That Invite Global Perspectives

Ajmera, Maya, and John Ivanko. 2000. *To Be a Kid.* **Watertown, MA: Charlesbridge.**

Large, colorful photographs celebrate kids as they play and learn, spend time with family and friends, and discover their environment and world. Two to three photographs of children from different parts of the world are depicted on each page for the various activities. Supported by the Global Fund for Children.

Foreman, Michael. 2009. *A Child's Garden: A Story of Hope.* **Somerville, MA: Candlewick.**

A young boy's home and world is reduced to rubble with a barbed-wire fence that separates him from flowing streams and green hills, until he sees a tiny green sprout that holds the promise of transforming his bleak landscape. This picturebook by a British author is set in an unnamed war-torn country.

Garay, Luis. 1997. *Pedrito's Day.* **New York: Orchard.**

Pedrito, a young shoeshine boy in Nicaragua, longs for the day when he has enough money for a bicycle. When he loses his *tia's* money after stopping to play with a group of boys, he faces a difficult decision of whether to tell a lie or replace the money from his own savings.

Skarmeta, Antonio. 2003. *The Composition.* **Illus. Alfonso Ruano. Toronto, ON: Groundwood.**

Pedro faces a difficult decision when an army captain asks children to write a composition on what their family does at night in order to win a highly coveted soccer ball. Set during a time of dictatorship in Chile, his decision has life-and-death consequences for his family.

Winter, Jeanette. 2009. *Nasreen's Secret School*. New York: Simon and Schuster.

A young girl has not spoken a word since her parents disappeared after being detained by the Taliban in Afghanistan. In despair, her grandmother risks everything to enroll Nasreen in a secret school for girls where she discovers the life-changing power of literacy and love.

References

Bennett, Milton. 2004. "Becoming Interculturally Competent." In *Toward Multiculturalism: A Reader in Multicultural Education,* ed. James Wurzel. Newton, MA: Intercultural Resource Corporation.

Byram, Michael. 1997. *Teaching and Assessing Intercultural Communicative Competence.* Bristol, PA: Multilingual Matters.

Case, Robert. 1991. "Key Elements of a Global Perspective." *Social Education* 57 (6): 318–325.

Choo, Suzanne. 2013. *Reading the World, the Globe, and the Cosmos.* New York: Peter Lang.

Cushner, Kenneth. 2015. "Development and Assessment of Intercultural Competence." In *The Sage Handbook of Research in International Education,* ed. Mary Hayden, Jack Levy and Jeff Thompson. Thousand Oaks, CA: Sage.

Fennes, Helmut, and Karen Hapgood. 1997. *Intercultural Learning in the Classroom.* London: Cassell.

Fleck, Ludwick. 1935. *The Genesis and Development of a Scientific Fact.* Chicago, IL: University of Chicago Press.

Hanvey, Robert G. 2004. *An Attainable Global Perspective.* New York: The American Forum for Global Education.

Hoopes, David. 1979. "Intercultural Communication Concepts and the Psychology of Intercultural Experience." In *Multicultural Education,* ed. Margaret Pusch. Chicago, IL: Intercultural Press.

Kniep, Willard. 1986. "Defining a Global Education by Its Content." *Social Education* 50 (6): 437-446.

Kramsch, Claire. 2011. "The Symbolic Dimensions of the Intercultural." *Language Teaching* 44 (3): 354–367.

Mansilla, Virginia, and Anthony Jackson. 2011. *Educating for Global Competence.* New York: Asia Society.

Merryfield, Merry. 2002. "What a Difference a Global Education Can Make." *Educational Leadership* 60 (2): 18–21.

Oxfam. 2006. *Education for Global Citizenship*. Oxford, UK: Oxfam.

Short, Kathy G. 2009. "Critically Reading the Word and the World: Building Intercultural Understanding Through Literature." *Bookbird* 47 (2): 1–10.

Sleeter, Christine. 1991. *Empowerment Through Multicultural Education*. Albany, NY: SUNY Press.

Strauss, Anselm, and Juliet Corbin. 1998. *Basics of Qualitative Research*. 2nd ed. Thousand Oaks, CA: Sage.

Children's Books Cited

Ada, Alma Flor. 2002. *I Love Saturdays y domingos*. Illus. Elivia Savadier. New York: Atheneum.

Ajmera, Maya, and John Ivanko. 2000. *To Be a Kid*. Watertown, MA: Charlesbridge.

Altman, Linda Jacobs. 1993. *Amelia's Road*. Illus. Enrique Sanchez. New York: Lee and Low Books.

Brown, Peter. 2009. *The Curious Garden*. Boston: Little Brown.

Cowley, Joy. 1999. *The Video Shop Sparrow*. Illus. Gavin Bishop. Honesdale, PA: Boyds Mills.

Foreman, Michael. 2009. *A Child's Garden: A Story of Hope*. Somerville, MA: Candlewick.

Garay, Luis. 1997. *Pedrito's Day*. New York: Orchard.

Kerley, Barbara. 2009. *One World, One Day*. Washington, DC: National Geographic.

Mandelbaum, Pili. 1990. *You Be Me, I'll Be You*. La Jolla, CA: Kane/Miller.

McDonald, Megan. 1996. *My House Has Stars*. Illus. Peter Catalanotto. New York: Orchard.

Shin, Sun Yung. 2004. *Cooper's Lesson*. Illus. Kim Cogan. San Francisco, CA: Children's Book Press.

Skarmeta, Antonio. 2003. *The Composition*. Illus. Alfonso Ruano. Toronto, ON: Groundwood.

Williams, Karen Lynn. 1990. *Galimoto*. Illus. Catherine Stock. New York: Lothrop.

Winter, Jeanette. 2009. *Nasreen's Secret School*. New York: Simon and Schuster.

Afterword

Moving Forward

The work we have shared in this book grows out of years of dialogue with each other and engagements with students that range from exciting to frustrating, depending on the day. We constantly reconsider our approaches, knowing we will continue to outgrow our current understandings and thus need to reframe our beliefs and their enactment in practice. We give ourselves permission to be inquirers engaged in a continuous cycle of action, observation, and reflection.

The work of Choo (2013) around nationalistic, world, global, and cosmopolitan approaches to teaching literature has challenged us to consider where our work and framework fits within this larger picture. Her discussions focus on the integration of world literature into high school classrooms, but her critique of these approaches forced us to reflect on our work in K–8 classrooms through a different lens.

Nationalistic approaches focus on books commonly referred to as "the canon," books considered classics within Western traditions that are used in many high school literature courses (Choo 2013). A nationalistic emphasis is also found in elementary basal anthologies and in programs such as Junior Great Books. These approaches ignore global connections and work against intercultural understanding because of their isolationism and ethnocentricism when only Western books are used in schools.

World approaches provide a sampling of representative books from around the globe—an anthology of readings—within a focus on universals across cultures. The emphasis is on breadth rather than depth, and some cultures and traditions are considered "better" than others. Both nationalistic and world approaches are problematic, because students read from within a Western perspective as the norm, with a focus on assumed universals across cultures.

In elementary classrooms, the world approach can often be seen in experiences where teachers or librarians put together a set of global books and each week or month read a book from a different country. The book is often accompanied by a cultural celebration or activity or an International Day with booths of activities and costumes for each country. Many of us are teacher educators and have realized that our courses on global literature fall into this approach when we organize the course syllabi around regions of the world. The problem with a world approach is that this brief touch on a succession of countries falls into the tourist trap of gaining superficial information, resulting in stereotypes and generalizations about global cultures. Although many of us started with this superficial introduction to many countries, our work with the framework for a curriculum that is intercultural was motivated by our desire to move beyond a world approach.

Global approaches focus on each person as a member of an interconnected global community—connected to others through global citizenship, a shared humanity that comes first—followed by other significant identities, such as national ones (Choo 2013). Whereas a world approach goes from part to whole, a global approach moves from whole to part, recognizing that first and foremost we are citizens of the human race and within that global citizenship have multiple points of reference and identity.

A global approach includes an understanding of humanity as both the universal and the particular, emphasizing what connects us as human beings as well as what makes each of us unique. This focus on both the particular and the universal has been at the heart of our work in classrooms. We recognize that if we focus only on the universal, on the qualities and needs we share as human beings, we fail to recognize the uniqueness that makes each cultural community and person distinctive and adds to the cultural richness of our world. On the other hand, if we focus only on the particular, we are in danger of exoticizing a culture as strange or weird, instead of seeing difference as resource (Ruiz 1984).

A global approach is interdisciplinary with an emphasis on developing the capacity of learners to think critically about cultural representations within texts and to consider the multilayered and multidimensional complexities of the world. The majority of our work in this book fits within a global approach as we explore the different ways in which such an approach can play out in classrooms and find spaces for global literature within mandates and standards. Our teaching of global literature in teacher education has also shifted to raising issues of availability, access, authorship, and authenticity across cultures and to intercultural understanding through literature as a critical perspective and social responsibility—instead of a survey of children's books from around the world.

Although a global approach has characterized our work with curriculum and global literature, cosmopolitanism has challenged us to dig deeper into how we suspend our beliefs and enter into dialogue with an open mind. Rizvi (2009) argues that the focus shifts to citizenship as an orientation, rather than membership to a physical place in the world. This orientation involves a willingness to engage the other, to imaginatively enter into their world, to focus on difference over uniformity, and to value diversity within sameness.

The purpose of engaging with literature through a cosmopolitan orientation is to develop a responsibility to the other through narrative imagination, allowing us to perceive the world through their eyes—not ours. We read to gain a sense of obligation and responsibility to others and to become more conscious of and committed to others, rather than to personally connect to the text. Reading for pleasure is no longer the focus of attention as we read; instead we read to move beyond self to otherness and for responsible engagement to the other.

Choo (2013) argues that this orientation is one of "hospitable imagination" in which we are fully open to the other without putting limits on our willingness to imagine their experiences and ways of thinking. The work that we share in this book is a step toward this orientation of openness, but we are still exploring what it means in practice to take on the perspective of the other without limits and to fully invite the other into our imaginations.

We are excited about the challenge of pursuing these ideas as we continue working in classrooms with children and teachers. Viewing intercultural understanding as an orientation rather than a field of study supports a stance of becoming, of always being engaged as learners in challenging our current understandings of global literature, interculturalism, and curriculum.

We engage in this work because we believe that children are our future, but only if we influence their present. Children's engagements with literature have the potential to transform their worldviews through understanding their current lives *and* imagining beyond themselves. Children do need to find their lives reflected in books, but if what they read only mirrors their views of the world, they cannot envision alternative ways of thinking and being. These experiences need to be embedded within a curriculum that is intercultural, or the potential to challenge readers to critically confront issues of power and responsibility in the world is diminished or lost. A curriculum and literature that are intercultural offer all of us, educators and students, the potential for enriching and transforming our lives and views of the world.

References

Choo, Suzanne. 2013. *Reading the World, the Globe, and the Cosmos*. New York: Peter Lang.

Rizvi, Fazal. 2009. "Global Mobility and the Challenges of Educational Research and Policy." *Yearbook of the National Society for the Study of Education* 108 (2): 268–289.

Ruiz, Richard. 1984. "Orientations in Language Planning." *NABE Journal* 8 (2): 15–34.

Appendix A

Award Lists and Resources for Locating Global Literature

Américas Award

http://claspprograms.org/pages/detail/37/Amricas-Award

This award annually names two winning titles and a list of recommended titles as high-quality children's and young adult literature that portray Latin America, the Caribbean, or Latinos in the United States. Given by CLASP, Centers for Latin American Studies Programs.

Children's Africana Book Award

http://africaaccessreview.org/

Africa Access Review recognizes authors and illustrators of K–12 books about Africa each year. The award chooses books in two categories: Young Children and Older Readers. A list of all award winners and honor books is available.

Hans Christian Andersen Award

http://ibby.org/

The International Board on Books for Young Readers (IBBY) sponsors the Hans Christian Andersen Award, the highest international award for an author or illustrator whose complete works have made a lasting contribution to children's literature. A list of award winners and nominees of outstanding authors and illustrators from around the world is available.

Jane Addams Children's Book Award

www.janeaddamspeace.org/jacba/

This annual award is given to children's books that promote the cause of peace, social justice, world community, and the equality of all sexes and races.

Middle East Book Award

www.meoc.us/meoc/book-awards

The Middle East Outreach Council gives an annual award that recognizes a picturebook, youth literature, and youth nonfiction about cultures of the Middle East, including the Arab world, Israel, Iran, Turkey, and Afghanistan. This award is affiliated with the Middle East Studies Association.

Mildred L. Batchelder Award

www.ala.org/alsc/awardsgrants/bookmedia/batchelderaward

The Batchelder Award is given to the most outstanding children's book originally published in a language other than English in a country other than the United States, and subsequently translated into English for publication in the United States. Award and honor books, including past winners, are included on the American Library Association website.

Notable Books for a Global Society

www.clrsig.org/nbgs_books.php

The Children's Literature and Reading Special Interest Group of the International Literacy Association (ILA) annually selects twenty-five outstanding K–12 trade books that enhance student understanding of people and cultures throughout the world. Current and past NBGS award book lists are available on the site.

Notable Social Studies Trade Books for Young People

www.socialstudies.org/notable

Selected by the National Council of Social Studies and the Children's Book Council, this K–8 bibliography highlights books that emphasize human relations and are sensitive to a diversity of groups and cultural experiences.

South Asia Book Award

http://southasiabookaward.org/

This annual award goes to two children's or young adult books about South Asia or South Asians in the diaspora from the South Asia National Outreach Consortium.

USSBY Outstanding International Books

www.usbby.org/

This award, sponsored by the United States Board on Books for Young People, is given to the best international books published in a country other than the United States and released in the United States during a calendar year. Books are separated into four age groups from pre-K to grade twelve.

Worlds of Words

http://wowlit.org/

This website has a searchable database of global children's and adolescent literature available in the United States. In addition, it has a blog, vignettes from classrooms that are using global and multicultural literature, book dialogues, and critical book reviews.

Appendix B

Global Resources for Teachers and Children

Asia Society

http://asiasociety.org/education

The Asia Society promotes understanding and partnerships between Asia and the United States. This educators' site provides resources on global competence and how-to guides related to global education, reports, blogs, plus a newsletter of resources.

Barefoot World Atlas

www.barefootbooks.com

In this app of an interactive three-dimensional globe, children can explore the regions and countries of the world, discovering hundreds of fascinating features. The music changes as children travel from region to region, and children can play a variety of puzzles to test their knowledge of facts and figures.

Duolingo

https://www.duolingo.com/

Students can learn more than twenty-one languages with this free tool or app. Each lesson includes a variety of speaking, listening, translating, and multiple-choice challenges. Students race against a clock to earn points. In classrooms, teachers can watch their students' progress on a dashboard.

ePals

www.epals.com/#/connections

Classroom teachers and students can connect, communicate, and collaborate with other students around the world through pen-pal letters. Teachers find connections by selecting student age ranges, languages, and average class sizes. Each year ePals challenges schools to solve a real-world problem.

Free Rice

www.freerice.com/

Children play trivia games of vocabulary, math, or chemistry, and for every answer they get right, ten grains of rice are donated to the World Food Program to help end hunger. Schools, classes, and students can play for free, competing against each other.

Google Earth

https://www.google.com/earth/

Teachers and students can explore geography or a community through Google Earth. Teachers can use keyhole markup language (KML) files to directly link to specific spots on Google Earth. In addition, there are many resources and user guides for educators.

International Children's Digital Library

https://itunes.apple.com/us/app/icdl-free-books-for-children/
id363731638?mt=8

This library contains thousands of children's books from more than sixty countries and languages, all available for free. Teachers can create their own bookshelf and find books for ages three to thirteen in many different languages.

Kids Can Make a Difference

http://kidscanmakeadifference.org/

These resources help kids learn about the root causes of hunger and poverty and ways to take action in their communities and world. A program of iEARN (International Education and Resource Network).

Learn Around the World

http://learnaroundtheworld.com/

This site helps learners virtually travel and visit places around the world. Teachers and students determine the direction of the virtual expedition where they can learn content, view video conferences or broadcasts, read trip logs, and view artifacts and photographs.

Primary Source

www.primarysource.org/

Primary Source is for teachers and provides professional development courses and resources on global education. In addition, a range of resource guides and online materials are available.

Reach the World

www.reachtheworld.org/

K–12 students and teachers connect with a volunteer world traveler who is studying and exploring the globe with the goal of developing knowledge, attitudes, values, and thinking skills that will help them be responsible citizens.

Skype

www.skype.com/en/

Children can have a Skype conversation with anyone in the world, including a classroom in a faraway country or an author of global children's or young adult books.

Teaching for Change

www.teachingforchange.org/

This website for teachers and parents focuses on building social justice in classrooms through professional development, online resources, and publications that focus on connections to world issues and encourage taking action as global citizens.

Appendix C

Cultural Authenticity as Author and Reader Responsibility in Children's and Young Adult Literature

This appendix contains questions that readers can ask about the connection of cultural authenticity to both the author's responsibility in creating a text and a reader's responsibility to question his/her responses to that text. Social responsibility is thus positioned in the transaction of the reader and the potential text in the construction of an interpretation of a text.

Cultural Authenticity as Author Responsibility

Cultural authenticity in connection to author responsibility addresses the extent to which a book reflects the core cultural beliefs and values and depicts the accurate details of everyday life and language for a specific cultural group. Given the diversity within any cultural group, there is never one image of life within any group, and so the themes and underlying ideologies are often more significant for analysis. Readers from the culture of a book need to be able to identify and feel affirmed that what they are reading rings true in their lives, and readers from another culture need to be able to identify and learn something of value about cultural similarities and differences. Evaluating authenticity involves considering complex issues, not making a simple yes-or-no decision about a book.

- **Literary qualities**

  How well does the author tell the story? Is it high-quality literature?

- **Origin of book**

  What is the origin of the book? Who was the original publisher, and in what country? Who is the author? Illustrator? Translator? What are their backgrounds?

- **Authorship**

  How do the author's experiences connect to the setting and characters in this book? What are the experiences and/or what is the research on which the book is based? Why might the author have chosen this story to tell?

- **Believability**

  Is this story believable? Could it happen? In what ways does it feel real? Are the characters larger than stereotypes but less than "perfect" heroes?

- **Accuracy of details and authenticity of values**

  What are possible issues of accuracy in the details of the book? What values are at the heart of the book? How do these values connect to the actual lives of people within the culture? Does this book reflect a specific cultural experience, or could it happen anywhere?

- **Perspectives**

  Whose perspectives and experiences are portrayed? Who tells the story? What is the range of insider perspectives?

- **Power relationships**

  Which characters are in roles of power or significance within the book? Who takes action? How is the story resolved? Where does the story go, and how does it get there? Who takes it there? Why?

- **Audience**

  Who is the intended audience? Is the book written for children from that culture or to inform children from other cultural backgrounds about that culture?

- **Relationship to other books**

  How does this book connect with other books about this cultural experience?

Does the collection of books reflect a range of perspectives and experiences within the culture?

- **Response by insiders**
  How have insiders responded to this book?

- **Connections for your readers**
  What are the possible connections for students? Is the book accessible?

For more discussion of these issues, see *Stories Matter: The Complexity of Cultural Authenticity in Children's Literature*, edited by Dana Fox and Kathy G. Short (NCTE 2003).

For reviews that focus on cultural authenticity of books, see

- *WOW Review* (wowlit.org),
- *Kirkus Reviews* (www.kirkusreviews.com),
- *Oyate* (http://oyate.org/) (reviews of books on Native peoples), and
- *Africa Access Review* (http://africaaccessreview.org/).

Cultural Authenticity as Reader Responsibility

Cultural authenticity in connection to reader responsibility addresses links between readers and global literature. Both books and readers embody distinct worldviews of beliefs and values that influence the transaction between a reader and a text. Readers from a background similar to the culture of a book may more readily identify with the situation or character and thus be more "open" to the author's perspective. Because of this cultural match, readers may determine that the text is culturally authentic. Someone who does not share that cultural background may have more difficulty understanding the situation or the reasons a character acts in a particular way, or even deny the authenticity or reality of the situation in the text.

A further consideration of reader responsibility and cultural authenticity is acknowledging that, in their attempt to understand the text, readers may find that attempting to understand the characters or situation is not the same as agreeing with the author or the book, but rather a way of gaining a greater understanding of the world and those within it. A reader's response to a book is complex and based on the juxtaposing contexts of the reader's culture and the culture represented in the author's text.

- **Reading context**

  What is the reader's purpose for reading the book? Who selected the book, and why was it selected? What stance (thoughts and feelings) does the reader take toward the book before reading? In what ways could the political environment or the difference between the time of publication and the time of reading create different stances toward the story?

- **Reader's context**

  What about this book resonates with the reader's own experience? What creates discomfort within the reader? In what ways could the reader's background create a positive or negative response to the book? What actions can the reader take to better understand the book? How can a reader remain open to understanding the book if he or she holds values that conflict with those of the author or the characters within the book?

- **The use of language**

  How does the author tell the story? Is the language accessible? In what ways is language usage similar to or different from the reader's language?

- **Origin of book**

  What is the origin of the book? How does the book's origin relate to the reader's origin? Who is the author? Illustrator? Translator? What are their backgrounds, and how do these relate to the reader's background?

- **Authorship**

  How does the author's telling of a story connect with readers' experiences? What gaps exist between the author and the reader, and what impact might those gaps have on the reader's understanding of, or response to, the text? How do those gaps position the reader?

- **Audience**

  Who is the intended audience of this book? How does the reader relate to this intended audience? Is the book written for children from that culture or to inform children from other cultural backgrounds about that culture?

- **Resonance**

  How does this story relate to the reader's experience or understanding of the world? Does the reader's value system allow him or her to accept or reject the characters or situation in the book? In what ways does the story feel real to the reader? If the story is portraying a specific cultural experience, what do readers learn about that culture?

- **Connecting to characters**

  Are the behaviors of the characters acceptable according to the reader's value system? What values does the reader possess that might make it difficult or easy to relate to the characters?

- **Perspectives**

  Whose perspectives and experiences are portrayed? How do these perspectives relate to the reader's own views? Do readers understand the range of insider perspectives? How can a reader check to see if the story could actually happen?

- **Relationship to other books**

  How does this book connect with other books about this cultural experience? Does the collection of books reflect a range of perspectives and experiences within the culture?

- **Response by insiders**

  How have insiders responded to this book?

- **Connections for your readers**

  What are the possible connections for readers? Is the book accessible? What can readers do when the connection is weak? What happens when the connection is so strong that readers see only their own perspective? How do readers allow authors to speak through their books, especially if the connection is weak or creates conflicting feelings in the reader?

These are just some questions to address with students as readers. To understand an author and/or the culture represented within the story, students should be encouraged to read other books from the same cultural group, region of the world, or country to build their knowledge. Remember that the book is just one of a number of possible stories from a particular place. The TED Talk "The Danger of a Single Story," by Chimamanda Adichie, which can be found at the following URL, is one way to start discussions with older readers on reader responsibility: https://www.ted.com/talks/chimamanda_adichie_the_danger_of_a_single_story.

Appendix D

Dialogue Strategies

Cultural X-Rays (Short 2009)

Cultural x-rays help students recognize their many cultural identities, develop understandings of culture, and raise awareness of how and why culture matters to them.

Materials

- Cultural x-ray (outline of a body with a large heart inside)
- Crayons or colored pencils
- Children's literature in which characters explore their cultural identities, particularly books where characters explore multiple identities

Procedures

- After reading and discussing picturebooks in which the characters explore their cultural identities, discuss the aspects of culture that influence each character's life and thought. You may want to create cultural x-rays for specific characters from these books that are particularly engaging for children.
- Each student creates a personal cultural x-ray highlighting what is outside as well as inside his or her cultural being. Students respond to these questions: What am I? What is important to me? What do I look like?

- o On the outside, students create labels to describe the behavior, appearance, and aspects of their identities that others can observe or easily determine (age, family, sex, language, religion, family composition, places they have lived).

- o On the heart shape inside the x-ray, students place the values and beliefs they hold in their hearts that may not be evident to others around them. Questions students can ask: What values have I gotten from my family? What are my beliefs?

- o Then students use a mirror to fill in the body shape, reflecting their actual physical appearance.

Cultural X-Rays of Personal Cultural Identity, Alejandro and
Natali, Fifth Grade

Graffiti Boards (Short, Harste, and Burke 1996)

Graffiti boards help students quickly capture their initial thinking and express their feel-ings about a text. Students respond by sharing current experiences, past events, quotes from the book, or ideas and comments.

Materials

- A large sheet of chart paper
- Markers, crayons, or pencils of various colors

Procedures

- Students engaged in a shared experience such as reading a picturebook or a text set of books are invited during the experience and afterward to sketch and write in small groups on a large sheet of paper.
- In small groups students choose a corner of a large piece of paper and begin jotting down words or phrases, sketching images, sharing feelings, or webbing their thinking. Students work alone and quietly. There is no particular organization, and everything is completed in graffiti fashion.
- When everyone is finished responding on the graffiti board, students share their thinking, using the graffiti board as a reference point or reminder.
- An adaptation with young children is to put a long sheet of mural paper on the floor so that all of the children can sit around it. They listen to the story read aloud and participate in an initial discussion, and then respond on the graffiti board as the book is read aloud again.

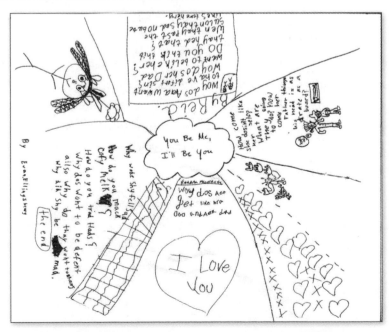

First-Grade Graffiti-Board Responses to *You Be Me, I'll Be You*
by Pili Mandelbaum (1990)

Sketch to Stretch (Short, Harste, and Burke 1996)

Sketch to stretch encourages students to think about the meaning of a story and to move to a symbolic depiction of that meaning, not an illustration of events in the story. They each sketch their individual meanings, generating new insights to share with a small group of students.

Materials

- A children's book or text selection
- Pencil, paper, crayons, colored pencils, etc.

Procedures

- After reading a picturebook, chapter from a novel, or selection of text, students have a brief discussion about that text. They are then asked, "What does this story mean to you?" and visually sketch the meaning.
- There are multiple ways to represent the meaning of an experience, and students can experiment with their interpretations. Students are encouraged not to draw an illustration of events from the story but to think about the meaning of the story and find a way to visually sketch that meaning. If they struggle with sketching the meaning, it may be helpful to have them draw their connections to the story.
- When the sketches are complete, each student shows his or her sketch to the others in a small group and shares his or her thinking related to the sketch.
- Another option is to show the sketch without making comments and have the participants study the sketch and say what they think the artist is attempting to convey. The artist has the "last word," to share his or her own intentions and thinking about the sketch.

Sketch to stretch by a second grader. This is his understanding of the concept of taking action, stopping to consider the consequences of doing something.

Consensus Boards (Short 2009)

Consensus boards give students time to explore their individual responses to a text, share that thinking with one another, and talk critically around a specific issue. After sharing their thinking about a broad range of connections, students come to consensus on the tensions and issues that they want to explore further through investigation and dialogue.

Materials

- Texts that are challenging and invite inquiry and multiple interpretations
- Markers
- A large consensus board created from chart paper that covers the table and has a center circle or square with 4-5 sections marked from that center to each corner of the paper

Procedures

- Students engage in an experience with a text by reading or listening to that text.
- During and after the experience, each student in a small group takes a section of the consensus board and jots, sketches, or webs responses to the text. Some students may need to first listen to the text and then respond during a second reading.
- Students share their responses with one another and think together about their interpretations of the text in their small groups.
- After sharing, students consider the tensions or issues that they might want to explore further and come to consensus on one or two tensions to think about as a group. These tensions are recorded in the center of the board.
- The group then decides on strategies for investigating this tension before their next group meeting, such as revisiting the text to locate quotations on the issue, writing or sketching their thinking about the issue, or creating a web of their connections and ideas.

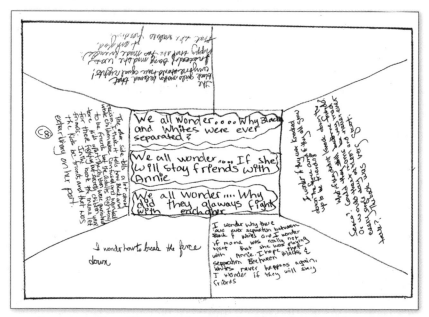

Consensus Board Response by Fifth-Grade Students to *The Other Side* **by Jacqueline Woodson (2001)**

Other response strategies can be found in *Creating Classrooms for Authors and Inquirers* by Kathy G. Short and Jerome Harste, with Carolyn Burke (Heinemann 1996).

Index